people types

& tiger Stripes

THIRD EDITION
BY GORDON LAWRENCE

CENTER FOR APPLICATIONS OF PSYCHOLOGICAL TYPE, INC.

Published by Center for Applications of Psychological Type, Inc.
Gainesville, Florida

Printed in the United Stated of America.

Designed and produced by Special Publications Inc.,
P.O. Box 4649, Ocala, Florida 34478

Library of Congress Cataloging in Publication Data

Lawrence, Gordon. 1930-   82-1243
        People types and tiger stripes   AACR2

        1. Teaching   2. Individualized instruction

3. Study Method of. I. Title

LB 1025.2.L38 1982 371.l'02

Library of Congress Catalog Number 93-072233

ISBN 0-935652-16-7

ACKNOWLEDGEMENTS

Of the many people who contributed ideas for the book and critiques of it, foremost is my wife Carolyn. She is my partner in many ways, and I am deeply grateful to her. Her influence is in every chapter.

I appreciate very much the depth of knowledge, editorial skills, practicality, and many helpful suggestions of those who read the manuscript: Nancy Barger, Sue Clancy, Pat Guild, Linda Kirby, Ray Moody, Elizabeth Murphy, Judy Provost, and Naomi Quenk. For their personal support, advice, and work on bringing the book into being, my thanks to Mary McCaulley, Jerry Macdaid, and David Parrett.

So much of what I have written in the book reflects the seminal work of Isabel Myers and Mary McCaulley; my work builds on theirs, and I feel privileged to extend what they have accomplished.

CONTENTS

Introduction ix

PART 1 — BASIC APPLICATIONS

CHAPTER 1: PEOPLE TYPES AND TIGER STRIPES
Patterns of Mental Habits.. 1
Exercise: Thinking About Mental Habits 2
Types Come From Patterns 4
Why Types and Patterns are Important 5
The Myers-Briggs Type Indicator 5
Jung's Theory of Psychological Types 7
The Mental Processes 7
The Third Dimension: Extraversion and Introversion 10
The Fourth Dimension: Judging and Perceiving 11
The Sixteen Types 12
Dynamics of Type and the Learning Process.................................. 15
Questions Often Asked About Type 16
Talk About Type Concepts 22
Exercise for Discussing Type Concepts 23
Check Your Knowledge of Type Concepts 24
Type Concepts Test.. 28
Answers to the Type Concepts Test... 30

CHAPTER 2: TYPE, MOTIVATION, AND LEARNING STYLE
Introduction: The Process of Studying Type Theory....................... 33
Type as a Way of Classifying Behavior.. 35
Type and Motivation 37
Type and Learning Style.. 39
Summary of Research on Type and Learning Style 40
Summaries of the Learning Preferences.. 43

CHAPTER 3: USING TYPE CONCEPTS IN PLANNING INSTRUCTION
The Sixteen Types are not Equally Represented 47
School Instruction Fits Some Types Better Than Others................. 48
Planning Instruction to Honor the Rights of Every Type 53
Exercise: Four Work Settings 54
Tips for Using Type in Planning... 57

Plan a Unit of Instruction Using Type Concepts 63
Examples of Class Projects Successful With All Types of Students 65
Using Type in Classroom-bound Instruction 70

CHAPTER 4: TYPE AND TEACHING STYLES
What Research Reveals About Type and Teaching Preferences 71
Teachers' Choices of Levels and Subjects 72
The Teacher in the Classroom 74
Exercise: Examining and Adjusting Teaching Styles 79
Type and The Teaching Team 81
Type and Human Relations by Isabel Briggs Myers 84

CHAPTER 5: TYPE IS A FOUR-LETTER WORD:
USES AND ABUSES OF THE MBTI
Misuse Arising from MBTI's Appearance 87
Confusion About Scales and Scores 89
Wrong Uses of the MBTI 92
Reliability, Validity, and Practical Effectiveness 93
The User Affects Reliability and Validity 94
The Ethics of Using the MBTI 95

CHAPTER 6: TYPE AND STEREOTYPE
Why Do We Stereotype? 97
Type and Stereotype 98
Persona, Shadow, and Stereotype 101
An Activity for Identifying Stereotypes 102
What We Can Do 104

CHAPTER 7: TAKING TYPE INTO ACCOUNT IN EDUCATION
by Isabel Briggs Myers 105

PART 2 — ADVANCED APPLICATIONS

CHAPTER 8: THE DYNAMICS OF THE TYPES
A Type is More Than Four Preferences 111
Type Theory is About Perception and Judgment 112
Dynamic Relationships of the Mental Processes 113
The Attitudes: Extraversion and Introversion 118
J and P Reveal the Dynamics 122
The Third and Fourth Mental Processes 125

The Practical Benefits of Knowing Type Dynamics 129
Type Concepts Test — Part Two 131
Answers to the Type Concepts Test — Part Two 133

CHAPTER 9: TYPE AND CURRICULUM REFORM

Taking Type Preferences Into Account in Curriculum Work 127
The Extraversion and Introversion Preferences 138
The Sensing and Intuition Preferences 140
The Thinking and Feeling Preferences 141
The Judgment and Perception Preferences 142
Using the Type Preferences in Curriculum Making 143
Curriculum Assumptions that Need to be Changed 144
Achievement vs. Development 145
Type Development 148
Taking Type Development Into Account in Curriculum Work 149
Influencing the System 150
Kinds of Mind 152
Engaging All the Types Through Their Strengths 153

CHAPTER 10: DEVELOPMENTAL NEEDS AND TYPE CONCEPTS

Looking at Development Through the Lenses of Type 157
Observing and Analyzing Development Problems 158
The Zig-Zag Analysis 161
Type Development Analysis 163
Case Studies in Type Development Analysis 166
Exercise: Analyzing Student Difficulties 171
The Contribution of Type Development to the
   Teaching of Character Development 172
Exercise: Type Strengths and Trouble Spots 174
Observation as a Way to Identify Chatacteristics 176

CHAPTER 11: KINDS OF MIND

Are the 16 Types 16 Kinds of Mind? 185
Mind as Verb 186
The Types as Kinds of Mind 187
How Can We Keep Track of 16 Different Kinds? 188
Four Kinds of Mind 190
ST, SF, NT, NF Mental Priorities 192
ST, SF, NT, NF Interactions 193
Discovering the Biases of One's Mind-set 194

CHAPTER 12: INTRODUCING TYPE INTO AN ORGANIZATION

Ourselves and Our Situations...206
Describing and Analyzing the Situation 207
Deciding on Possible Entry Points...215
Deciding on Strategy — The Long View...218
Deciding on Tactics — An Action Plan 219
Ethical Guidelines for Using the MBTI 221

EPILOGUE — NEXT STEPS 221

APPENDIX: INTRODUCTION TO TYPE

by Isabel Briggs Myers...225

INTRODUCTION

Thirteen-year-old Lisa. Lisa is a problem for her teachers. She's bright enough, but she seems to value popularity above everything else. Talkative, friendly and gregarious, she relies on her friends to make decisions for her and she patterns her behavior after theirs. Adults see her as flighty, unsure of herself and her own point of view. Her work and conversations are often trite and shallow. While she is conscientious and wants to please, sometimes her classmates and teachers are annoyed by her "helpfulness;" they wish she would mind her own business. When criticized by a teacher or her friends, she seems deeply hurt and resentful.

Lisa frustrates her teachers; this is not because she disrupts class or resists assignments. The problem is that they realize her personal development is not going well and they feel powerless to do anything about it. Perhaps, through their planning meetings, they can focus on a strategy to help Lisa develop some perspective and "a mind of her own." But at least 50 more of the students they see every day need attention as much as Lisa does. There is not the time to work out a strategy for each of them.

Thirty-three-year-old Lisa. Lisa is a problem for her boss. She's bright enough for her job, but she seems to value popularity above everything else. Talkative, friendly, and gregarious, she relies on her work-mates and friends to make decisions for her and she patterns her behavior after theirs. They see her as flighty, unsure of herself and her own point of view. Her work and conversations are often trite and shallow. While she is conscientious and wants to please, sometimes her co-workers and boss are annoyed by her "helpfulness;" they wish she would mind her own business. Whenever they criticize her work, she seems deeply hurt and resentful.

Lisa frustrates her boss; this is not because she slacks off or resists assignments. The boss realizes her personal development problems are interfering with her work and feels powerless to do anything about it. Improvement on those problems would certainly benefit her work performance, but helping her with them is outside the boss's responsibility.

Do you see in Lisa's behavior a pattern you recognize? Probably every classroom has a "Lisa," as do many workplaces. All of us in the

helping professions have encountered her. As you might suppose, I wrote the two descriptions to make the point that personal development problems not dealt with in childhood and youth follow the person into adult life.

What this book is about. This book presents ways to recognize the basic ingredients in behavior that make up a motivation pattern, and to then make an educated, shortcut prediction about what strategy will work best with the Lisas and the wide variety of other people we teach and supervise. It is about helping all of them identify their resources, not just the ones in trouble. The focus of the book is one method for identifying mind-sets, learning styles, and motivation patterns, and using the patterns in planning instruction and other helping processes. The objective is helping people find and use their strengths to strengthen weaknesses.

Behind the book lies a long, personal search by the author to find practical and effective means of matching instruction to basic differences in students. A variety of approaches exists. Many of them merit attention. The approach presented here is based on Carl G. Jung's ideas about psychological types, as made practical through the work of Isabel Briggs Myers.* Theirs is a remarkable theory that offers a fresh perspective on people's patterns of dealing with their world.

This book includes readings and instructions for activities that explain the theory and guide you in making applications of it. The book may be used to guide a workshop or group study, or it may be used by individuals. The activities that are designed for small groups can be accomplished by individuals with the occasional assistance of a colleague. The book is addressed to teachers and others in helping professions, but many others — including parents and bosses — should be able to translate the ideas and activities to their own framework. Because most of my own work has been in education, the examples I use are mainly from school and college settings.

---

*Jung, Carl G. (1921-1971). Psychological Types, *Princeton: Princeton University Press. Myers, Isabel Briggs (1980).* Gifts Differing. *Palo Alto, California: Consulting Psychologists Press.*

NEW FEATURES OF THE THIRD EDITION

The third edition has six new chapters, doubling the content of the second edition. I have widened the scope beyond learning styles, the theme of the earlier editions. In the years since the second edition, Myers' self-report instrument for identifying people's types, the Myers-Briggs Type Indicator® (MBTI®),** has become the most widely used instrument of its kind. It is used extensively in career guidance, personal counseling, team building in organizations, and many other applications besides those in schools that I wrote about in the earlier editions. So I have included new material for MBTI users in all settings.

Readers of the earlier editions will recognize Chapters 1, 2, 3, 4, and 10, which are revised but basically the same, with some elaborations and new exercises I have developed and examples I have encountered since then. The other chapters are new. The new materials include:

- introducing type into an organization
- type and curriculum reform
- ethical pitfalls in using type and how to avoid them
- stereotyping, how to spot it and give it up
- practical ways of introducing type to people
- exercises on adapting teaching styles
- consideration of the types as 16 distinct kinds of mind
- deeper layers of understanding of type theory
- more examples of using type in schools and colleges
- type development and how to foster it
- summaries of research involving the MBTI in studies of learning styles

This edition is divided into two parts Part one has seven chapters on basic applications of type concepts, including the beginning theory needed for guiding sound uses of type. Part two has five chapters, one on the deeper aspects of type theory, and four on advanced applications. My purpose was to provide materials useful to all readers, whatever their prior knowledge of the work of Jung and Myers.

** *Myers-Briggs Type Indicator and MBTI are registered trademarks of Consulting Psychologists Press, Inc., Palo Alto, CA.*

PEOPLE TYPES AND TIGER STRIPES

People's habits tell a lot about them. Not just their "good" and "bad" habits, but also such habits as what they pay attention to, what they care about, and how they decide things. These are mental habits. Do you know any people with mental habits like these? Chris is quick to notice people's feelings, and tries to stay out of arguments. Jan likes to argue, likes to explain things, and sometimes doesn't notice people's feelings. John's father wants him to keep a careful record of how he spends his weekly allowance. John says record keeping isn't important to him. Pat wishes her mother would watch the clock more and get to places on time. Pat's mother wishes Pat would relax and not get an ulcer over being five minutes late. Some mental habits are very deep in a person. Trying to change them is like trying to change the stripes on a tiger — like trying to change the grain in a piece of wood. The information that follows is about mental habits — the kind we probably can't change but can learn to use better.

PATTERNS OF MENTAL HABITS

The deep mental habits come in patterns, in combinations. Described below are eight patterns you can use to study yourself, your friends and family. Pick out your own patterns. There are no better or worse patterns. Think carefully and try to pick the patterns that really describe you best. This exercise is not a test. It is simply a way for you to start looking at the patterns in yourself. After you have completed the exercise, you will be able to see how the eight sets form into patterns of people types, and you can get an idea of which type may be yours.

EXERCISE: THINKING ABOUT MENTAL HABITS

Which pattern describes you better, E or I?

E	I
E *likes action and variety*	I *likes quiet and time to consider things*
E *likes to do mental work by talking to people*	I *likes to do mental work privately before talking*
E *acts quickly, sometimes without much reflection*	I *may be slow to try something without understanding it first*
E *likes to see how other people do a job, and to see results*	I *likes to understand the idea of a job and to work alone or with just a few people*
E *wants to know what other people expect of him or her*	I *wants to set his or her own standards*

    E's interest turns mostly outward to the world of action, people and things. I's interest turns more often to the inner world of ideas and private things. Everyone turns outward to act and inward to reflect. You must do both, but you are more comfortable doing one or the other, just as right-handers are more comfortable with the right hand, but do use the left one.

    Circle the **E** or the **I** in the margin to show which pattern fits you better.

    E stands for extraversion, which means outward turning.

    I stands for introversion which means inward turning.

Which pattern describes you better, S or N?

S	N
S *pays most attention to experience as it is*	N *pays most attention to the meanings of facts and how they fit together*
S *likes to use eyes and ears and other senses to find out what's happening*	N *likes to use imagination to come up with new ways to do things, new possibilities*
S *dislikes new problems unless prior experience shows how to solve them*	N *likes solving new problems, and dislikes doing the same thing over and over*

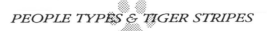

S	N
S enjoys using skills already learned more than learning new ones	*N likes using new skills more than practicing old ones*
S is patient with details but impatient when the details get complicated	*N is impatient with details but doesn't mind complicated situations*

S pays most attention to the facts that come from personal experience. **S** can more easily see the details, while **N** can more easily see the "big picture." **N** pays most attention to meanings behind the facts. **S** and **N** are two kinds of perception, that is, two ways of finding out or giving attention to experiences. **S** stands for sensing and **N** stands for intuition. Everybody uses both their sensing and their intuition to find out things. You use both, but you use one more than the other.

Circle the **S** or the **N** in the margin to show which pattern fits you better.

Which pattern describes you better, T or F?

T	F
T likes to decide things using logic	*F likes to decide things using personal feelings and human values*
T wants to be treated with justice and fair play	*F likes praise, and likes to please people, even in small matters*
T may neglect and hurt other people's feelings without knowing it	*F is usually very aware of other people's feelings*
T gives more attention to ideas or things than to human relationships	*F can predict how others will feel*
T can get along with little harmony	*F values harmony; feels unsettled by arguments and conflicts*

T makes decisions by examining data, staying impersonal and cool. **T** stands for thinking judgment. **F** makes decisions by paying attention to personal values and feelings. **F** stand for feeling judgment. You make **T** and **F** judgments every day, but you use one kind of judgment more than the other.

Circle the **T** or **F** in the margin to show which pattern fits you better.

Which pattern describes you better, J or P?

J	**P**
J likes to make a plan, to have things settled and decided ahead	**P** likes to stay flexible and avoid fixed plans
J tries to make things come out the way they "ought to be"	**P** deals easily with unplanned and unexpected happenings
J likes to finish one project before starting another	**P** likes to start many projects but may have trouble finishing them all
J usually has mind made up	**P** usually is looking for new information
J may decide things too quickly	**P** may decide things too slowly
J wants to be right	**P** wants to miss nothing
J lives by standards and schedules that are not easily changed	**P** lives by making changes to deal with problems as they come along

Circle the **J** or **P** in the margin to show which pattern fits you better. **J** stands for judgment and **P** stands for perception. **J** people run their outer life with settled judgments. **P** people run their outer life in an open, perceiving way.

TYPES COME FROM PATTERNS

Now you can put together the four letters of the patterns that describe you best. Draw a circle here around the same letters you circled in the margins above.

E I   S N   T F   J P

Now write your four letters here: ___ ___ ___ ___

The four letters together make up a whole pattern called a type. It may be your type. There are 16 different "people types" as shown by the 16 combinations of the letters. Find yours.

ISTJ	**ISFJ**	**INFJ**	**INTJ**
ISTP	**ISFP**	**INFP**	**INTP**
ESTP	**ESFP**	**ENFP**	**ENTP**
ESTJ	**ESFJ**	**ENFJ**	**ENTJ**

Each type is different from the others in important ways. As you come to understand the type ideas better, you will see how type affects your life with your friends and family, at school or in a job.

If you are a teacher, the activity you have just completed is one you may want to use with students. With young students in mind, I wrote it in as simple language as I could. You may photocopy and reproduce the activity for students, giving credit to this publication. Use it only as a discussion starter, as a first step in thinking about type. It is not an instrument developed by research.

WHY TYPES AND PATTERNS ARE IMPORTANT

This book shows how an understanding of type is important to teachers and other professionals concerned with instruction, training, and guidance. In my own work to understand student motivation and learning style, I have come to the conclusion that type is fundamental. It is crucial in explaining why certain approaches to instruction or supervision work with some people and not with others. The fact that a person prefers sensing perception over intuitive perception, or prefers an active (extraverted) approach to problem solving over a reflective (introverted) one, is not just an interesting curiosity. It is information that some professionals have used to make dramatic improvements in the effectiveness of their work.

THE MYERS-BRIGGS TYPE INDICATOR®*

The four dimensions of type (EI, SN, TF, and JP) and the ideas behind the sixteen types represent the lifelong work of Isabel Briggs Myers. In 1962 Educational Testing Service published the Myers-Briggs Type Indicator, a paper and pencil instrument she developed with Katharine Briggs, her mother, over a twenty year period. Regarded as a research instrument, it did not have wide circulation or usage until Consulting Psychologists Press assumed responsibility for publishing it in 1975. The Indicator was developed specifically to carry Carl Jung's theory of type (Jung, 1921-1971) into practical applications.

The rest of this book will be more useful to you if you have taken the Indicator and are aware of your own profile. The Indicator was written to be taken by people who have not yet studied about type. Spontaneous responses probably give a more accurate profile, so the time to take the Indicator is before you proceed with the book. If you have not yet taken it, inquire about a local source that can administer it and give you information about your type. Persons qualified to

Myers-Briggs Type Indicator and MBTI are registered trademarks of Consulting Psychologists Press, Inc., Palo Alto, CA.

order instruments from Consulting Psychologists Press (CPP) may order the Indicator from them. The address is: 3803 Bayshore Road, Palo Alto, CA 94303. Phone: 800-624-1765. They also may order from The Center for Applications of Psychological Type (CAPT), 2815 N.W. 13th Street, Gainesville, FL 32609. Phone: 800-777-2278. Both will provide a catalog of MBTI materials and other related resources. The question booklets are reusable. There are two means of scoring the responses: by handscoring keys or by a computer scoring service that provides each person with a printout of his/her type profile and an interpretation of it. Hand scoring keys and computer scoring are available from both sources.

CPP and CAPT also distribute *Introduction to Type* by Isabel Myers (published by CPP) a booklet that gives a basic explanation of type concepts. Because *Introduction to Type* is a primary resource for interpreting your results from the Indicator, a version of it has been reproduced in this book as an Appendix. If your responses to the Indicator are scored by the computer service, your printout will show your MBTI results and a description of the reported type. If your response sheet is handscored, look up the description of your four-letter results in *Introduction to Type* (the Table of Contents on page A-1 will show you where to find the description of the matching type. Notice that two descriptions are on a page, with characteristics in common shown first and contrasts between the two types shown at the bottom.)

Finding your own preference type

Look again at the four type preference letters you chose while reading the "People Types and Tiger Stripes" activity. If they are not the same as the type derived from the Indicator, use *Introduction to Type* to find the matching description, and compare the two. Decide which description fits you best. Keep in mind that the Indicator is a carefully researched instrument and the "People Types" exercise is not. Don't expect to understand type concepts quickly. Their meanings will present themselves to you at times and in circumstances that will surprise you.

For now, read *Introduction to Type*, all 18 pages, with special attention to pages A-2–A-6. If your work situation seems to call for you to be a different type than what you see yourself to be in your life outside of work, make an estimation of your work-self type using pages A-17 and A-18. After using these descriptions you should be better able to decide which of the preference types is your "best fit." Try on your hypothesized type and test its usefulness to you.

JUNG'S THEORY OF PSYCHOLOGICAL TYPES

The great Swiss physician-psychologist, C. G. Jung, developed one of the most comprehensive of current theories to explain human personality. Where other observers saw people's behavior as random, Jung saw patterns. What he called "psychological types" are patterns in the way people prefer to perceive and make judgments. In Jung's theory, all conscious mental activity can be classified into four mental processes or functions — two perception processes (sensing and intuition) and two judgment processes (thinking and feeling). What comes into consciousness, moment by moment, comes either through the senses or through intuition. To remain in consciousness, perceptions must be used. They are used — sorted, weighed, analyzed, evaluated — by the judgment processes, thinking and feeling.

THE MENTAL PROCESSES

Perceiving processes: Sensing and intuition*

Sensing (S) is the term used for perception of the observable by way of the senses. **Intuition (N)** is the term used for perception of meanings, relationships and possibilities by way of insight. **Sensing (S)** types use sensing and intuition, but prefer, and therefore develop, sensing. With good type development, the expertise in sensing can lead to a differentiated awareness of present experience, acute powers of observation, a memory for facts and detail, and a capacity for realism, for seeing the world as it is. Traits characteristically developed as a consequence of a preference for sensing include a reliance on experience rather than theory, a trust of the conventional and customary way of doing things, a preference for beginning with what is known and real, and then moving systematically, step by step, tying each new fact to past experience and testing it for its relevance in practical use. To most sensing types, "real intelligence" is characterized as soundness, accuracy and common sense.

---

*These descriptions of the processes of perception and judgment are adapted by permission from: M. H. McCaulley (1978). Applications of the Myers-Briggs Type Indicator to Medicine and Other Health Professions. HRA Contract 231-76-0051, DHEW. Gainesville, FL: Center for Applications of Psychological Type.

Sensing types (S) are attracted to careers and settings where skillful application of well-learned knowledge is more important than developing new solutions; where working with tangibles is more important than using theory and insight; and where dealing with the immediate situation and using sound, conventional wisdom is more important than making bold breakthroughs.

Intuitive types (N) use sensing and intuition, but prefer and therefore develop intuition. With good type development, intuition provides insight into complexity, an ability to see abstract, symbolic and theoretical relationships, and a capacity to see future possibilities, often creative ones. Attitudes characteristically developed as a result of a preference for intuition include a reliance on inspiration rather than on past experience, an interest in the new and untried, and a preference for learning new materials through an intuitive grasp of meanings and relationships. To most intuitive types, "real intelligence" is shown by insight in grasping complexities, and flashes of imagination or creativity.

Intuitive types (N) are attracted to careers and settings where it is more important to find the pattern in complex systems than it is to deal with the practical details; where creating new knowledge is more important than applying existing knowledge, where working with theory and imagination is more important than dealing with tangibles; and where intellectual challenge is more important than the enjoyment of the pleasures of everyday events.

Judgment processes: Thinking and feeling

Thinking (T) is the term used for a logical decision-making process, aimed at an impersonal finding. **Feeling (F)** is a term for a process of appreciation, making judgments in terms of a system of subjective, personal values. Both thinking and feeling are considered rational processes because they use reasoning to arrive at conclusions or decisions.

Thinking types (T) use both thinking and feeling but prefer to use thinking for making judgments. With good type development, expertise in thinking leads to powers of analysis and an ability to weigh facts objectively including consequences, unintended as well as intended. Attitudes typically developed from a preference for thinking include objectivity, impartiality, a sense of fairness and justice, and skill in applying logical analysis. Thinking types are attracted to areas where tough-mindedness and technical skills are needed.

Feeling types (F) use thinking and feeling but prefer to reach judgments through feeling. With good type development, feeling leads to development of values and standards, and a knowledge of what matters most to themselves and other people. Attitudes typically resulting from a preference for feeling include an understanding of people and a wish to affiliate with them, a desire for harmony, and a capacity for warmth, empathy and compassion. Feeling types are attracted to areas where understanding and communication with people are needed, and find the interpersonal skills more interesting than the technical skills.

Preferences among the mental processes

Everyone uses both of the perceiving processes — **sensing (S)** and **intuition (N)**, and both of the judging processes — **thinking (T)** and **feeling (F)**. But everyone prefers one of each pair over the other. That makes four preference pairs: sensing plus feeling **(SF)**, sensing plus **thinking (ST)**, intuition plus **feeling (NF)**, and intuition plus thinking **(NT)**. Myers called the **SF** combination sympathetic and friendly, the **ST** practical and matter-of-fact, the **NF** enthusiastic and insightful, and the NT logical and ingenious. See page A3 of the Appendix for her descriptions of the four combinations. In Chapter 11 of this book, Kinds of Mind, is a discussion of the patterns represented in the four combinations.

Jung observed that in each person's preferred pair one of the processes is dominant. It has the leadership in the personality; it serves as the centerpost, and the other processes are helpers in the person's mental framework. Using my own preference pair as an example, intuition plus thinking **(NT)**, you know more about me when you know that intuition is dominant, and my thinking process is a helper to the dominant, intuition. People with intuition dominant see the world in terms of possibilities. Possibilities come into my mind continually, and I evaluate them mainly with my second preference, thinking. In the **NT** combination, when thinking is dominant, logical order is the first concern, and the intuition process serves the dominant **T** by supplying possibilities for making an orderly system work well.

The nature of the dominant process and other aspects of the dynamics of the 16 types are discussed in Chapter 8.

THE THIRD DIMENSION:
EXTRAVERSION AND INTROVERSION

Jung identified a third dimension of personality structure: extraversion-introversion. He invented these terms. He created them from the Latin components, and assigned to them quite specific meanings. These meanings have been distorted, if not corrupted, in American common usage. Staying close to the Latin, extraverting means outward-turning and introverting means inward-turning. We all do both regularly, every day. We turn outside of ourselves to act in the world, and we turn into ourselves to reflect. Of course, action without reflection is blind and may be fruitless; and reflection that does not lead to action may be futile. Both extraverting-action and introverting-reflection are essential. However, each person is not equally "at home" in action and reflection. Those who prefer extraverting often say "When in doubt, act." Those who prefer introverting are more likely to say "When in doubt, reflect on the matter more deeply."

To extravert is to think out loud, to reveal half-thought ideas, to process one's experiences outwardly, as a means of doing one's best mental work. To introvert is to keep ideas inside, where the best mental work goes on, and polish the ideas until they are ready to be exposed. So people who prefer extraverting, whom we call extraverts, are seen as more outgoing, and those who prefer inner processing, whom we call introverts, are seen as reserved. Extraverting means looking outward for interests, values, and stimulation. Introverting means looking inward for these.

Extraverting and introverting also refer to how the dominant process — **S, N, T,** or **F** — is used. A person whose preference is for extraversion most often uses the dominant mental process outwardly, where it is visible to others. A person whose preference is for introversion most often uses the dominant process inwardly, privately. It is no surprise that people who prefer extraverting are easier to get to know; they show their dominant process most readily. It takes longer to get to know the ones who favor introverting, who reserve their dominant for the inner life.

THE FOURTH DIMENSION: JUDGING AND PERCEIVING

Briggs and Myers elaborated Jung's ideas of psychological type and showed a fourth dimension that is present, but not highlighted in the descriptions already given. The fourth dimension is the attitude taken toward the outer world. When a judgment process (**T** or **F**) is used in running one's outer life, the natural drive is to have things decided, judged, settled, planned, organized, and managed according to plan. In this personality pattern, the drive is always toward closure, toward having a settled system in place. This is the judging attitude toward the outer world, represented by the letter **J** as the fourth letter of the type designation, ___**J**.

When a perception process (**S** or **N**) is used to run one's outer life, the natural drive is toward keeping things open to new perceptions. The person wants to stay flexible, so as to adapt to changing circumstances, and to experience life as widely as possible. In this personality pattern, the drive is always toward keeping plans and organization to a necessary minimum so one can respond to new perceptions and adapt flexibly to new circumstances. This is the perceiving attitude toward the outer world, represented by the letter **P** as the fourth letter of the type designation, ___**P**.

Thus the fourth letter of the type designation is a ___**J** or a ___**P**. As we get to know a person, the **JP** aspect of his or her type is often the first to be noticed. A person's planful or spontaneous nature is quickly apparent.

Directing one's outer life in a planful way, as **J**s do, seems readily understandable. What is the **P** way? Being receptive and spontaneous do not appear to be ways of directing one's life. They appear reactive and not proactive. Aren't the **P** types proactive? The analogy of steering a sailboat or skateboarding may fit here. These are activities that require many adjustments in a short span of time, actions that appear spontaneous and impulsive rather than based on judgment. Actually, many judgments are happening very quickly. And each adjustment, the steering required, quickly takes into account the changing conditions and how they interact with the steerer's intentions. There are good reasons to believe that the perceiving types tend toward occupations that require this kind of steering, adjusting to changing events; occupations such as fine artist, artisan, journalist, craftsman, laborer, actor, and psychologist.

To summarize briefly, in Jung's theory of psychological types, all conscious mental activity occurs in two perception processes (sensing and intuition) and two judgment processes (thinking and feeling). Everyone uses all four processes, but we differ in how much and how well we use each of them. In every person, one of the processes is dominant and that process indicates the basic way the person addresses life. If a person uses the dominant process mainly in the world of people and things, that person's orientation is called extraverted. The person who uses the dominant process mainly in the inner, private world of ideas and thoughts has an introverted orientation. Briggs and Myers added the fourth dimension, and a **J** or **P** at the end of the set of letters that is the shorthand designation of each type. The **J** means a judging, planful way of running one's outer life. The **P** means a perceiving, spontaneous outer life.

THE SIXTEEN TYPES

The MBTI has four scales corresponding to the four dimensions of type theory, as shown in the figure.

The MBTI uses a shorthand designation for the eight characteristics: E for extraversion, I for introversion, etc., as in the figure. Note that N is used for intuition because I has already been used for introversion. While type is reported and explained in four parts, it is not merely a combination of parts. Nor is it static, as the term "type" often connotes. Type is a dynamic system, and each type is an integrated pattern. The dynamics of the types is the subject of Chapter 8.

The accompanying page of brief descriptions of the sixteen types highlights the strengths of each type, and the similarities and differences of the types.

Myers wrote extensive descriptions of each type, and at least a one-page description is given to people when their type is reported from the MBTI, for example, as shown in *Introduction to Type*, Appendix A of this book. Condensing the type descriptions into one table results in considerable oversimplification, so these brief description highlights should be used cautiously.

In the four letter formula for each type, two letters appear in bold type, **ENTJ** for example. This type is referred to as the extraverted thinking type with intuition. The two middle letters are the preferred mental processes of this type. The process in bold type, **T** in this case, is the dominant process. In the table, the types are displayed to show the opposites across from each other — that is, types with all four letters different. For example, **ENTJ** and **ISFP**, at the top, differ in all four letters. The areas of strength of the one are the other's areas of weakness. People with opposite preferences have the most difficulty communicating with each other. To find common ground, they must make use of their less preferred and less trustworthy mental processes. But opposites stand to gain the most from each other, because each represents to the other the direction in which the greatest opportunity for growth lies. What one person uses well and naturally, the other person uses less well and with effort. Thus, they can complement and support each other, and help each other to grow. Maturity in terms of type is the capability to use all the processes, whatever process is needed, whenever it is needed.

FOUR PREFERENCES ARE SCORED TO ARRIVE AT A PERSON'S TYPE

Does The Person's Interest Flow Mainly To	
E — *The Outer World of Actions, Objects and Persons?*	*The Inner World of Concepts and Ideas?* — **I**
EXTRAVERSION	**INTROVERSION**

Does The Person Prefer To Percieve	
S — *The Immediate, Real, Practical Facts of Experience and Life?*	*The Possibilities, Relationships and Meanings of Experiences?* — **N**
SENSING	**INTUITION**

Does The Person Prefer To Make Judgments or Decisions	
T — *Objectively, Impersonally, Considering Causes of Events & Where Decisions May Lead?*	*Subjectively and Personally, Weighing Values of Coices & How They Matter To Others?* — **F**
THINKING	**FEELING**

Does The Person Prefer Mostly To Live	
J — *In a Decisive, Planned and Orderly Way, Aiming To Regulate & Control Events?*	*In a Spontaneous, Flexible Way, Aiming To Understand Life and Adapt To It?* — **P**
JUDGMENT	**PERCEPTION**

BRIEF DESCRIPTIONS OF THE SIXTEEN TYPES

ENTJ
Intuitive, innovative ORGANIZER; analytical, systematic, confident; pushes to get action on new ideas and challenges.

ESTJ
Fact-minded, practical ORGANIZER; assertive, analytical, systematic; pushes to get things done and working smoothly and efficiently.

INTP
Inquisitive ANALYZER; reflective, independent, curious: more interested in organizing ideas than situations or people.

ISTP
Practical ANALYZER; values exactness: more interested in organizing data than situations or people: reflective, a cool and curious observer of life.

ESTP
REALISTIC ADAPTER in the world of material things; good natured, tolerant, easy going; oriented to practical, first hand experience: highly observant of details of things.

ESFP
REALISTIC ADAPTER in human relationships; friendly and easy with people, highly observant of their feelings and needs: oriented to practical, first hand experience.

ISTJ
Analytical MANAGER OF FACTS AND DETAILS; dependable, decisive, painstaking and systematic: concerned with systems and organization; stable and conservative.

ISFJ
Sympathetic MANAGER OF FACTS AND DETAILS, concerned with people's welfare; dependable, painstaking and systematic: stable and conservative.

ISFP
Observant, loyal HELPER; reflective, realistic, empathic; patient with details, gentle and retiring; shuns disagreements; enjoys the moment.

INFP
Imaginative, independent HELPER; reflective, inquisitive, empathic, loyal to ideals; more interested in possibilities than practicalities.

ESFJ
Practical HARMONIZER and worker-with-people; sociable, orderly, opinioned; conscientious, realistic and well tuned to the here and now.

ENFJ
Imaginative HARMONIZER and worker-with-people; sociable, expressive, orderly, opinioned, conscientious; curious about new ideas and possibilities.

INFJ
People-oriented INNOVATOR of ideas; serious, quietly forceful and persevering; concerned with the common good, with helping others develop.

INTJ
Logical, critical, decisive INNOVATOR of serious ideas; serious, intent, highly independent, concerned with organization; determined and often stubborn.

ENFP
Warmly enthusiastic PLANNER OF CHANCE; imaginative, individualistic; pursues inspiration with impulsive energy; seeks to understand and inspire others.

ENTP
Inventive, analytical PLANNER OF CHANCE; enthusiastic and independent; pursues inspiration with impulsive energy; seeks to understand and inspire others.

The sixteen types are arranged on the page so that the four with the same dominant process are together in quadrants. The four with thinking dominant are in the upper left quadrant, and the four with feeling dominant in the upper right; the four with sensing dominant in the lower left, and the four with intuition dominant in the lower right. This arrangement of the quadrants provides a way to begin examining the relationships between learning style and Jungian preference type.

DYNAMICS OF TYPE AND THE LEARNING PROCESS

In my judgment, the most essential relationship between type and learning style or work style can be seen in the nature of the dominant mental process in each personality. Refer again to the brief descriptions of the sixteen types and consider the differences represented by the quadrants, beginning with the types with thinking dominant. The young thinkers in school are energized by logically organized material; they thrive on things that can be analyzed, and resent anything that must be "learned" which does not fit logically into their mental systems. They respond best to a teacher who is well organized, but they resist and resent the teacher whose organization is not logical. If they do not find logical orderliness in either the material or the teacher, there is no way for them to bring their best energies and effort to the learning tasks.

The types with feeling dominant are in the upper right quadrant of the table. As the young feeling types start a new school year, they test the situation with two paramount criteria: Does the teacher care about me? Is the subject matter something I can give my heart to? If a caring relationship is formed with the teacher, it can carry the young feeling types through many school tasks that don't interest them. When attachments to the teacher and school subjects are both achieved, these children produce at their best. With both conditions absent, they lose their primary motivation, and any adjustments in instructional procedures and physical conditions are likely to make little difference.

Young sensing types, represented in the lower left quadrant, may appreciate logical order and harmonious working relationships, but their learning motivation does not depend primarily on either. Above all else, they respond to what they see as practical and functional. Their criteria are: Can this teacher and this material show me something useful? Is it real, practical, and clear? Will I learn some skills that my senses can master and put to good use now? These are the students most likely to become lost when the teacher skips steps in explanations and directions, leaves large gaps for students' imagination to close, teaches abstractions without checking to see whether they connect with concrete realities in the students' lives, and teaches "facts" and "skills" that can only be put to use at some indeterminate time in the future. These are the students who do their best mental work when their senses are fully engaged ("I think best with my hands . . .").

The last group, the intuition dominant students, are in the lower right quadrant. These students crave inspiration above all else. They are fully engaged only when their imaginations are fired with intriguing ideas and plans. For them, routines quickly become dull. Unless the teacher or the material inspires them, boredom sets in and drives them to seek out something — anything — to relieve the boredom and to reestablish the inspirational spark. Often they resort to daydreaming, to reading off-task material, or to undermining the teacher. Their energy flows wherever inspiration is. When inspired, they are the most innovative of all types.

If teachers and others in the helping professions were to learn just one thing about psychological types, the thing most important to understand is the power of the dominant process. If the best learning is to happen, thinking types must pursue logical order; feeling types must follow their hearts; sensing types must strive to engage their senses in the mastery of practical skills; and intuitive types must follow whatever inspires. To capture the interest of diverse students requires real artistry in teaching. Understanding the power of the dominant mental process makes that task a little easier.

The most essential thing to know about the motivations of types is that thinking dominant types do their best work when pursuing logical order; feeling types do their best work when their heart is in it; sensing types do their best work when their practical skills are needed and valued; and intuitive types do their best work when pursuing an inspiration.

QUESTIONS OFTEN ASKED ABOUT TYPE*

How does a person get to be a type?

Jung believed that we are born with a predisposition for one type. Environmental factors are very important, since they can foster type development, or get in its way. One of the four mental processes (**S**, **N**, **T**, or **F**) and one attitude (**E** or **I**) are your natural bent, according to Jung, and these natural preferences make up the heart of type.

Some of these questions and answers are adapted from an unpublished document written by Mary McCaulley, and are use here with her permission.

Type may not be clear in young people; that is, the dominant process may not yet be developed enough to organize and integrate the personality. The first task of a young person in type development is to have one of the processes emerge as leader in the personality. A later task is to gain balance by developing the auxiliary process. The other two processes also have to be developed, at least passably, because all four processes are needed every day of our lives. In middle life, some people begin to focus on their third and fourth processes and can become very skillful in them.

How do you develop a mental process?

By using it purposefully to achieve something you think is important. A good example comes from the use of sensing. Development of sensing provides a direct and keen awareness of physical realities and excellent powers of observation. If you are sitting on a train, watching the scenery go by, you are using your sensing but not particularly developing it. If you are driving yourself around a strange city, you will probably concentrate your sensing to notice and remember landmarks — this process develops your sensing. Of course, this kind of focus and effort requires both perception and judgment, the dominant helping the auxiliary to develop, and vice versa.

Doesn't type fence you in?

Not if you understand it. An understanding of type frees you in several ways. It gives you confidence in your own direction of development — the areas in which you can become excellent with the most ease and pleasure. It can also reduce the guilt many people feel at not being able to do everything in life equally well. As Isabel Myers put it, "For most people, really understanding their own type in particular, and other people's types in general, is a releasing experience rather than a restricting one. It sets one free to recognize one's own natural bent and to trust one's own potential for growth and excellence, with no obligation to copy anyone else, however admirable that person may be in his or her own different way." Finally, acknowledging your own preferences opens the possibility of finding constructive values instead of conflicts in the differences you encounter with someone whose preferences are opposite yours.

Are types kinds of personalities?

Many things go into the makeup of a personality — genetics, family life, life circumstances outside the family, society's expectations and requirements, and many learned traits; psychological type is just one aspect of personality. Because people's types express themselves in so many parts of their lives, the types are often called personality types. But type is not synonymous with personality. With people who are likely to be put off by the term psychological, I refer to the types as personality types.

Are the types essentially different sets of traits?

No. Type and trait represent different ways of looking at our psychological natures. The types can be identified by their differences in traits, and they are described by their traits. For example, in the table "Brief Descriptions of the Sixteen Types," the descriptive words and phrases used for each type represent traits. But the type preference categories are not traits. Rather, they are mind-sets, distinct ways of processing experiences, that become visible as traits. For example, extraversion as a type preference is an either-or category, not a trait that is measured as more or less, or degrees of skillfulness. Because this question is too complex for a good short answer, a portion of Chapter 2 covers it more fully.

Can you change your type?

Scores in the Myers-Briggs Type Indicator can be changed depending on how you answer the questions. Score changes can result in a report of a different type. Jung seemed to believe that each person has a true type that he or she may not yet have discovered. The true type does not change, although it may seem to, as one focuses on developing different mental processes at different stages of one's life. Behaviors can change, of course, but the roots of them remain the same.

However, there are many reasons you might take the MBTI two different times and come out different types. You might still be discovering your preferences, and trying them on for size. Or you might be working especially hard to develop one of the mental processes, so that you report it on the MBTI with stronger than usual emphasis. Or, you might take the MBTI one time as your "job self," responding as you see yourself acting on the job, and you might take it another time as your "home self," responding as you see yourself in your home environment. If your type differs in two reports, this fact may lead to interesting information about yourself. As you cast your thoughts back to your frame of mind when you were answering the questions, consider how it may have affected your reporting of yourself, and may or may not reflect your true type.

How do you discover your true type?

Start with what you are sure about. Read all the type descriptions that include the preferences you are sure of. At this point, you may find a type that you know is yours. If you are still puzzled, start observing yourself. For example, if you are undecided about thinking or feeling, start noticing how you make decisions. Are decisions better if you trust your heart (**F**) or your head (**T**)? Notice when activities take a lot of energy and effort. See if you can identify which mental process you were using. It is often true that preferred processes seem effortless, and less preferred processes are more tiring. For example, if watching details closely for a long time makes you feel tired, cross, or nervous, you might investigate whether other sensing activities are also hard for you. You could then look to see if intuitive activities come more easily. If they do, you could consider whether intuition might be your preferred process. To test these ideas, you could ask yourself if your hunches, flashes of inspiration and other intuitions are generally accurate or trustworthy.

What is the best type to be?

For you, the type you really are. Jung's theory says your best satisfactions in life will be those that come through the strengths of your type.

Is everyone of the same type alike?

No. There are many individual differences within each type, because many things influence personality besides type. Some people are at a higher level of type development than others. Even in people of the same type who are well-developed, there are big differences. Take an ESFJ for example. You would expect all the ESFJs to share a wish for people around them to be happy, and would work to achieve harmony. Some ESFJs might be interested in education and be teachers; others might become family doctors and others salespersons. Still others might find their way of helping in volunteer work, or in being a good parent. All these activities offer effective ways of using feeling in the outer world, as extraverted feeling types are predicted to do.

Can you guess someone's type, and is that a good thing to do?

When we are trying to understand, influence, manage, or teach someone else, we often do not know the person's type. As soon as we learn type concepts, we see the value of estimating people's types so as to reach them better. Making a wild guess about someone's type is easy and fun, yet often inaccurate, and sometimes the guess seriously defeats its own purpose. If I make a wrong guess about a person's type and act as if it were a truth about the person, I may be increasing rather than closing the communication gap between us.

Accurately guessing someone's type is a skill that takes a long time to develop. Type concepts have been important in my life for over 20 years, and I am continually learning new ways to recognize characteristics of type, and correcting misconceptions I have been carrying. People who know type concepts well will tell you that the learning never ends.

When you do want to guess someone's type preferences, to improve communication between the two of you, treat your guess as a hypothesis to be checked out, then listen carefully and be ready to change your guess. This book will give you many ideas of behaviors to listen and watch for that are indicators of type preferences.

Do some types make better teachers than others?

All sixteen types are represented among teachers who have answered the MBTI. Each type has its characteristic strengths and limitations. Each makes special contributions to teaching. Any type can become a good teacher. Students also come in all sixteen types. At times, all students need the support of being with a teacher who is like them in type, because understanding comes more easily between similar types. At times, every student needs the challenge of being with a teacher of a different type. Finding the right balance between support and challenge for students is an important task for those who plan instruction. If a faculty has a mixture of types, and knows about the characteristic strengths of different types, then students can be better served.

What types commonly become teachers?

To understand the proportions of the different types among teachers, it is first useful to know the distributions of the types in the general population. The best estimate is that in the general population, extraverts outnumber introverts in a proportion of two or three to one;

sensing types outnumber intuitive types in approximately the same ratio. Women come out about 66% feeling types, and men come out about 60% thinking types. In the general population, judging types outnumber perceiving types with about 55% **J** and 45% **P**. The table shows the MBTI preferences of teachers at various teaching levels.

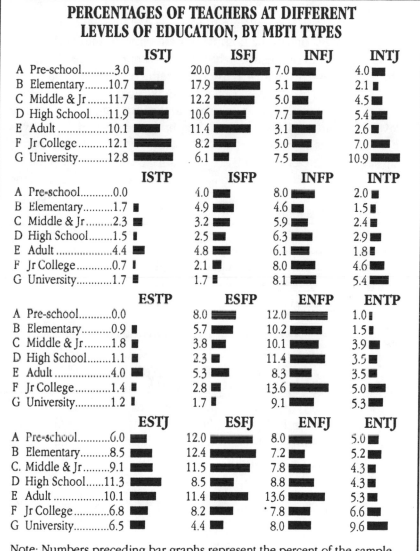

PERCENTAGES OF TEACHERS AT DIFFERENT LEVELS OF EDUCATION, BY MBTI TYPES

	ISTJ	ISFJ	INFJ	INTJ
A Pre-school	3.0	20.0	7.0	4.0
B Elementary	10.7	17.9	5.1	2.1
C Middle & Jr	11.7	12.2	5.0	4.5
D High School	11.9	10.6	7.7	5.4
E Adult	10.1	11.4	3.1	2.6
F Jr College	12.1	8.2	5.0	7.0
G University	12.8	6.1	7.5	10.9

	ISTP	ISFP	INFP	INTP
A Pre-school	0.0	4.0	8.0	2.0
B Elementary	1.7	4.9	4.6	1.5
C Middle & Jr	2.3	3.2	5.9	2.4
D High School	1.5	2.5	6.3	2.9
E Adult	4.4	4.8	6.1	1.8
F Jr College	0.7	2.1	8.0	4.6
G University	1.7	1.7	8.1	5.4

	ESTP	ESFP	ENFP	ENTP
A Pre-school	0.0	8.0	12.0	1.0
B Elementary	0.9	5.7	10.2	1.5
C Middle & Jr	1.8	3.8	10.1	3.9
D High School	1.1	2.3	11.4	3.5
E Adult	4.0	5.3	8.3	3.5
F Jr College	1.4	2.8	13.6	5.0
G University	1.2	1.7	9.1	5.3

	ESTJ	ESFJ	ENFJ	ENTJ
A Pre-school	6.0	12.0	8.0	5.0
B Elementary	8.5	12.4	7.2	5.2
C. Middle & Jr	9.1	11.5	7.8	4.3
D High School	11.3	8.5	8.8	4.3
E Adult	10.1	11.4	13.6	5.3
F Jr College	6.8	8.2	·7.8	6.6
G University	6.5	4.4	8.0	9.6

Note: Numbers preceding bar graphs represent the percent of the sample falling in that type. In bar graphs one inch represents 20% of sample.

These data came from the data bank which is a product of the scoring services of the Center for Applications of Psychological Type in Gainesville, Florida. The table shows occupations recorded by teachers from around the country whose MBTI answer sheets were sent in for scoring.

Extraverts (in the lower half of the table) and introverts are about equally represented at all levels of teaching. Considering that 2/3 or more of the general population is composed of extraverts, it appears that teaching is one of the occupations attractive to introverts.

Intuitive types (in the two right-hand columns) made up about half of the teacher samples. With intuitive types being outnumbered in the general population two to one, teaching as an occupation seems to be attractive to intuitive types, particularly in the upper grades and college levels. In nearly all the intuitive bar graphs the proportion of intuitive types increases as grade level rises. This is consistent with type theory: sensing types preferring work that is pragmatic and concrete, intuitive types preferring the abstract and theoretical. Note that four of the sensing types — ISTP, ISFP, ESTP and ESFP — are under-represented among the teacher samples; more about this later.

Feeling types (in the two middle columns) are in the majority through high school, with thinking types outnumbering feeling types in the samples of college teachers. At all levels judging types (in the top row and bottom row) outnumber perceiving types — at a ratio of about two to one, higher than the general population.

TALK ABOUT TYPE CONCEPTS

I have explained the Myers-Briggs Type Indicator and type concepts to many people. After getting an explanation and having the opportunity to ask questions, the next best step for most people in learning about type is talking about the concepts with family, colleagues, and friends. You are likely to get the most out of this book if you are part of a group of four or five colleagues using the book together. This is a good point to begin your discussions, if you have not started talking already. Convene a meeting. Each person should bring to the meeting his or her MBTI profile and this book. In addition the group will need several apples, at least one for each person, or a bag of peanuts in the shell. Here are some suggestions for the agenda of your meeting. Keep your own notes for possible further use.

EXERCISE FOR DISCUSSING TYPE CONCEPTS

A. Share your reactions to your MBTI profiles. If you know each other well, you may want to guess each other's type letters.
B. The object of this meeting is to help each other understand the concepts of "people types." Raise questions you have about the concepts. Your group may want to review specific portions of *Introduction to Type*, or previous parts of this book.
C. Discuss opposites and dominants, using the "Brief Descriptions of the Sixteen Types."

Exercise: Eat An Apple *

Now you can stop wondering what the apples are for. They are to help you get a deeper insight into the four mental processes — sensing, intuition, thinking and feeling. Follow these activity instructions:

A. This activity is to help you distinguish the mental processes of perception (intuiting and sensing) and judgment (thinking and feeling). Work in pairs, with one partner being a recorder. The recorder should mark off four sections on a sheet of note paper. Label one section Sensing, one Intuition, one Feeling, and one Thinking. As both partners talk, the recorder should make notes in each section, as indicated below, starting with sensing. Each person selects and eats an apple (or peanut), paying attention to each of the four processes separately, one at a time. Take three or four minutes for each process.
  1) As you eat the apple, list your sense impressions of the apple and its parts: skin, flesh, carpels, seeds — noting colors, shapes, textures, tastes, muscular movements and tensions. List facts only.
  2) List your intuitions that come to you during the experience. Memories and associations: Who or what do apples make you think of? Can you recall other ways of enjoying apples? baked? jellies or ciders? games? other? Do you recall apples in stories, myths, poems, proverbs, or superstitions? Do you find yourself speculating about this particular apple?
  3) Can you think about apples? Did your sense impressions or your intuitions lead you to make any logical conclusions about this apple? About apples in general? "I'd say this apple has been in cold storage. I say that because . . ."

The idea for this activity was suggested by Alan Bundick.

4) List your feeling judgments: How you felt about trying this experiment; how you felt about choosing the particular apple you did; how you felt about eating the apple you chose.

B. Each recorder read to the others in the group what was written in the sensing section. Get concurrence that all items were sensory data. Then read each of the other three similarly.

C. The group then discusses this question: In what ways is the set of data recorded under **Sensing** fundamentally different from the kinds of things listed under **Intuition**? Do all members of the group agree? Do the two sets of data help to show why people who perceive with their senses more than with their intuition, and who dwell more on sensory data than intuitive data, are fundamentally different from intuitive types (and vice versa)? Can you see why they would be more tuned to concrete facts, in the "here and now," and less tuned in to abstractions, imaginings, possibilities and speculations? Now consider the notes under **Feeling** and **Thinking**. How are these two kinds of judgment statements basically different? Do they help to show the real differences between **F** types and **T** types?

CHECK YOUR KNOWLEDGE OF TYPE CONCEPTS

Before going on to applications of type to education and other settings, you may wish to see how well you grasp the concepts. To close the chapter I have included a word list you can use to review the ideas: Words to Help Understanding of Type Concepts. Following that is a Type Concepts Test and an answer key with which you may check your responses.

Don't be discouraged by the fact that learning about the types is a long, slow process. Fortunately, there are ways to put type concepts to work bit by bit as we learn them. Long before the complexities of all the types emerge in our understanding, we can use the concepts without distorting them or making them trivial. Each or any of the type dimensions — EI, SN, TF and JP — can be considered separately. If you have a basic grasp, say, of E and I, you can put it to work. For example, in a brief exchange with someone, guessing E or I may be useful as you decide whether you want to help the person process a thought aloud or allow time for the person to process the thought quietly inside.

In this EI example, all the 16 types are sorted into just two categories. That is the simplest way of using type ideas. Often, however, it

is far more revealing and useful to sort the types into four categories, as I do in Chapter 3 in presenting IS, ES, IN, and EN groupings as a practical way of looking at work settings likely to bring out peoples' best work.

After you have completed the Type Concepts Test and are reasonably sure you understand type concepts, the following activities will make a practical check of your understanding.

First, you might find several people (colleagues, family, students, etc.) who are interested in taking the Myers-Briggs Type Indicator. Arrange for a qualified person to administer it to them and explain the theory to them, with you serving as a helper in the explanations. If appropriate, have them check their comprehension with the Type Concepts Test. (This activity is less cumbersome than it sounds.) Typically, people who learn about type want to talk with someone about it. This activity encourages you to talk about type concepts with care, and thereby will test your comprehension of the theory and your ability to use the terminology appropriately.

Second, you can select a professional colleague to be a partner. Select a colleague whose type is different from yours. Arrange to observe each other informally in several different situations. Then discuss with each other the ways that type shows up in everyday behavior. You will want to use the booklet *Introduction to Type* — especially pages A-17 and A-18 — to get ideas of what to observe, and as a resource in developing your capacities to observe each other.

EXTRAVERSION When extraverting, I am . . .
Oriented to the outer world
Focusing on people and things
Active
Using trial and error with confidence
Scanning the environment for stimulation

SENSING PERCEPTION When using my sensing I am . . .
Perceiving with the five senses
Attending to practical and factual details
In touch with the physical realities
Attending to the present moment
Confining attention to what is said and done
Seeing "little things" in everyday life
Attending to step-by-step experiences
Letting "the eyes tell the mind"

THINKING JUDGMENT When reasoning with thinking, I am . . .
Using logical analysis
Using objective and impersonal criteria
Drawing cause and effect relationships
Being firm-minded
Prizing logical order
Being skeptical

JUDGMENT When I take a judging attitude, I am . . .
Using thinking or feeling judgment outwardly
Deciding and planning
Organizing and scheduling
Controlling and regulating
Goal oriented
Wanting closure, even when data are incomplete

INTROVERSION When introverting, I am . . .

Oriented to the inner world
Focusing on ideas, concepts, inner impressions
Reflective
Considering deeply before acting
Finding stimulation inwardly

 INTUITIVE PERCEPTION When using my intuition I am . . .

Perceiving with memory and associations
Seeing patterns and meanings
Seeing possibilities
Projecting possibilities for the future
Imagining; "reading between the lines"
Looking for the big picture
Having hunches; "ideas out of nowhere'
Letting "the mind tell the eyes"

 FEELING JUDGMENT When reasoning with feeling, I am . . .

Applying personal priorities
Weighing human values and motives, my own and others
Appreciating
Valuing warmth in relationships
Prizing harmony
Trusting

 PERCEPTION When I take a perceiving attitude, I am . . .

Using sensing or intuitive perception outwardly
Taking in information
Adapting and changing
Curious and interested
Open-minded
Resisting closure to obtain more data

TYPE CONCEPTS TEST*

Record your multiple-choice responses on a separate sheet and check your answers with the key that immediately follows the test. Some of the items have *more than one* correct answer.

1. Type theory is concerned with the valuable differences in personality that result from
   a. basic mental health
   b. environmental influences
   c. the way people perceive and judge
2. By extravert is meant
   a. a gregarious type who talks a lot
   b. a shallow person
   c. one who prefers to focus on people and things
3. By introvert is meant
   a. one who prefers to focus on ideas and concepts
   b. one who is aloof and unsociable
   c. a neurotic
4. By sensing type is meant
   a. one who is sensitive and empathic
   b. one who is sensuous
   c. one who prefers to perceive through the five senses
5. By intuitive type is meant
   a. one who has prophetic powers
   b. one who values imagination, inspirations and possibilities
   c. one who has extrasensory perception
6. By thinking judgment is meant making judgments
   a. by means of all the mental processes
   b. Logically and impersonally
   c. taking into account all the data
7. By feeling judgment is meant
   a. immature, emotional judgments
   b. irrational and illogical judgments
   c. judging on the basis of human motives and values
8. Sensing plus thinking people are mainly interested in
   a. facts which can be collected and verified by senses and analysis
   b. possibilities which reveal themselves in new data and experiences

---

This test was originally developed by Anna Nuernberger.

c. problems which allow them to use their ingenuity

9. Sensing plus feeling people are mainly interested in
   a. the impersonal and logical handling of other people
   b. making decisions about facts which take into account how people feel
   c. problems that allow them to use their imagination

10. The intuition plus feeling people are most interested in
    a. projects that involve them with equipment and tools
    b. possibilities for people
    c. facts about projects

11. The intuition plus thinking people
    a. enjoy practical problems
    b. are interested in possibilities which they approach with impersonal analysis
    c. choose projects that do not require executive or technical ability

12. The "tendencies" of the types
    a. are the way people are and nothing can be done about it
    b. are the talents you can aspire to realize, and the warnings of what to guard against
    c. are among the most useful learnings you can experience from understanding type theory

13. Certain types
    a. will have trouble with other types
    b. can be of more use to you than other types
    c. will be easier to understand than other types

14. In conflicts, you can use your understanding of type
    a. by being sensitive to the other person's type
    b. by being certain that the other person is aware of your point of view
    c. to understand what it is that one of you sees and values more highly than the other

15. In education, you can use your understanding of type
    a. to plan more effective learning situations according to type
    b. by expecting a person to focus on processes intrinsically comfortable to him
    c. to plan situations which exercise all the processes and give children broad choices in developing their own type preferences

ANSWERS TO THE TYPE CONCEPTS TEST

1. c. the way people perceive and judge. (Sensing and intuition are the perceiving processes; thinking and feeling are the judgment processes.)

   a. *Basic mental health is assumed to be associated with good type development, but it is not the basis of the theory.*

   b. *Environmental influences can indeed affect the way types develop, but they are not the main concern of type theory.*

2. c. one who prefers to focus on people and things

   a. *and b. answers may reveal prejudices you need to look at. Introverts may see extraverts as over-talkative and shallow, because introverts have little way of knowing how satisfying the company of others can be to extraverts.*

3. a. one who prefers to focus on ideas and concepts

   b. *and c. choices may indicate either that you do not understand the meaning of the word introvert, or that you have a prejudice that can affect your dealings with introverts. If you are an introvert yourself, you may lack the allegiance to your own type which is necessary for an effective and happy personality.*

4. c. one who prefers to perceive through the five senses.

   a. *and b. are not correct. Being a sensing type brings with it no assurance that one will be sensitive, empathic, or sensuous.*

5. b. one who values imagination, inspiration and possibilities.

   a. *and c. are not correct. Having a preference for intuition over sensing is no assurance that one has, or can attain, prophetic powers or extrasensory perception.*

6. b. logically and impersonally

   a. *In general language, thinking is often used to describe all the mental processes. In type theory, thinking is restricted to judgments made in a logical, impersonal way.*

   c. *Sensing perception is more associated with seeing all the data.*

7. c. judging on the basis of human motives and values. (A feeling judgment is one that comes to a rational conclusion by weighing the different human values and motives involved.)

   a. *and b. are not correct. Emotion in the dictionary is defined as "a strong surge of feeling marked by an impulse to outward expression, often accompanied by complex bodily reactions." When considering type, it is important to distinguish emotion (the visible expression of affect) from feeling, which is used to*

indicate a rational process of making decisions. Feeling judgment needs to be distinguished from emotional reaction. Feeling judgment can be mature or immature. Mature feeling insures that transitory pleasures do not outweigh long-term important values. Feeling is rational, but not intended to be logical, since logic is an aspect of thinking.

8. a. facts which can be verified by senses and analysis.

 b. and c. refer to activities more interesting to persons preferring intuition rather than sensing perception.

9. b. making decisions about facts which take into account how people feel.

 a. Impersonal and logical handling of people tends to be more interesting to thinking types.

 c. Problems which allow use of imagination are more interesting to intuitive types.

10. b. possibilities for people

 a. The sensing plus thinking people are more interested in equipment and tools.

 c. Sensing types are more interested than intuitives in facts about projects.

11. b. are interested in possibilities which they approach with impersonal analysis

 a. Sensing people are more likely to enjoy fact problems.

 c. People with the intuition, thinking, and judging combination are often interested in executive assignments.

12. b. are the talents you can aspire to realize, and the warnings of what to guard against. (The talents stem from the activities of the dominant and the second favorite processes; the warnings concern the consequences of lack of development of the other processes.)

 c. are among the most useful learnings you can experience from understanding type theory. Both b. and c. are correct choices.

 a. This answer is partially correct. The theory does assume that each person has some processes and attitudes that are more comfortable, and that these preferred processes suggest the person's best road to growth. The answer is wrong in assuming that nothing can be done about it. The essence of type development is in learning to use all one's processes in increasingly skillful and appropriate ways.

13. a., b., and c. are all correct answers for Question 13.
   a. will have trouble with other types. (People who are of very
      different types may have trouble getting along, especially if
      they do not understand type differences. They can be of great
      help to each other if they learn to respect their preferences
      and their different communication styles.)
   b. can be of more use to you than other types (Generally, peo-
      ple who are very much alike have little trouble in agreeing
      what should be done, but since they have similar abilities and
      deficits, they will be less help to each other than to people of
      somewhat different types.)
   c. will be easier to understand than other types. (Similar types
      typically, but not always, find it easier to understand each
      other.)
14. a. by being sensitive to the other person's type
   b. by being certain that the other person is aware of your point
      of view
   c. to understand what it is that one of you sees and values more
      highly than the other (All three answers are correct. If differ-
      ences are identified, understood and respected, they can be
      discussed rather than fought over.)
15. a. to plan more effective learning situations according to type
   b. by expecting people to focus on processes intrinsically com-
      fortable for them
   c. to plan situations which exercise all the processes and give
      children broad choices in developing their own type prefer-
      ences (All three choices are correct. Although all of us use all
      four mental processes, exercise both perception and judg-
      ment, and experience both the outer and inner worlds in
      varying degrees, we learn best when we can learn according
      to the strengths of our own type.)

2

TYPE, MOTIVATION, AND LEARNING STYLE

INTRODUCTION: THE PROCESS OF STUDYING TYPE THEORY

Learning about type takes time. Not just the time given to reading about it in this and other books. It takes time to soak in, to show its value, and to get integrated into one's view of human nature. A keen interest in it speeds the process, but it seems to follow a progression that won't be rushed very much.

From my first contact with the Myers-Briggs Type Indicator and Jung's idea of the psychological types, I saw type theory as an important contribution to my area of work — the improvement of teaching and curriculum work. The outcomes of formal education depend so much on understanding student differences in motivation, interests, learning styles, and aptitudes. I was very grateful to be introduced to a theory that was yielding useful insights into these differences in students.

Even though my beginner's understanding was just on the surface of the rich and deep theory, many applications of type to teaching showed themselves to me from the first. Though the 20+ years since then, my understanding has evolved and deepened in a progression that other people learning about type have also experienced. Your understanding of type may follow a similar pattern. It does take time.

A progression of understanding

At the beginning I saw the usefulness of type in terms of the separate dimensions: EI, SN, TF, and JP. While application to my work was my initial motivation, I soon found my uses of type were superficial until I began to study the meanings of type differences in my own family and among other people I was closest to. I needed to explore with them the personal experiencing of our own type preferences — how daily life is experienced differently through the extravert's and introvert's viewpoint, etc. — before I could get beyond the surface, in applications to my work. We had to ask of each other uncounted questions, and then try out and agree on language about introversion and extraversion that fairly represented these two ways of being in the world, with a minimum of stereotyping. Similarly, we developed our understandings of SN, TF, and JP.

Some questions I asked were about their learning styles and interests, and problems in classrooms. After having the responses of those most close to me, I felt ready to frame questions for people I did not know or know well. At that point, I was still focused on the four separate dimensions of type. I began to look for evidence of type preferences in action in classrooms, in my own and other peoples' classrooms where I could be an observer. New understandings about type seemed to come best to me through these kinds of direct experiences at work and at home.

The approach to learning about type I have described so far may be more an extravert's way than an introvert's. But I believe that starting in the inner circle of family and friends and gradually working out to the wider circles is a general approach for learning about type that will be effective for most people.

In those days, when I started teaching people about type, I concentrated on the four dimensions. If we think of the four dimensions as the first layer of type theory, I stayed in that layer a long time. I knew there was more to type theory, but until I understood the more complex aspects of type by seeing them reflected in my family life, I didn't see their importance in my work.

Deeper layers

Next in my progression was recognizing the power of the dominant process, as I suggested in the table in Chapter 1: "Brief Descriptions of the Sixteen Types," and the accompanying paragraphs. Soon after, I saw that the orientation of the dominant, extraverted or introverted, made dramatic differences in peoples' basic motivations and their approach to communication with others. Several years passed before I could call quickly to mind the dynamics of each of the 16 types. Type dynamics is the topic of

Chapter 8. Learning about type requires time, a gestation period. Allow it the time needed.

In my work I have studied many theories concerned with explaining human nature. None has been richer or more rewarding than type theory. The deeper I go into it, the more it reveals. Its value does not fade or become overshadowed by more comprehensive ideas, as have most of the other theories I have encountered. I believe you will find it worth all the effort you give to studying it and using it. I hope this book substantially speeds your process of understanding type. But be aware that you get from one layer of understanding to another only as you make applications of the ideas and let the results show you deeper aspects to study.

TYPE AS A WAY OF CLASSIFYING BEHAVIOR

Carl Jung saw his psychological types as a distinctive way of classifying human behavior. His research showed him that many of our behaviors cluster in patterns that seem to reveal different frames of mind, distinctly different ways of processing our experiences. His theory of psychological types stands apart from other modern theories of psychology. While all psychology is concerned with behavior traits, Jung distinguished types from traits.

Type preferences are not traits

For example, extraversion can be seen as a type preference or as a trait. Jung devised the term to characterize a type preference, as the polar opposite of introversion. It is an either-or category. Like pregnancy — one is either pregnant or not; no one is a little pregnant or a lot. The Myers-Briggs Type Indicator sorts people into one category or the other. Traits, on the other hand, are not sorting categories, they are characteristics that are measured. Treated as a trait, extraversion would be measured; a person would have a lot of it, a little of it, or some quantity in between. You can take a psychological test that includes extraversion and introversion as traits. It is possible for someone to score equally high on both traits, meaning that the person may be equally skilled at extraverting and introverting, has both skills readily available when needed. Or score higher on one and lower on the other. Or low on both, suggesting that these traits are not well developed. That is not what type is about.

Just as there are no types better than other types, there is no such thing as too much or too little of a type preference. When someone says, "She's too extraverted" or "He's an extravert off the wall," extraversion is being treated as a trait. What is meant in this shorthand language is not that the person has too high a score on E as a type preference. Rather, it means that the person has traits such as talkativeness, gregariousness or self-disclosure that aren't being managed well.

The preference scores you get from taking the MBTI are not a measurement of skillfulness, maturity, balance, or any other quality. The MBTI scores have two parts, a letter and a number on each of the four scales. The letter, such as E for extraversion, reports which of two polar-opposite categories your answers sorted you into. The number part of the score suggests how much you prefer one over the other.

Of course, the type preferences have traits that tend to cluster with them; for example, introverts valuing privacy more that extraverts, having greater capacity for sustained concentration, etc.

It is natural for people who prefer introversion to be more developed in skill traits such as sustained concentration because they cultivate their introverting side and spend more time using such traits.

When explaining type, we use clusters of traits to help define the type preferences. Throughout the book, wherever there are lists associated with the type preferences, the terms listed represent traits. For example, decisiveness and a need for closure and planning are traits that go with the J type preference, and flexibility, adaptability, and a need for openness are traits that go with the P type preference.

Mistaking type preferences as traits

People often mistakenly treat a type preference as a trait. For example, someone who comes out J on the MBTI may say, "I really have to work on my P; I need to be more flexible and spontaneous. Next time I take the MBTI I hope I score as a P." The person sees J and P as traits, something that can be worked on and changed, as one might take some training on assertiveness to become more assertive. The person who came out J may indeed work on the traits of spontaneity and flexibility. But if the type report is correct and the person uses mainly a judgment process in running his or her outer life, no amount of work on traits associated with the P preference will change him or her to having a perceiving process running the outer life. For the J person, working on traits such as spontaneity has to be done from a J mind-set. The J has to plan when and how to be spontaneous, how to allow time and opportunity for it. The type preference does not change; the person remains a J who is getting better at traits that do not come naturally to a J.

In summary, type preferences are not traits, or even clusters of traits. They are preferred ways of being in the world, different mind-sets, different ways of experiencing life's daily events and processing the experiences. The 16 type designations represent 16 different patterns of organization of mental energy. It follows, then, that the types also represent different patterns of motivations, interests, learning styles, and aptitudes.

TYPE AND MOTIVATION

Motivation is a key issue in every theory about human nature. Because this is a book for practitioners rather than for theorists, I don't try to show this view of motivation in relation to other views. I just address the practical question: What does type theory tell us about peoples' motivations in their everyday lives? Motivations and learning styles are discussed in this chapter as they appear in school and colleges. Readers concerned with peoples' motivations and learning styles outside formal education, such as trainers who work in organizations, will see that the type differences described here are consistent in all aspects of life, wherever the learning happens, and not just in classrooms.

Schools across the United States, urban and rural, big and small, report that students' lack of motivation for school tasks is one of the most persistent and perplexing problems. Student motivation is, of course, very complex, having its roots in family life, peer relationships and societal pressures that lie beyond the teacher's range of influence. But teachers do have the power to affect student motivation in some respects; and one key to that power can be seen in the type concepts.

Four aspects of motivation

Type theory suggests that we break down motivation into four parts, corresponding to the four dimensions of type:

1. The extraversion-introversion preference shows the broad areas of a person's **natural interests**. Extraverted people are, by nature, continuously alert to events outside themselves, turning outward to pick up cues, ideas, expectations, values and interests. This inclination to scan the environment gives them a variety of inter-

ests. In contrast, introverted people naturally look inward for resources and cues, and pursue fewer interests more deeply. Attending more often to the inner storehouse of perceptions and judgments, introverts take a reflective approach to life, while extraverts take an active, trial-and-error approach. Of course, extraverts often do look inward and introverts often do turn outward. All four pairs of preferences described in this section refer to habitual, but not constant tendencies.

2. The sensing-intuition preference reveals basic **learning style** differences. In learning situations, sensing people attend most often to the literal meaning they find in concrete experiences. They learn best by moving step-by-step through a new experience, with their senses as engaged as possible. Intuitive learners' attention is drawn most often to things that stimulate imagination, to possibilities not found in sensory experience. Their minds work by skips and jumps, looking for patterns wherever the inspiration takes them. The other three dimensions of type also have learning style preferences associated with them, but the SN differences are the most basic.

3. The thinking-feeling dimension shows patterns of **commitments and values**. People who prefer thinking commit to activities that respond to logical analysis, and to situations where human factors don't have to be a primary concern. People who prefer feeling commit to personal relationships and to situations that call on their harmonizing ability.

4. The judging-perceiving dimension shows **work habits**. People with a judging attitude are drawn toward closure, wanting a clear work plan to follow. Disliking unsettled situations, they may sometimes lock into a course of action without looking at enough of the relevant data. People with a perceiving attitude resist closure, wanting to keep all channels open for new data. Disliking fixed plans, they may sometimes postpone decisions, leaving much to be done in a rush as a deadline closes in on them.

By taking these four natural motivation patterns into account in planning instruction, by working with them rather than against them, teachers can better direct student energies toward learning. This chapter and the next two show how type concepts can be used to help focus our own and others' mental energies for effective learning and working.

TYPE AND LEARNING STYLE

Motivation and learning style are overlapping categories. When we are focused on how people effectively approach learning tasks, motivation is a part of learning style. Psychological type and learning style overlap also. Type and learning style are certainly not synonymous. Type preferences reveal a lot about learning preferences, but some learning strategies are independent of one's type.

What is meant by learning styles? The term is used variously and loosely in educational literature. I have tried to pin it down with a definition. I use "learning styles" broadly to cover four aspects of psychological makeup:

A. Cognitive style in the sense of preferred or habitual patterns of mental functioning: information processing, formation of ideas, and judgments.

B. Patterns of attitudes and interests that influence what a person will attend to in a potential learning situation.

C. A disposition to seek out learning environments compatible with one's cognitive style, attitudes and interests, and to avoid environments that are not congenial.

D. Similarly, a disposition to use certain learning tools, to use them successfully, and avoid other tools.

Researchers tell us that all of us change some of our learning strategies from situation to situation, from teacher to teacher. Other strategies we want to keep the same in all situations if we can. Type preferences fall in this latter category. There is ample evidence that they remain the same through all situations. Even in those situations that call on us to produce behaviors quite different from our usual ways of acting, our type preferences don't change. So the aspects of learning style that are a reflection of one's type can be expected to persist across situations. That expectation is confirmed by the research on learning styles that involved the MBTI.

Those of us who use type theory as a tool to help us teach and advise students make many assumptions about the ways that students of different types want to learn or ways they do learn most effectively. To see whether our assumptions from type theory were supported by empirical evidence, I examined all the published reports of research — now more than 130 — that used the MBTI in studies of learning, teaching, and academic aptitudes. I first examined the research reports in 1984 (published in Volume 8 of the *Journal of Psychological Type*), and updated the review recently. About one-fourth of the studies gave some indirect evidence of learning style preferences, and another fourth actually tested learning style hypotheses.

Over eighty per cent of the studies analyzed learning style differences by examining the four MBTI scales separately rather than by using the 16 preference types. That choice was dictated, in many cases, by sample size; obtaining adequate numbers for the 16 categories takes a fairly large sample. For that reason, most of the results I have summarized here are given by the four scale categories.

With a very few exceptions — where research results were ambiguous or unclear — all of the research outcomes support type theory as presented by Isabel Myers. I have combined and summarized the results in table form. The four tables report what learning style behaviors or clearly reported preferences were associated with the type preference categories in the research. Readers who understand type and observe learning styles may feel that some important learning preferences are missing in these lists. For example, in Table 2., under ES types, there is no mention of the preference for action; and in Table 3., under SF types, a preference for group projects is not included. What you see here is what the researchers reported, which is not as encompassing as the anecdotal evidence of teachers who are experienced in using type.

Following the tables are narrative summaries that are easier to read but are less compact. They incorporate the research conclusions and are somewhat expanded by observations by teachers who know type theory and type behaviors well.

TABLE 1. LEARNING PREFERENCES
ASSOCIATED WITH DIMENSIONS OF MBTI TYPE

EXTRAVERSION
- talking, discussion
- psychomotor activity
- working with a group

INTROVERSION
- reading, verbal reasoning
- time for internal processing
- working individually

SENSING
- tasks that call for carefulness, thoroughness, and soundness of understanding
- going step-by-step

INTUITION
- tasks that call for quickness of insight and in seeing relationships
- finding own way in new material

- tasks that call for observing specifics
- tasks that call for memory (recall) of facts
- practical interests (independent of intelligence)

- tasks that call for grasping general concepts
- tasks that call for imagination

- intellectual interests

THINKING	FEELING
- teacher's logical organization - objective material to study - depth and accuracy of content - personal connection to content	- personal rapport with teacher - learning through personal relationships

JUDGING	PERCEIVING
- work in steady, orderly way - formalized instruction - prescribed tasks - drive toward closure, completion	- work in flexible way, follow impulses - informal problem solving - discovery tasks - managing emerging problems

TABLE 2. LEARNING PREFERENCES ASSOCIATED WITH MBTI TYPES BY QUADRANTS

IS__TYPES	IN__TYPES
- demonstrations - labs - computer assisted instruction - films, audio-visual aids	- serious reading - tutorials - independent study - systematically organized courses

ES__TYPES	EN__TYPES
- television - reports to class on topics selected by students - scheduling my time - having a schedule and sticking to it - orderly work on goals set in advance	- reading - self-instruction - courses that put me on my own initiative - working on group projects - meeting a lot of people - opportunities to be creative and original

TABLE 3. LEARNING PREFERENCES ASSOCIATED WITH MBTI TYPES BY MENTAL PROCESS COMBINATIONS

_ST_ TYPES
- demonstrations

- labs

- television
- having a plan and sticking to it
- having a study schedule

_SF_ TYPES
- student-led demonstrations or presentations
- instruction with personal involvement
- television
- films and audiovisuals

_NF_ TYPES
- learn through personal relationships
- dislike impersonal, didactic instruction
- highly value faculty feedback
- low-friction student-led discussions
- opportunities to be creative and original

_NT_ TYPES
- organized teacher lectures

- self-instruction

- reading, researching
- systematically organized discourses

TABLE 4. LEARNING PREFERENCES ASSOCIATED WITH MBTI TYPES BY PERCEPTION AND ATTITUDE COMBINATIONS

_S_P TYPES: Structured exploratory observation, hands-on
_S_J TYPES: Structured, didactic, well-organized, sensory-rich instruction
_N_P TYPES: Low structure, inductive instruction
_N_J TYPES: Moderate to high structure, "serious" instruction

SUMMARIES OF THE LEARNING PREFERENCES

HOW THE E AND I PREFERENCES AFFECT LEARNING

EXTRAVERSION

Cognitive style: The extraversion preference is associated with a cognitive style that favors:
- learning by talking and physically engaging the environment,
- letting attention flow outward toward objective events,
- talking to help thoughts to form and become clear,
- learning through interactions, verbal and non-verbal.

Study style: The extraversion preference is associated with a study style that favors:
- acting first, reflecting after,
- plunging into new material,
- starting interactions needed to stimulate reflection and concentration,
- having a strong, interesting, external-extraverted reason for studying, beyond learning for its own sake,
- avoiding distractions that will cut into their concentration,
- studying with a friend,
- studying to prepare to teach someone.

Instruction that fits E's: The extraverting types do their best work with:
- opportunities to "think out loud"; for example, one-to-one with the teacher, classroom discussions, working with another student, action projects involving people,
- learning activities that have an effect outside the learner, such as visible results from a project,
- teachers who manage classroom dialogue so that extraverts have ways to clarify their ideas before they add them to class discussion,
- assignments that let them see what other people are doing and what they regard as important.

INTROVERSION

Cognitive style: The introversion preference is associated with a cognitive style that favors:
- quiet reflection,
- keeping one's thoughts inside until they are polished,
- letting attention flow inward,
- being engrossed in inner events: ideas, impressions, concepts,
- learning in private, individual ways.

Study style: The introversion preference is associated with a study style that favors:
- reflecting first, acting after (if necessary),
- looking for new data to fit into the internal dialogue that is always going on,
- working privately — perhaps checking one's work with someone who is trusted,
- reading as the main way of studying,
- listening to others talk about the topic being studied, and privately processing what they take in,
- extraverting just when they choose to.

Instruction that fits I's: I's like learning situations that let them:
- work internally with their own thoughts: listening, observing, lab work, reading, writing,
- processing their experiences at their own pace,
- present the results of their work in forms that let them keep their privacy,
- have ample time to polish their work before needing to present it,
- have time to reflect before answering the teacher's questions.
- tie their studies to their own personal interests, their internal agenda.

SENSING

Cognitive style: The sensing preference is associated with a cognitive style that favors:
- memory of facts,
- observing specifics,
- processing data step by step,
- starting with the concrete, then moving to abstract,
- being careful and thorough,
- aiming toward soundness of understanding,
- staying connected to practical realities around them,
- being attentive to what is in the present moment.

Study style: The sensing preference is associated with a study style that favors:
- a sequential, step by step approach to new material,
- beginning with familiar, solid facts,
- moving gradually toward abstract concepts and principles;
- approaching abstract principals and concepts by distilling them out of their own personal, concrete experience.

Instruction that fits S's: S's do best with instruction that allows them to hear and touch as well as see (or only read about) what they are learning. They like:
- hands-on labs,
- relevant films and other audiovisual presentations,
- materials that can be handled,
- computer-assisted instruction,
- first-hand experience that gives practice in the skills and concepts to be learned,
- teachers who provide concrete learning experiences first in any learning sequence, before using the textbook,
- teachers who show them exactly what is expected of them,
- teachers who do not move "too quickly" through material, touching just the high spots or jumping from thought to thought,
- assignments that do not expect them to generate possibilities not based on solid facts,
- skills and facts they can use in their present lives.

Being naturally observant of details in the here and now, they tend to overlook the big picture, general meanings, and implications for the future.

They believe the adult world has specific skills and facts they should be taught, and they are disappointed in any teacher who expects them to discover them for themselves.

INTUITION

Cognitive style: The intuition preference is associated with a cognitive style that prefers:
- being caught up in inspiration,
- moving quickly in seeing associations and meanings,
- reading between the lines,
- relying on insight more than careful observation,
- relying on verbal fluency more than on memory of facts,
- focusing on general concepts more than details and practical matters.

Study style: Intuitives typically adopt a study style that includes:
- following inspirations,
- jumping into new material to pursue an intriguing concept,
- finding their own way through new material, hopping from concept to concept,
- attending to details only after the big picture is clear,
- exploring new skills rather than honing present ones,
- reading.

Instruction that fits N's: The intuitive types do their best work with:
- learning assignments that put them on their own initiative, individually or with a group,
- real choices in the ways they work out their assignments,
- opportunities to find their own ways to solve problems,
- opportunities to be inventive and original,
- opportunities for self-instruction, individually or with a group,
- a system of individual contracts between teacher and students.

Intuitive types like beginnings a lot more than endings, because beginnings are fired with the fascination of new possibilities. When they have study assignments they can be enthusiastic about, they are much more likely to carry them to the finish line.

In high school and beyond, they generally like experiences rich with complexities, which may include stimulating lectures.

After a concept or skill is understood to their satisfaction, they may find continued practice boring, shift over to new inspirations, and never achieve complete mastery.

They get frustrated with the teacher who paces instruction "too slowly."

HOW THE T AND F PREFERENCES AFFECT LEARNING

THINKING

Cognitive style: The thinking preference is associated with a cognitive style that favors:

- making impersonal judgments, aiming toward objective truth,
- keeping mental life ordered by logical principles,
- analyzing experiences to find logical principles underlying them,
- staying free from emotional concerns while making decisions,
- naturally critiquing things, aiming toward clarity and precision.

Study style: Thinking types typically adopt a study style that includes:

- having objective material to study,
- compartmentalizing emotional issues to get clear thinking on the task at hand,
- analyzing problems to bring logical order out of confusion,
- wanting to get a sense of mastery over the material being studied.

Instruction that fits Ts: The thinking types do their best work with:

- teachers who are logically organized,
- subjects and materials that flow logically and respond to logic,
- feedback that shows them their specific, objective achievements.

FEELING

Cognitive style: The feeling preference is associated with a cognitive style that favors:

- making value judgments concerning human motives and personal values,
- attending to relationships,
- personalizing issues and causes they care about,
- staying tuned to the quality of the subjective tone of relationships and seeking harmony in relationships,
- attending to the quality of their own emotional life,
- naturally appreciating people and their accomplishments.

Study style: Feeling types typically adopt a study style that includes:

- learning through personal relationships rather than impersonal individualized activities,
- learning by helping and responding to other peoples' needs,
- studying with a friend,
- wanting to choose topics to study that they care deeply about.

Instruction that fits Fs: The feeling types do their best work with:

- teachers who value a personal rapport with students,
- assignments that have a goal of helping people,
- feedback that shows warm appreciation for the student and his or her effort, and gives corrective suggestions in that context,
- personalized assignments.

JUDGMENT

Cognitive style: The judging preference is associated with a cognitive style that favors:
- having a clear structure in a learning situation from the beginning,
- aiming toward completions and getting closure,
- having life organized into an orderly plan.

Study style: Judging types typically adopt a study style that includes:
- planful and scheduled work, drawing energy from the steady, orderly process of doing their work,
- wanting to know exactly what they are accountable for and by what standards they will be judged,
- treating assignments as serious business, and persisting in doing them.

Instruction that fits Js: The judging types do their best work with:
- pre-planned structure, and a teacher who carefully provides it,
- predictability and consistency,
- formalized instruction that moves in orderly sequences,
- prescribed tasks,
- milestones, completion points, with little ceremonies to honor successful completions.

PERCEPTION

Cognitive style: The perceiving preference is associated with a cognitive style that favors:
- open exploration without a pre-planned structure,
- staying open to new experience,
- managing emerging problems with emerging structures,
- the stimulation of something new and different.

Study style: Perceiving types typically adopt a study style that includes:
- spontaneously following their curiosity,
- studying when the surges of impulsive energy come to them,
- studying to discover something new to them,
- finding novel ways to do routine assignments so as to spark enough interest to do the assignments.

Instruction that fits Ps: The perceiving types do their best work when:
- they can pursue problems in their own way,
- they have genuine choices in assignments, as with a system of individual contracts in which the student can negotiate some of the activities,
- assignments make sense to them,
- their work feels like play.

Do these learning style patterns ring true for you? Discuss them with friends and colleagues whose type preferences are different from yours.

The obvious question that comes to mind is, How can so many differences be accommodated in one classroom? In the next chapter, we will consider applications of these learning style differences in the daily business of classrooms.

3

USING TYPE CONCEPTS IN PLANNING INSTRUCTION

THE SIXTEEN TYPES ARE NOT EQUALLY REPRESENTED

The sixteen types are not equally represented in the school population. It is hard to estimate the distributions of types in the general population because different occupations and different educational levels have their own characteristically different type distributions. The estimates given below are composites from several data sets of students and adults.

Extraversion 66% ---------- ---------- *Introversion 33%*
Sensing 66% --------------------------- *Intuition 33%*
Thinking (female) 33% ---------- *Feeling (female) 66%*
Thinking (male) 60% -------------- *Feeling (male) 40%*
Judgment 55% ------------------------- *Perception 45%**

This means many more students are ESFJ, for example, than are INFJ, and more are ENFJ than INFJ. The uneven distribution of the first two type dimensions, EI and SN, is a crucial fact for teachers, as can

| IS 8 | IN 4 |
| ES 15 | EN 8 |

be seen in the diagram following. A typical classroom of 35 students would have this distribution of types:

The distribution might be different for elective courses because students' type preferences often influence their choices of electives. The distribution

---

These and other statistics presented in the chapter are from Myers, I.B. and McCaulley, M.H. (1985). Manual: A Guide to the Development and Use of the Myers-Briggs Type Indicator. Palo Alto, CA: Consulting Psychologists Press, Chapter 4.

is different in college samples; in general, college students are more evenly divided between E and I and between S and N.

SCHOOL INSTRUCTION FITS SOME TYPES BETTER THAN OTHERS

If a classroom has four times as many ES__ types as IN__ types, what does that mean to the teacher? The question brings us to the second key fact: most school instruction gives an advantage to some types and handicaps others.

Consider these three descriptions; do you regard them as typical of school instruction patterns?

1. Students work individually on their own tasks, each with his/her own set of materials or books. Quiet is expected so each one can concentrate and think through the work individually.

2. When new concepts or rules are introduced, the teacher or textbook tries to follow a sequence of first presenting the concept verbally, defining it; then giving examples, illustrations and/or demonstrations; and finally (at least sometimes) giving students an opportunity to use the concept or rule.

3. The main medium of instruction is words, spoken or written symbols. A student's successful manipulation of words in a dialogue or on tests is the primary way that teachers have of judging a student's achievement. In the case of mathematics and some science knowledge, the symbols of instruction are abstractions representing things other than words.

Are the three descriptions typical? Yes, so much that they seem to be essential. Yet they clearly favor certain types of students. The first one is a natural format for introverts, who prefer to do most of their work quietly inside their own heads, to keep ideas inside until they are polished and ready to be exposed. Extraverts, two-thirds of the students, really do their best thinking with their mouths open. Their thoughts come more clear as they hear them spoken. The most natural setting for extraverts, the one in which they learn best, is one that allows them to think out loud and to act — that is, to do, make, move, produce — rather than just read and recite words about such

actions. The testing of ideas and skills in the outer world tells the extravert whether the half-formed ideas and skills are worth having. The introvert, on the other hand, prefers to test ideas against private criteria, in the inner world of the mind — a process that is much easier for schools to manage.

The second classroom practice described above, that of presenting abstractions first and applications after, appeals to the intuitive's learning style, not to the sensing type. Abstractions, such as definitions, theories, lists of procedures and rules, help intuitive types get into a topic because they want to see the abstract meaning, the relationships to prior knowledge, the "big picture," before they take on new concrete experience.

An example from a student

A conversation that I had with a student at a diesel mechanics school will illustrate the conventional intuitive bias of instruction; that is, abstractions first and concrete experience after. The student was complaining about paper and pencil tests, saying he did much better with "hands-on" tests in the shop. "I think better with my hands." When asked to give an example, he told of being given a defective alternator he was to take apart, fix and reassemble. He was given a diagram to guide him in the operation. "I studied the diagram and studied it until I thought I would puke. I couldn't understand it. So I threw down the diagram. I took the alternator apart, carefully laying it down in a pattern. Then I saw the problem, fixed it, and reversed my pattern to put it back together. It worked perfectly." Did he look at the diagram afterwards? "Yes." Did he understand it then? "Yes, sure. It made sense then." To this sensing type student, the abstract diagram made sense as a map of the complex territory only after he first put his senses to work in understanding the territory. It seems likely that similar diagrams he encounters in the future will be more useful to him.

Probably the young man was an ES__ type. His best learning came when he could use a combination of senses, actively operating on the realities of his tangible environment. Note that he did not follow the prescribed sequence of instruction, beginning with the abstraction, the diagram.

Contrast this student's experience with that of an ENFP, a type with intuition dominant. He was disgusted with his community college auto mechanics class. It convened for two weeks without books. "All we

do is stand around the cars and take parts off and put them back on."
He was ready to quit. His mother, knowing about type, urged him to
stay until the books arrived. When they came and he then had the
words and other symbols he needed to understand the principles, he
could begin to understand the machines.

Type and the skills of reading

How extensively are standard instruction practices biased toward
introversion and intuition? No careful analysis has been made, but the
bias is widespread. Probably the young child first encounters it in the
teaching of reading. Of course, reading is primarily an introverted
activity; it is done quietly by oneself. And it is fundamentally an intuitive activity, involving abstractions — the printed symbols. But reading need not be taught as if all students were introverts and intuitives.
The skills of reading can be and are mastered by students of all types,
and students of all types can leave school with a positive attitude
toward reading.

Tragically many students are alienated by their first encounters with
reading instruction. Type theory points to the probability that most of
the alienated children are extraverted and sensing types. There are
data showing that the dropout rate is much higher among sensing
children. Isabel Myers obtained type data from 500 people who did
not finish 8th grade; 99% of them were sensing types.

What setting for reading instruction appeals to ES__ types? They
learn best through action, with many chances to talk. Reading aloud
with a partner is useful. They can be asked to recall a concrete experience that is worth recording, or the teacher can provide such an
experience. If the child wants to report an experience to someone
not present, he or she can dictate it and see it transcribed; this
process demonstrates writing and recording as activities that are
interesting and useful.

To the sensing types, exercises such as reading "sight words" may
seem like learning nonsense syllables; it is more useful to help them
decode printed language through phonics and word attack skills. Most
S children need explicit practice in matching sounds to letters until
they have mastered them all and are no longer mystified by the
printed symbols. When their first excursions into reading begin with
putting sounds to letters and letter combinations, they are more likely
to experience reading as enjoyable.

Once the basics are mastered, sensing students will benefit greatly from exercises that focus their attention on the meaning of what they have read; interpretation of meanings requires the use of intuition, and sensing children are less likely to do this easily without careful teaching.

While adult reading is mostly a silent, individual activity, type theory suggests that reading should be taught to most children as a social process. First in a small group with other children at the same level of decoding skills, sounding out letters and words as other children listen and follow along. Then reading aloud in the same groups from stories that contain the mastered words. Then writing together and reading aloud; sharing stories, writing scripts to be acted; quizzing a partner on vocabulary and spelling; teamwork in writing and critiquing letters, reports and newspapers they write to be read by people whose opinions matter to the writers; reading aloud to younger people or to anyone else who will listen; and any other such activities that demonstrate reading as a social transaction. The content of reading, as much as possible, should be words from the students' lives that have a direct connection to their concrete experiences. These techniques, from mastery of the code through writing for the benefit of others, will help eliminate the bias of instruction that disadvantages the ES__ types.

Type and testing

Correcting the biases of instruction that harm ES__ children is perhaps the most crucial unrecognized problem of American education. No doubt the biases are largely unconscious, unintended. In my experience, most textbook writers are intuitive types, as are the writers of standardized tests. Most are probably unaware that their products reflect their own intuitive way of viewing the world, their way of approaching learning tasks. Writers of pencil and paper intelligence tests, also intuitives, most likely are unaware that their tests have a bias toward the kind of intelligence they value most, intuitive intelligence (manipulating symbols, drawing inferences, and the like).

Considering the biases, there is no surprise in the fact that IN__ students as a group score highest on intelligence tests, followed by EN__, IS__, and ES__, in that order. Why do sensing types, on average, score lower that intuitive types? First because the symbols of language have to be translated into meaning. That is done by intuition. On paper tests, a double translation is needed, printed symbols into words, and words

into meanings. It is a slower and less confident process for sensing types. The second reason is because the tests concern abstractions. Sensing types are more at home with the facts of a situation. As Isabel Myers has noted, they do not automatically link idea to idea, as intuitive types tend to do, but want to test ideas against known facts, a process that takes more time. Aiming for this kind of thoroughness, the sensing types are especially unfairly evaluated by timed paper-and-pencil tests.

In my notes of conversations with her, I found an anecdote Myers told that suggests an aspect of sensing intelligence not reached by such tests. "Speaking of where sensing people are bright and an intuitive may stub his toe, at one time somewhere we had a refractory lock which was hard to turn. I was struggling and getting nowhere and Chief [her husband, a sensing type] said, 'Can't you feel what's going on in there?' And I said I couldn't. That must have meant some sensation there carried a very instructive meaning to which I was absolutely oblivious. I'm sufficiently intelligent, but not on that side." Myers' contrast of her intuitive intelligence with that of her husband's sensing intelligence highlights for me the inadequacy of paper-and-pencil tests to measure some aspects of sensing knowledge.

My experience tells me that the unconscious bias toward intuitive intelligence stretches from Kindergarten through graduate school. There is an assumption, certainly from secondary education on, that intuition is a higher form of mentality than sensing, that brighter people grow beyond their dependence on sensory processing to the "higher stage" of abstract processing. This view is incorrectly rationalized by citing theories of cognitive development such as those of Piaget and Kohlberg. Those theories do not address the mental preferences of sensing and intuition as Jung characterized them. Mixing the two theories of cognitive development together is like combining apples and oranges.

I am reminded of a T-shirt I got from a friend who knows I am left-handed. It reads, "Everyone is born right-handed. Only the greatest overcome it." I hope this book adequately makes the case that the sensing preference is not something to be outgrown or overcome. I strongly believe that the record of American education in the twentieth century is, among other things, a record of neglect of sensing intelligence, an intelligence typified by the young diesel mechanics student who bypassed the prescribed instruction process and solved his problem his way — and the kind of intelligence possessed by the majority of American students.

However, the biases in instruction — the teaching, textbooks, and testing — that handicap the extraverted sensing students do not make the instruction ideal for the introverts or intuitives. Introverts with a sensing preference are not benefitted by instruction with an intuitive bias. And many intuitives have told me of the boredom and frustration they have felt when instruction was too cut and dried, too pro-grammed, and not giving them enough elbow room for their intuitions to range through the material in a satisfying way. Many intuitives said the instruction they experienced was biased against them.

PLANNING INSTRUCTION TO
HONOR THE RIGHTS OF EVERY TYPE

Certainly, all students have a right to a learning setting that will offer them their best opportunity to develop. That is an ideal everyone subscribes to, and everyone knows it is still beyond our reach. Type theory provides some new insights into how to improve learning set-tings to serve all students better.

Trying to improve our conventional instruction practices using type theory or any other ideas takes hard work and a lot of time. Having helped many people get started using type in schools and colleges, I know it can be done and is worth the effort. Such a broad and long-term task has to be accomplished one classroom at a time, in small steps. I have included in this chapter ideas for using type that represent many steps, small and large. They can only be undertaken one or a few at a time. Start small, and confirm for yourself that each step is an improve-ment. If you start on a grand scale while you are just beginning to understand type concepts, you are likely to undermine your own plan.

Start small, perhaps just planning ways to get more physical activity and constructive dialogue into your instruction plans. Or find more con-crete experiences to supplement the abstractions presented in our text-books. Consider starting lessons with concrete experiences before the students open the textbook to read about the subject of the lesson. In this chapter and Chapters 9 and 10 you will find a progression of ideas that may take several years to gradually introduce into a classroom or curriculum. Start with one or two ideas where·your understanding of type seems most secure.

This section provides a number of ways for you to begin using type concepts in planning instruction. The first of these is an exercise entitled Four Work Settings. The exercise is made up of four checklists. Use them

first to identify your own most preferred and least preferred work or learning settings. Follow the directions for the exercise. You may want to mark

EXERCISE: FOUR WORK SETTINGS

Directions

Step One: Put a check mark beside those items that are true for you, on all four lists.

Step Two: Go back over all four lists. Draw a circle around the check marks for those items that are strongly true of you.

PATTERN A
I AM LIKELY TO DO MY BEST WORK IN SITUATIONS THAT:

___ make practical sense to me

___ have a clear organization in them

___ are practical and realistic

___ let me know just what is expected of me

___ let me work at a steady speed, step-by-step

___ require accuracy and careful attention to details

___ require patience

___ don't have many surprises in them

___ let me use my practical experience

___ let me use my memory for facts

___ let me think through a problem by myself before I have to act on it

PATTERN B
I AM LIKELY TO DO MY BEST WORK IN SITUATIONS THAT:

___ will produce practical results, useful products

___ involve other people or take group effort

___ let me work toward goals step by step in an orderly way

___ are real and not just dealing with theory

___ give me a clear picture of what other people are doing and what they regard as important

___ have realistic schedules that don't expect too much too soon

___ let me learn from first-hand experience, on the job

___ let me use the practical skills and facts I possess

___ give me a regular work schedule, but give me some variety and time to socialize, too

___ let me work with concrete things, hands-on materials

___ let me "think out loud" with other people

the checklist items lightly in pencil, so that you can erase the marks later
and use the pages as masters to photocopy for your students to respond to.

PATTERN C
I AM LIKELY TO DO MY BEST WORK IN SITUATIONS THAT:
___ let me work in my head with my own ideas
___ let me work toward solutions in my own way
___ give me a chance to be creative
___ let me set my own standards of quality
___ let me work hard when I feel like it, and go easy when I need to
___ don't burden me with too many routines
___ have important ideas behind them
___ give me ample time to think out my ideas before I have to act
___ let me use my hunches and inspirations
___ let me follow my curiosity
___ let me work in depth on things of importance to me

PATTERN D
I AM LIKELY TO DO MY BEST WORK IN SITUATIONS THAT:
___ put me on my own initiative
___ let me plan and carry out new projects
___ involve other people in solving problems, such as group projects
___ let me create new ways of doing things
___ let me try out my ideas to see if they work, to see how other people
react to them
___ don't require a detailed accounting of how I use my time
___ pose problems needing more attention to the broad picture than to
details
___ provide variety and minimize routine
___ let me figure out how to put theory into practice
___ let me make mistakes without penalties and learn from the mistakes
___ challenge my imagination

What do responses to the exercise mean?

Look back over your responses and see what patterns you find. As you may have discovered, the A list describes IS__ preferences for work situations. The B list, ES__ preferences; the C list, IN__ preferences, and the D list, EN__ preferences. You probably put the most check marks on the list that matches your type, and the most circled check marks on that list. Very likely you also put the fewest check marks on the list opposite your type — as ES is opposite IN and IS is opposite EN.

Now answer three questions, to your own satisfaction:

1. Does the list with the most marks reflect work conditions that are usually highly important to me?
2. Would I probably work less productively under the other three sets of conditions?
3. Do the four lists apply as appropriately to schoolwork situations as to other kinds of work situations?

Most people answer yes to all three questions, including young people. Some adults spread check marks across two or three of the lists. Their maturity gives them the flexibility to work well in a variety of situations. Young people may be less adaptable, more polarized toward one pattern. For such students, attention to matching of schoolwork situations to students' types becomes more urgent.

If the 16 types are distributed in your classroom as they are in the general population, you may find nearly half of your students choosing list B, with less choosing A and D, and very few choosing C. The four lists were written to apply to any work situation, not just to the classroom. They do not refer to "learning situations" or "learning style" because those terms call to mind the usual features of the classroom (lecture, workbooks, audio-visual materials, etc.), and those features make it difficult to look more broadly at learning situations. (Later in this chapter is a list of classroom features that different types prefer.)

Four teaching preferences, four teaching biases

You may find it helpful to go back through the four lists and respond to each item as if it were a question beginning thus: "In my teaching, do I typically provide learning situations that..." Be critical and mark only the items that describe what you regularly have provided for students. From this analysis you can identify what you prefer and what learning structures you are most likely to neglect. A major step in learning to use type in our planning is recognizing that our most preferred ways of teaching are the least preferred ways of learning for some students.

Through the years, I have often asked students in my classes — every three weeks or so — to give me a brief evaluation of the various aspects of the course, indicating the most valuable and least valuable to them, and giving suggestions for improvement. From the classes in which we used the MBTI, I learned quickly and dramatically that the _S_J types had a hard time with my (ENTP) way of structuring our work. They pinpointed blind spots in my planning. It should have been no surprise to me that I was teaching the way I like to be taught. But my image of myself as a good teacher kept me from seeing the areas I was neglecting. Their evaluations spurred me to get more serious in understanding what was needed to balance my own inclinations. I still find lots of room for improvement and continue to be surprised at blind spots that turn up. If the Four Work Settings exercise turned up a blind spot for you, it may be a good place to start in using type concepts in your planning.

TIPS FOR USING TYPE IN PLANNING

Here is a procedure for planning instruction that begins with the four lists you have analyzed. When thinking about instruction plans, keeping 16 types in mind is difficult if not impossible. It is simpler to start with a model that sorts the types into four sets — IS, ES, IN, and EN — as represented in the four lists you have just used. This approach need not abandon the TF and JP dimensions. Rather, they can be used as ways of making adjustments in the four basic models, adjustments to fit the needs of individual students, or of small groups. Making adjustments for TF and JP is discussed later in the chapter.

The four-sets approach is not the simplest way to start using type concepts in your planning. If you want to start at a more basic level, other options follow these paragraphs.

I suggest five steps in planning instruction with the help of the IS, ES, IN, EN lists.

1. Begin with a careful consideration of your own most natural teaching style. Chapter 4, Type and Teaching Styles, may help you identify relationships between your teaching style and your type. It also offers ways to examine the contrasts

between your teaching style and the learning needs of students whose type preferences differ from yours.

Your basic instruction plan should let you work from your strengths. Your energy for teaching comes in part from the satisfaction of exercising your type preferences. We cannot work well outside the framework of our own types. But we can find teaching styles that accommodate the essential needs of our own types and at the same time provide a good learning environment for students of other types. The analogy of planning a long trip for a van full of family members may help you think about your instruction plan. The drivers have to look after their needs and protect their comfort zone, but the trip will be drudgery for everyone if the needs and interests of passengers are overlooked.

2. Consider next the needs of ES__ students, because they are the types most often neglected in instruction plans. Check your plan by using the items of the ES list as criteria.

3. Develop alternative activities, variations that will appeal to IS__, EN__, and IN__ students. Using the items of those three lists, see what variations you can make in your basic plan and still stay within your comfort zone.

4. If you want to plan adjustments to accommodate TF and JP differences, you will find suggestions for that later in the chapter.

5. Double-check your plans by referring to the tables and lists in Chapter 2 that show learning preferences associated with the type preferences (Have I provided for Es?, for Is?, etc.)

Plan for the type preferences rather than for individuals

You will notice that my suggestions for planning do not include giving attention to the types of individual students. How reasonable is it for the teacher to expect to keep in mind the types of all the students? I know a few elementary teachers who do it, and some college teachers who can because of small class sizes. A more reasonable expectation is that we plan to teach to type preferences, without regard to which students are which types. When we do, students have the opportunity to attend to their own individual differences, and address their own needs, often with less assistance from us.

I believe the way for most teachers to begin teaching with type in mind is to use the type preferences in the planning of lessons. In most

situations, the teacher does not need to first administer the Type Indicator to the students. When the teaching plan takes type into account, the students will respond positively, even when the teacher does not know the types of particular students. I generally recommend to teachers that they learn the types of difficult, enigmatic students, the ones for whom regular planning and teaching are not working well. In Chapter 10 are suggestions of how to use type in making a plan specific to one student.

Teaching students about type

Some teachers find a lot of value in teaching their students about type and using the language of type with them ("We need to do some serious introverting right now, so let's not distract each other;" "Would one of you sensing people help me explain this more clearly?"). In that case, they probably should take the Type Indicator, be given a full explanation of the type concepts, and be coached in constructive, ethical uses of type. For some students, knowing about type is extremely important to them as they work to make sense of their lives.

Using the preferences as a checklist

When I am planning a unit or lesson, I go through a mental checklist of type preference pairs, starting with SN. I start there because these perception processes have the most to do with how students encounter new material. I want to use some kind of advance organizer at the beginning to make a bridge to the new material from the concepts and viewpoints they now hold. Intuitive type students need a "big picture" organizer that shows them the conceptual context we will be working in. Sensing type students need an organizer that relates to their own concrete experience. I want to provide both to help them link old to new. Good teachers have always known how to use examples and analogies that reach both sensing and intuitive minds. The homely but powerful analogies in the parables of Jesus are good illustrations of this technique.

The EI preferences are next on my checklist. How can I plan an active, at least dialogue-active, way to get them started in processing the new material? Then, how do I build in a reflection component that appeals to extraverts as well as introverts? The TF dimension reminds me that I need two approaches to build their commitment to studying the subject.

USING TYPE CONCEPTS   *59*

The JP dimension is especially important for me. Being a perceiving type, unless I plan carefully I tend to neglect the needs of my J students for a clear structure right from the beginning. In a carefully constructed handout, I tell precisely what is expected of the students. For the P types, I put into the handout suggested options for reaching the expected outcomes, and allow students to negotiate with me another option they may want to propose. I have students write individual plans and present them to me for approval or negotiation.

Improving classroom routines with type concepts

Even the most routine aspects of classroom instruction can be infused with some concrete action to make them more appealing to extraverts and sensing types. For example, when drill on reading and writing and other skills is needed, the class can be shifted into two-person teams. Team members can choose each other (for example, by writing first, second and third choices on a piece of paper, from which the teacher selects partners) or can ask to be assigned to someone by the teacher. Teams should keep the same membership for several weeks, with the teacher cancelling a team or changing team composition as needed. During team time, members can decide whether to, and when to, work together or separately; and how much time to spend in either arrangement. Some teachers give the students the option of handing in joint work or separate products. The point is that two kinds of accountability need to be maintained. Individual students are responsible for their own work, and are responsible to the teacher.

Secondly, the team members are accountable to each other. If the team members have been taught the concepts of type, and if they know each other's types, they can use their understanding of type to communicate more easily in the process of trying to be accountable.

Of course, students in the K-12 grades can get quite noisy when talking in small groups or pairs. You can deal with that by teaching them quiet voice. Demonstrate quiet voice, speaking just loud enough for the voice to carry clearly for about two feet. By having them talk to a partner with the volume turned way down, the class will realize that everyone can understand his or her partner without raising voices, and the low rumble of talking in the background doesn't interfere. Until they develop the habit of quiet voice, the talking will escalate from time to time to intrusive levels. When this happens, simply stop the dialogues, and require everyone to work separately without talking. That is punishment enough to encourage them to work on their self-discipline. They want to talk and will train themselves in quiet voice so that the privilege of talking doesn't get taken away.

Adjusting instruction for TF differences

If you have made or revised a basic instruction plan in terms of **ES, EN, IS,** and **IN** preferences, you then can consider the TF and JP dimensions as a means for seeing if the plan has a logical structure and flow to it **(T)**, promotes a warm and respectful interpersonal learning climate **(F)**, is business-like **(J)**, and has playful elements in it **(P)**. You can use this list of "needs" that are usually associated with TF and JP differences.

Thinking types need order, if order is taken to mean that logic rules the situation. They resent order that is not logical. The teacher should prompt Ts to take leadership in analyzing confused situations, to use their logic to make the situations orderly, and to spell out logical consequences.

Thinking types need to achieve, to have a sense of mastery, to know some things deeply and do them well This need is a natural ally to the school's objectives. Many T children don't know what they can master, what skills they can develop to the mastery level, and they need very specific help in this. Without help, some of them will find mastery in anti-social behavior, because the need for mastery is much stronger than the need to please people — including teachers. For the majority of the Ts, mastery is most likely to be found in technical areas, many of which are unfortunately unavailable for students to explore until they reach high school.

Thinking types need to endure, to persist, to prevail in things they are committed to. They want to have the last word in arguments. They may choose the wrong things to persist in, and they often need help in identifying the values that really are most worthy of their stick-to-it determination. Teachers can avoid useless confrontation with T students by recognizing early signs of persistent resistance and redirecting the students' thinking power into careful analysis of the situation, looking for cause and effect relationships. (Teacher: "We seem to disagree. Tell me how you see the problem... Have you thought about it from this angle?")

Feeling types need approval and personal support more than they need to achieve, to prevail, or to be "right." In some F students

the need is very strong. Teachers who emphasize independent, individualized activities for students should be especially careful that they have not cut off F students from one of their main sources of motivation: the sense that their work is valued and appreciated. They want warm, not cool or impersonal acknowledgement of their work.

Feeling types need to be needed, to know they are helpful to peers and adults. They are turned off by assignments that seem to have no particular value to anyone except themselves in some impersonal, remote sense (as with memorization of many facts and skills that are found in textbooks). Receiving the teacher's personal support and approval does not adequately substitute for the student's need to be helpful. So feeling types are most likely to profit from work in a harmonious group — when the task involves group members in helping each other, with a division of labor and shared responsibility. Examples would be group projects, tutoring, team learning and drilling with a partner. Projects that have a goal of being helpful to people outside the classroom are especially motivating to F students. They may even warm up to more remote materials if the human side is presented first. Fs want content they can personally relate to, stories of people, ethical issues, etc.

Feeling types strongly need friendship. They value harmony and will give in on disagreements because they want to preserve satisfying personal relationships. If the teacher will give them the opportunity to call attention to disharmony in the classroom, F students can be very helpful in leading the class toward an improved classroom climate. Most important of all to many F students is the opportunity to work with a friend. Friends who work together generally will stay on task if they know they will be separated when they abuse the opportunity. Peer affiliation is probably the most powerful force inside middle schools and high schools. The wise teacher harnesses it and doesn't try to fight it.

Adjusting instruction for JP differences

Judging types need structure and predictability much more often than do perceiving types. IS_J students need them most. If J students have not worked out their own structure for schoolwork, the teacher must provide it. They value an orderly sequence of studies. Js can be comfortable with some variety and spontaneity if they know that an underlying structure is intact or that the structure actually calls for those things.

Judging types need milestones, completions, and a sense of closure. Progress charts and tangible records are useful. Ceremonies, even little ones, to mark successful completions are valued, as are traditions generally. Persistence is a related J trait, and ceremonies that honor successful persistence will be especially appreciated. (In contrast, persistence does not come easily to Ps, but they need to develop it; the ceremonies are likely to benefit them too.)

Judging types need a system of accountability that is clear and made known in advance. They want to know what they are accountable for, when, how, and by what standards they will be judged. Js will learn out of a sense of duty, for a while at least; but that is not a good substitute for clear expectations made known in advance.

Perceiving types need variety, novelty, and change. As McCaulley and Natter note, the typically structured classroom "can make the perceptive types feel imprisoned, with the result that they spend energy needed for study trying to get freedom. More flexible classrooms are naturally more suited to these students."

Perceiving types need autonomy and a real choice. The need is especially strong in _N _P types. They work much better at tasks they have chosen. They will accept structure and a system of accountability if they have choices within the structure, and especially if they have had a hand in deciding and protecting the structure. For example, a system of individual contracts, in which a student can negotiate some activities, is a structure Ps would enjoy planning and supporting.

Perceiving types need opportunities to be spontaneous and free-wheeling, to follow their curiosity. The teacher alert to this need will find tasks for Ps that let them explore and find new facts or possibilities for the class to use.

PLAN A UNIT OF INSTRUCTION USING TYPE CONCEPTS

Here are steps you can take to try out the ideas of type in your classroom. If you have a colleague or two with whom you can share your plan, this planning sequence may be more helpful to you.

1. Select one classroom group of students with which to try using type concepts. As needed, coordinate your choice of students and your

instruction plans with other people. Even if you believe it is not appropriate for your students to answer the MBTI, you can still use type concepts in many ways to reach students of different types.

2. If your students are 12 years or older, decide whether to administer the Myers-Briggs Type Indicator to them. The Murphy-Meisgeier Type Indicator for Children® (MMTIC®)* is also available and has been validated for second through eighth grades. In most situations, teachers need to coordinate MBTI or MMTIC administration with the school counselor and obtain approval of the principal. If you decide to use the MBTI, precede the administering of it with an introduction to the idea, such as the "People Types and Tiger Stripes" activity in Chapter One. The introduction should serve to spark students' interest in the instrument so they will respond to it seriously. Some students will have difficulty with the MBTI because of its reading level. Reading the items aloud to them is an option. If you do read the questions to them, each student should have a copy of the Indicator to look at as you read. Tell the students the Indicator was created for adults, and there may be questions where they do not understand the words. In this case, they may omit the question. Do not interpret questions for the students. If you read questions aloud, take care to make sure your own type preferences don't show. Make each choice sound equally desirable. After they take the MBTI or MMTIC, be sure they have their profile interpreted and their questions answered. Nearly all the students will be keenly interested in their profiles.

3. Decide whether to have the students respond to the four lists entitled, "I Am Likely to Do My Best Work . . ." Steps two and three are intended to give you some evidence of the types of your students. Having information on that is not essential to this planning sequence, but it is helpful. If you have students who cannot read the Indicator or the other materials, it is possible to recognize characteristics of type in their behavior. In Chapter 10 is a set of observation checklists you can use to estimate students' types by observing the patterns in their behavior. The process is time-consuming but it may fit your needs. Once again, knowing each student's type is not essential to planning instruction with type concepts.

4. Prepare a plan of instruction — either a new plan you have not

---

* *Myers-Briggs Type Indicator and MMTIC are registered trademarks of Consulting Psychologists Press, Inc., Palo Alto, CA.*

implemented before, or a revision of a plan you have used before. This plan will incorporate type concepts. You may want to start with a single dimension of type, such as EI, or you may want to follow the IS, ES, IN, EN process described earlier in this chapter. Prepare it in sufficient detail so that your colleagues can read it and probably follow its intent without having to ask you for clarification on major points. If you prefer, you can prepare a joint plan with one or more partners. In either case, your plan should have a clear rationale based on type concepts.

5. If you need a formal evaluation plan, decide what data you can gather, as progress reports or a final report at the end of the unit, to show tangibly how well your plan worked. If you do succeed in making a better match between students and the learning setting, what would you expect to improve? Student time-on-task can be estimated by simple observation. Student interest can be sampled by a few questionnaire items. Student achievement can be documented by student products and by teacher-made tests. Organize these ideas into an evaluation plan.

6. Before you implement your plan, have your colleague(s) review it, critique its applications of type concepts, and make suggestions.

EXAMPLES OF CLASS PROJECTS SUCCESSFUL WITH ALL TYPES OF STUDENTS

Here are four examples of instruction plans that had a strong measure of concrete activity in them, and were (predictably) successful with ES students as well as the others. Note that the teachers who planned and conducted these activities did not consciously follow the six-step plan, but in retrospect all the features of the planning process can be seen.

The greenhouse project

Sixth grade students in Jacksonville, Florida, became interested in the processes of plant growth and got the idea of building a greenhouse so they could house the number of plants they wanted to grow, and could continue growing them throughout the winter. Concrete activity was at the center of the plan: presenting the idea to the principal, a field trip to a local greenhouse, letter writing to obtain information about greenhouse construction, dialogues with a nurseryman, a businessman and a construction foreman (a parent), and maintaining a

bulletin board related to the progress of the project.

Science and math became concrete and active, too. Students made charts and graphs for the plant experiments; plotted the sun's movement in relation to the school to help decide the best location for the greenhouse; made careful measurements and worked up plans concerning the size, shape, materials, and cost of the greenhouse; and the plant experiments themselves had many active aspects. All the students wanted to be involved in some way in the actual construction work: using the posthole diggers, sawing, hammering, and stapling the plastic covering on.

In analyzing the events as they evolved, we can see the students — particularly the ES__ and EN__ students — would be drawn to the physically active aspects of the projects. Virtually all parts of the project were performed by teams, with the more quiet and reflective activities coordinated with the active work. The library research on greenhouses and the sun's path, and design work would appeal especially to IN__s, as would the plant experiments themselves. Type theory suggests that IS__s would be attracted to the planning of details, learning from experienced adults, keeping accounts for the fund raising and calculating materials needed and the cost of them. Probably the IS__ students were also the most reliable in caring for the plants and recording the outcomes.

Adopted grandparent program

The adopted grandparent program at P. K. Yonge Laboratory School in Gainesville, Florida, began over 30 years ago and has been successfully adapted at many other schools. It was originated by a second grade teacher who worked with the administrator of a nearby nursing home to arrange visits of the children to the residents of the home. Her class "adopted" some of the residents and gradually built a strong relationship with them that was beneficial to the adults as well as the children. The residents were ones who volunteered to be involved and had lively minds. Many of them became frequent visitors and helpers at the school.

The children who chose to go regularly to the nursing home learned about companionship with very old people, the problems of living with infirmities, and death of loved ones. They arranged birthday parties for their adopted grandparents, made craft gifts for them, wrote poems, read to them, helped them eat, and had many other activities with them as they would with their own grandparents. The grandparents in turn gave the children individual attention and help they may not have received otherwise. Many former P. K. Yonge students consider their time with their adopted grandparents as a highlight of elementary school.

The inner-city housing project

Some Nashville junior high school social studies teachers planned a very successful unit for students of their inner-city school. Many of the students had the ability to do well in school but most were expected to drop out because of what was termed their "defeatist" attitude. Most of the students lived in apartment buildings that were poorly maintained. No one knew the landlord; rent checks went to a realty company, and requests about repairs mostly went unheeded.

When the teachers learned about the housing conditions, they proposed a project for the students to find out more about the situation and to try to do something about it. Students agreed, without much enthusiasm at first. Investigative teams were formed. After preliminary planning, some teams took a questionnaire, a note pad, and a camera to an apartment building to interview tenants and document the need for repairs. These teams kept records of how much rent was paid; what requests for repairs were made and when, and which were honored, and what repairs were still needed. Another team went to City Hall to find deeds and other documents that would show who the absentee landlords were.

After a file of facts, figures, and photographs was prepared for each building, one team made an appointment with the landlord and presented him with the file. In several buildings, the students' project resulted in repairs and had other positive spinoffs. Some students and their families became active in tenant cooperatives and earned wages or rent rebates for helping to care for their building.

Besides learning something about economics and local politics, the students more importantly gained a sense of their own capability to influence "the system" they had thought to be mysterious and inaccessible.

As with the greenhouse project and adopted grandparents program, the central events of this unit were active and concrete, and were sufficiently varied that all of the 16 types would find activities of high interest to them.

ISTJ

Linear learner with strong need
   for order (SJ)
Likes direct experience (S)
Likes audiovisuals (S); lectures (I)
Enjoys working alone (I)
Likes well-defined goals (S)
Prefers practical tests (S)

ISTP

Linear learner; needs help in
   organizing (SP)
Likes direct experience (S)
Likes lectures, audiovisuals (S)
Enjoys working alone (I)
Wants logically-structured,
   efficient materials (IT)

ESTP

Linear learner; needs help in
   organizing (SP)
Needs to know why before
   doing something (S)
Likes group projects, class reports,
   team competition (E)
Likes direct experience (S)
Likes audiovisuals (S)
May like lecture (T)

ESTJ

Linear learner with strong need for
   structure (SJ)
Needs to know why before doing
   something (S)
Likes direct experience (S)
Likes group projects, class reports,
   team competition (E)
Likes audiovisuals, practical tests (S)
May like lecture (T)

ISFJ

Linear learner with strong
   need for order (SJ)
Likes direct experience (S)
Likes listening to lectures (I)
Likes audiovisuals (S)
Enjoys working alone (I)
Likes practical tests(S)

ISFP

Linear learner; needs help
   in organizing (SP)
Likes direct experience (S)
Needs well-defined goals (S)
Needs harmony in group projects (E)
Likes audiovisuals, practical tests (S)
Enjoys working alone (I)
Needs sensitive instructor (IF)

ESFP

Linear learner; needs help in
   organizing (SP)
Likes direct experience (S)
Likes audiovisuals; practical tests (S)
Needs to know why before doing
   something (S)
Likes group projects, team
   competition, class reports (E)
Needs orderly, well-defined goals (S)

ESFJ

Linear learner with strong need for
   structure (SJ)
Needs to know why before doing
   something (S)
Needs well defined goals (S)
Values harmonious group projects,
   team competition, class reports (EF)
Likes audiovisuals; practical tests (S)
Likes direct experience (S)

INFJ

Can be global or linear (NJ)
Wants to consider theory first, then
  applications (N)
Enjoys working alone (I)
Prefers open-end instruction (N)
Needs harmony in group work (F)

INFP

Global learner; may need help in
  organizing (NP)
Likes reading, listening (N)
Wants to consider theory first, then
  applications (N)
Needs harmony in group work (F)
Prefers open-end instruction (N)
Enjoys working alone (I)
Likes autonomy (NP)

ENFP

Global learner; needs choices and
  deadlines (NP)
Likes seminars (EN)
Likes reading if can settle down long
  enough (EN)
Likes harmonious group projects, team
  competition, class reports (EF)
Likes autonomy (NP)
Needs help with organizing (NP)

ENFJ

Can be global or linear learner (NJ)
Likes seminars (EN)
Likes reading if can settle down long
  enough (ENF)
Likes harmonious group projects,
  class reports (EF)
Likes listening (N)
Likes pencil-and-paper tests (N)
Prefers open-end instruction (N)
Wants to consider theory, then
  applications (N)

INTJ

Can be global or linear (NJ)
Wants to consider theory first, then
  applications (N)
Enjoys working alone (I)
Prefers open-end instruction (N)
Good at paper-and-pencil tests (NT)

INTP

Global learner; needs help in coming
  to closure (NP)
Likes reading, listening (N)
Wants to consider theory first, then
  applications (N)
Good at paper-and-pencil tests (NT)
Prefers open-end instruction (N)
Enjoys working alone (I)
Likes autonomy (NP)

ENTP

Global learner; needs choices and
  deadlines (NP)
Likes autonomy (NP)
Likes seminars (EN)
Likes reading, listening (N)
Wants to consider theory, then
  applications (N)
Good at paper-and-pencil tests (NT)
Prefers open-end instruction (N)

ENTJ

Can be global or linear learner (NJ)
Likes seminars (EN)
Likes reading if can settle down long
  enough (EN)
Likes group projects, class reports,
  team competition (E)
Likes listening (N)
Likes pencil-and-paper tests (N)
Prefers open-end instruction (N)
Wants to consider theory, then
  applications (N)

The aluminum can project

Three middle school teachers had planned a year's theme of human ecology. One activity, suggested by the students, proved to be especially rewarding — collecting aluminum cans to be recycled. It not only led them into the issues of finite resources and recycling, but the income from the sale of the cans paid for the cost of busing them on several field trips: to a plant making aluminum extrusions, to a power plant to see how electricity is generated, to a small company that built solar heating units, to a sewage treatment facility, and to a bird sanctuary.

Among other things, students figured out techniques for saving energy at home and monitored their family's consumption of energy by charting the relative effect of various conservation measures. As they became aware of ecological problems in their community, the students also wrote letters to the editor of the newspaper and a group of them presented a proposal to the city council. These activities were the more dramatic highlights of a year of study, and they were strong motivating elements for the more typical activities: use of textbooks, films, resource persons, library report work, and some laboratory experiments.

The thread common to the four examples of instructional planning is the emphasis on making active (extraverting) and concrete (sensing) experiences the center of attention of students. Other activities, more conventional to classrooms, are sparked in that way and take on new importance for students who are not natural academicians.

USING TYPE IN CLASSROOM-BOUND INSTRUCTION

Of course, instruction cannot always be planned to incorporate the action, variety, and concrete experiences described in these examples. Type concepts can also help you plan better instruction when you are limited largely to the classroom and media center. The table entitled "Relating Type to Instructional Strategies" was developed by Margaret K. Morgan, of the University of Florida. It briefly shows what has been learned about the classroom learning styles of each of the 16 types. Note that in the table sensing types are described as linear learners, and intuitive types as global learners. Linear refers to the step-by-step sequential approach to learning tasks. The global approach involves intuitive leaps, seeking to see the whole of the task first. Also note the preferences of different types for various media of instruction. These preferences are confirmed by research reported by McCaulley and Natter. *

---

* M.H. McCaulley and F.L. Natter (1980). *Psychological Type (Myers-Briggs) Differences in Education*. Gainesville, FL: Center for Applications of Psychological Type.

TYPE AND TEACHING STYLES

When considering type and teaching preferences we find two main topics: how our types exert influence on our behavior as teachers, and how we may use knowledge of type to adjust our teaching styles to better fit the needs of students. This chapter is mainly about the former. Chapters 2 and 3 are mainly about the latter. While the whole book is about understanding the role of psychological type in people's behavior, this chapter is focused on teaching behavior specifically.

Let's review what the previous chapters have included about teaching styles. Chapter 2 deals with the influence that type has on our cognitive styles, our preferred work style, and the kind of instruction we prefer for ourselves. Chapter 3 gives us a way to consider how our own type may affect the kind of work settings we provide for our students. Yet to come are Chapters 10 and 11. Chapter 10 includes the zig-zag technique we can use to examine our problem-solving biases, which certainly have a bearing on teaching style. Chapter 11, Kinds of Mind, gives descriptions of the ST, SF, NF, and NT mind-sets, examples of how they influence teaching, and suggestions for guarding against mind-set bias in teaching.

WHAT RESEARCH REVEALS ABOUT
TYPE AND TEACHING PREFERENCES

Teachers and researchers who understand type concepts see ample evidence that teachers' types do indeed affect how they teach and what they prefer to teach. Much more needs to be learned about type differences in teaching styles, but research is already supplementing observation to provide some interesting facts about the ways different types of teachers behave in their classrooms.

The facts below come from four sources. One is "A summary of Myers-Briggs Type Indicator research applications in education" by J. Hoffman and M. Betkouski which appeared in *Research in Psychological Type,* 1981, Volume 3, pages 3-41. The second source is a study by R. DeNovellis and G. Lawrence, "Correlations of teacher personality variables (Myers-Briggs) and classroom observation data," reported in *Research in Psychological Type,* 1983, Volume 6, pages 37-46. In this study, trained observers recorded teacher and student behaviors in the classroom; the observers did not know the types of the teachers they were rating. Another source of information is research using the data bank of the Center for Applications of Psychological Type in Gainesville, Florida. And the fourth source is my own review of research studies that have been reported since the Hoffman-Betkouski review.

TEACHERS' CHOICES OF LEVELS AND SUBJECTS

Levels. Different types of teachers are attracted to different levels of schooling, and to teaching of different subjects. As shown in the table in Chapter 1, all types are represented in all levels of education, but in quite different proportions. More Ss than Ns teach in elementary and middle school grades; Ss and Ns are about equal in high school; more Ns than Ss are found in college and university teaching, with about two-thirds of university teachers being Ns. This pattern is consistent with type theory; the proportion of Ns increasing as the subject matter becomes more abstract.

More Fs than Ts choose the lower grades, while more Ts than Fs are found in post-secondary education, a distribution that is also consistent with type theory: the more impersonal curriculums of higher education attracting more Ts.

Of special interest in the table is the representation of the 16 individual types at the various levels of education. While the four NF types — INFJ, INFP, ENFP, and ENFJ — are about equally represented at all levels, the four SF types — ISFJ, ISFP, ESFP, and ESFJ — are three times as likely to be in pre-school and elementary grades as in higher education. The four ST types — ISTJ, ISTP, ESTP, and ESTJ — are fairly evenly distributed across the levels, but the NT types — INTJ, INTP, ENTP, and ENTJ — clearly tilt toward higher education. This distribution is also consistent with type theory: the SFs being more oriented to the concrete and personal teaching roles, and the NTs being drawn to the abstract subjects and academic roles.

A comparison of the table with estimates of the 16 types in the general population shows several striking contrasts. The IN__ types, who make up about 10% of the population, are very much over-represented among teachers at all levels. ISFJs are over-represented at all levels except the university, as are ISTJs at all levels except pre-school.

The four _S_P types are dramatically under-represented. While together they make up about 30% of the general population, only about 10% of teachers are of these four types. This can be a real problem for _S_P students; teachers who share a similar mind-set and who emulate the _S_P kind of good type development will be scarce. The explanation for the scarcity is not hard to find. Formal education is conducted mainly with an _N_J bent.

I have administered the MBTI to many school and college faculties, and I have seen the type tables of many more. It is very unusual for one or more types to be entirely missing from the faculty type table. But the distribution of the faculty among the 16 types is often mismatched with that of the students. In general, student tables show more extraverts, more sensing types, and more perceiving types than are represented in the faculty. Most striking of all in the faculty type tables is the relative absence of the _S_P types. The research can't show us a cause and effect relationship, but we can speculate that the generally lower grade point averages of the _S_P group, and the higher representation of these types among school dropouts, are affected by the mismatch of types between students and faculty. My own opinion is that the way the _S_P types see the world does not easily fit into the usual classroom practices of our schools and colleges. Some behaviors and viewpoints that are natural expressions of their types are often misunderstood and misinterpreted by their teachers. The _S_P learning style and instruction plans to accommodate it are discussed in Chapters 2 and 3.

Subjects. Teachers' choices of subjects to teach are predictable from type theory too. The sample list that follows shows that Ss are attracted to teaching of practical courses; Ns to courses emphasizing theories and ideas. Ts are attracted to teaching of mathematics, science and technical skills; Fs to language arts and fine arts.

Art, Drama, Music ....Half are _NF_ types
Coaching..Half are _S_J types
English...2/3 Ns, 2/3 Fs
Foreign Language ....70% Fs
Health ....Evenly distributed
Mathematics, 7-12 ....2/3 Ss
Science, 7-12 ....2/3 Ts
Special Education.............................Evenly distributed
Industrial, technical........................45% in two types: ISTJ, ESTJ

THE TEACHER IN THE CLASSROOM

Type Preferences and Teaching Styles

In this section about teaching styles and in the next three sections I have summarized what research has shown about the tendencies of teachers when they are sorted by types. The differences reported are statistically significant, but the differences may not be large.

Of course, a teacher's actual behavior in the classroom is influenced by many things besides his or her psychological type. Some of the statements describing your type will fit you, and others may not. A sign of a good teacher is the ability to flex one's teaching style to better fit the needs of those being taught. The style that results from the flex may not be the same as the natural inclinations of one's type.

Extravert-introvert differences. Extraverted teachers are more likely than their introverted counterparts to give students choices about what to study and how to go about learning tasks, and to engage them in classroom or school projects. Introverted teachers are more likely to structure learning activities through the materials they select for students. Extraverted teachers are more likely to be constantly attuned to the changes in student attention and activities. Introverted teachers are more attuned to the ideas they are trying to teach, and tend to center the control in themselves.

Sensing-intuitive differences. Sensing types tend to emphasize facts, practical information, and concrete skills. Intuitive types tend to emphasize concepts and relationships, and the implications of facts for understanding larger matters. Sensing type teachers tend to keep things centralized, and focus activities on a narrow range of choices. Intuitive type teachers are more likely to give a wide range of choices to students, form them into small groups more often, and expect independent and creative behavior from them. At the elementary and middle school levels, intuitive teachers are more likely to move freely around the room than their sensing counterparts.

Thinking-feeling differences. Thinking type teachers make relatively few comments about student performance, and these are likely to be objective statements. Feeling types are more likely to praise and criticize, support and correct, in words and by body language. Thinking types have students spend more of their time focused on what the teacher is doing or saying.

In elementary and secondary classrooms, feeling type teachers have students spend more time in their individual work; are more likely than thinking type teachers to move from student to student, attending to each student in their individual work, and usually seeking some dialogue; and seem better able to attend to more than one student at a time, in contrast to thinking types who typically deal with the class as a whole.

Judging-perceiving differences. The classrooms of judging type teachers are more likely to be orderly, with adherence to structure and schedules. Perceiving type teachers encourage more movement around the classroom, more independence, more open ended discussions, and more socializing in study groups.

Student Reactions to Teachers' Management Styles

The classrooms of I, S, and J teachers are likely to be quiet and orderly. When students in these classrooms get off task, they are apt to daydream, doodle, and do other passive, withdrawn things. In contrast, the classrooms of E, N, and P teachers typically have more movement and more noise. In these classrooms, students have a greater voice in decisions about activities. When students get off task, they are likely to do so actively and noisily. The E, N, and P teachers spend more time trying to get students settled down to work.

Structure and Flexibility in the Classroom

I__J teachers seem to need the most structure in the classroom; E__Js need somewhat less; I__Ps need less; and E__Ps need the least structure of all. In fact, E__P teachers often do things that will bring unpredictability into the classroom — encourage open ended discussions, ask students to create projects, permit socializing in study groups, etc.

TYPE AND TEACHING STYLES   *75*

Clearly, the amount of structure a teacher needs for personal equilibrium will suit the needs for external structure of some of the students in the classroom, and will not fit others at all. What are the implications of these differences for instruction? It is unrealistic to ask teachers to change their need for structure. There are two alternatives to the mismatch between student and teacher needs. First, students can be placed so as to obtain a better match between teacher style and student need for classroom structure. This is not a solution for use on a broad scale; grouping by types is not a good idea for reasons discussed elsewhere in the book. But in individual cases, especially in the early grades, students who need special support can be placed with a teacher whose structure style is most helpful to their growth.

The second way to deal with different structure needs is the teachers learning the techniques needed for varying structure — techniques that permit them to meet more students' needs, but yet do not force them beyond their own equilibrium.

As an example of the latter solution, one J mathematics teacher in a middle school was able to keep his natural style, but to redirect it more appropriately. He realized that his own need for order and control was resulting in overbearing supervision of his students. He redirected his need for order to an inanimate object: a chart showing all the students' names and all the sub-objectives of the course. He exercised his J by moving the markers on the chart as the students completed their tasks.

In another example, a P fifth-grade teacher, who realized he was too unstructured for many students, found a solution in individual student contracts. Students who needed more structure got more tightly-drawn contracts. He also arranged for election of class officers. Students debated and decided on a set of class rules, and the officers exercised J responsibilities for enforcing the rules.

Type and Questioning Styles

The kinds of questions teachers ask students, and the ways they ask them, usually reflect the teachers' own preferences for sensing or intuition. Sensing teachers are likely to start a sequence of questions with a request for facts and details; the responses they are seeking are predictable. Intuitive teachers are likely to start with questions that call for synthesis and evaluation: "What's the main theme (issue, problem) here?" "What are your impressions of...?"

Because intuitive teachers personally like questions that stimulate imagining and hypothesizing ("If you were . . ." "What might have happened if . . . ?"), intuitive teachers may assume that all students like, or should like, such questions to answer. Sensing students are put at a disadvantage with these questions, unless other questions that engage sensing come before them. "What did you see happening?" "Which facts are most important? . . . Why?" "Which facts give you clues why so-and-so did such-and-such?" This sequence of questions carries the student from the known to the unknown, from the givens to the speculative. It helps S students connect with the teacher's intention, and also models a good mental discipline for N students.

Sensing teachers may neglect to ask students to synthesize, to hypothesize, and to attend to the "big picture." Intuitive teachers may allow students to be too casual about the facts, so long as they have the concepts right.

While teachers instinctively lean toward questioning styles that reflect their type preferences, they can readily train themselves into questioning strategies that are fair and appealing to all types of students. That is one of the themes of Chapter 3.

Teachers Report Their Teaching Styles

Another kind of research involved teachers describing in detail the ways they view and conduct their teaching. The following are representative descriptions of the teaching process provided by teachers to L. L. Thompson and reported in her 1984 dissertation, "An investigation of the relationship of the personality theory of C. G. Jung and teachers' self-reported perceptions and decisions" (Ohio State University). The extensive interview data were sorted by teachers' type, and summarized by the four mental process combinations.

The role of the teacher is to:

ST: Set an example for students, be a role model, and share knowledge and experience

SF: Instruct, discipline, encourage, support, role model, and serve others

NF: Encourage, inspire, provide variety and creativity, and motivate students to develop

NT: Encourage, inspire, help students develop as citizens and persons

Ideas for teaching come from:

ST: State and local curriculum guides, textbooks, and experience

SF: Curriculum guides, manuals, textbooks, workshops, other teachers, and experience

NF: Concepts from content of subject taught; courses, reading, knowledge of student development, and "ideas from everywhere"

NT: Concepts from subject area, knowledge of students' needs and development, synthesis of ideas from many sources

Teaching is planned by:

ST: Making complete, detailed plans in advance for year and term with specific objectives

SF: Establish complete objectives and detailed teaching plans using yearly school calendar; taking students' abilities into consideration

NF: Structuring plans around general goals, themes, and students' needs; then adapting plans to students' needs week to week

NT: Making a plan according to an overall yearly structure; organizing by concepts or themes; determining details by student levels

Typical method of teaching is described as:

ST: Following daily routine, directing activities

SF: Following ordered daily pattern adjusted for person-centered interactions

NF: Using a flexible daily pattern depending on topic and student need

NT: Having a flexible daily routine that depends on topics and student need, with interaction based on expectations for order and learning

Students' work is evaluated by:

ST: Using points and percentages in a systematic way

SF: Using points and percentages, plus extra credit options

NF: Using a number of factors, only one of which is grades

NT: Using a number of factors

The teacher feels successful if:

ST: Student grades and behavior improve

SF: Student behavior and grades improve, and there is the feeling of having contributed to students' education

NF: Student learning and participation increase, and there is the feel-

ing of having made a personal contribution to students' education
NT: Students have increased involvement with learning

I have used the Thompson results as the basis for an exercise to demonstrate to teachers the reality of type differences and how they influence teaching style. My approach is to sort teachers into four groups by the process combinations — ST, SF, NF, NT — and have each group first give their own responses to the topical questions; after that, read the summaries on the same topics given above; and finally to have them discuss the implications for flexing their teaching styles to accommodate type differences in students. I stated the topical questions in these words:

- The role of the teacher is to:
- Ideas for teaching come from:
- I plan my teaching by:
- In regard to daily teaching routine, I:
- I evaluate students' work by:
- I feel successful in my teaching if:

EXERCISE: EXAMINING AND ADJUSTING TEACHING STYLES

We all can use help, practice, and constructive feedback in tuning-up our teaching techniques to do a better job with students whose types are most different from ours. Here is a discussion activity for teachers or prospective teachers. I have used it successfully to exemplify the improvement needs and the assistance process. The objective is to plan some teaching practices that will fit the needs of one's most opposite types and obtain feedback on the planned ideas. The activity organizes participants into groups by the type preference combinations that teachers say are most difficult to bridge across from teacher to student. Allow a minimum of an hour for the exercise.

1. Form four type-alike groups: _S_Js, _N_Ps, _N_Js, and _S_Ps.
2. Have each group:

    a. Read the list of teaching preferences reported by researchers that follows these instructions.

    b. Discuss and confirm and/or clarify the statements referring to the two type preferences they have in common: S&J, N&P,N&J, or S&P.

    c. Turn to Chapter 2 and read "Summaries of the Learning Preferences Associated with E, I, S, N, T, F, J, and P" — read-

ing only the descriptions of their opposites, as _N_P is opposite _S_J, and _N_J is opposite _S_P.

    d. Discuss and write on newsprint the changes the group members would be willing and able to make in their teaching practices to better engage and evaluate the students whose learning preferences are most opposite their own.

3. Combine opposites, the _S_J and _N_P groups joining, and the _N_J and _S_P groups joining.

    a. In each combined group, each sub-group use its notes to report what was produced in step 2, and invite clarifying questions from the other sub-group.

    b. In turn, each sub-group react and give constructive suggestions about the teaching practices that were intended for students of their type.

4. Reconvene as one group. Have a reporter for each work group tell the whole group what was accomplished in the work group. Debrief the exercise.

This exercise is especially effective when it is repeated with a variation. After participants prepare lesson plans designed to reach students of their opposite type preferences, repeat steps 2d., 3, and 4 to critique the lesson plans, participants begin to see that type-different colleagues can be an important resource to them in improving their planning.

Teaching Practices Summary to be Used in This Exercise

_S_J Teachers' Tendencies	_N_P Teachers' Tendencies
• emphasize facts, practical information, concrete skills	• emphasize concepts, relationships, implications of facts
• centralized instruction, focus activity on narrow range of student choices	• give students choices • use small group work • expect independent, creative work
• expect quiet and order	• expect student movement during study time, and some noise
• need clear classroom structure and schedules	• encourage open-ended discussions

- questioning style starts with request for facts and specifics, expecting predictable responses
- may neglect intuitive students' need to see the big picture first

- questioning style starts with request for synthesis, evaluation, big picture responses
- may neglect sensing students' need to start with observable specifics
- may be too casual about the facts if students get the concepts

_N_J Teachers' Tendencies
- emphasize concepts, relationships, implications of facts
- give students choices
- use small group work
- expect independent, creative work from students
- expect order, with adherence to structure and schedules
- allow noise if work is orderly
- questioning style starts with request for synthesis, evaluation, big picture questions
- may neglect sensing students' need to start with observable specifics

_S_P Teachers' Tendencies
- emphasize facts, practical information, concrete skills
- focus activity specifically on what students should accomplish
- expect students to be free to express themselves
- expect diverse learning styles
- expect movement and some noise during study time
- questioning style starts with request for observed facts and details, expecting predictable responses
- may neglect intuitive students' need to see the big picture first

TYPE AND THE TEACHING TEAM

For some teachers their work involves teamwork with other teachers. Of course, type differences are a fact to be reckoned with, along with other differences, as the team does its work. The combination of types on a teaching team often makes a difference in the team's productivity, compatibility and flexibility. A good mix of types is a strong asset to a team.

Look at the type table on the last page of *Introduction to Type* in the Appendix of this book. Does your team have a balanced mix of types, with three or four of the columns (ST, SF, NF, NT) represented?

Three or four quadrants, too (IS, ES, IN, EN)? Ideally a team would have all of the eight preferences represented. If your team lacks any of them, someone usually must take on the responsibility for the point of view and disposition that would come naturally a person with that preference.

Consider your own strengths as a team member. Read back through the information about teaching styles on the previous pages and their relevance to you. Analyze your own zig-zag. (See Chapter 10). Do these analysis give you a new angle for looking at your strengths and weaknesses? For looking at your contributions to your team? Does the zig-zag give you some ideas of how to use your strengths to strengthen a weakness?

Following is an activity I designed for members of teaching teams. It is useful for considering the mix and balance of types on any kind of team; with a little alteration I have used it in many different organizational settings besides schools. Your team may find it helpful as a way to start a dialogue about type-related issues affecting the team.

✎ Exercise: The Green-White Conflict

Here is a description of a conflict between two teachers. Using type concepts, analyze the conflict and consider what might be done to improve the relationship.

Understanding the Green-White conflict

Two members of a teaching team frequently seem to have misunderstandings. Mr. Green is often the "idea man" of the team, suggesting with enthusiasm that the team try this or that. Generally his ideas seem sound to the team, but in need of some refinement and attention to practical details. Mrs. White, another team member, is usually the first one to question Mr. Green's ideas, on grounds of practicality, and she states her position in such a blunt way that she sometimes causes hard feelings. At that point, Mr. Green "clams up," and his idea fades away without the team dealing with it further. Outside of team planning meetings, Green and White seem to get along quite well. Analyze the Green-White relationship by answering these questions:

1. What types are Green and White? Make a guess.

2. How can you explain the conflict in terms of type theory?

3. Assuming you are a member of their team and felt a need to help them, what would you say to Green? To White? Would you say it privately, or during team meeting? Write your remarks just as you would say them; put them in quotation marks.

4 . Do you identify with either Green or White more than with the other? Would you be comfortable in the role of peacemaker between these two? Do your responses to these questions relate to your own type?

The Green-White situation will yield many more insights if you can discuss it with a colleague or two. After you have discussed it, you can compare your analysis and action plan with the one below.

Possible actions for the Green-White conflict

Chances are that Mrs. White doesn't even know her blunt reaction (T) caused hard feelings. Quick to make a judgment (J) based on awareness of missing details (S), she is probably an _STJ. Choosing to speak to her in the meeting or in private would depend on your comfort in the two settings. There are advantages to talking directly about the conflict in the meeting, at the time it happens. When the problem is talked out in the meeting, there is less chance that members will wonder who talks to whom outside the meeting and who is seen as wrong or right, etc. In the meeting you might say, "We need fresh ideas, and we also need to look at them carefully for practicality and detailed planning. Let's look at Mr. Green's proposal as a beginning concept, and when we're clear about what he has in mind, let's analyze it for practicality."

If you chose to speak to Mrs. White privately, you might say, calmly and straight to the point, "I think you came across too strongly with Mr. Green. I'd say his feelings are a reality we have to recognize next time. Your knack for spotting quickly what is missing in a proposed plan is a real asset to the team, but I'll bet Mr. Green feels you never heard what he did say. He probably wouldn't be turned off if you said instead, "Your plan might work if we figured out how to deal with this and this and this."

Mr. Green, full of interesting possibilities (N) not thought out completely (P) was hurt by the critical analysis (F) and retreated too quickly to withdrawn silence. The retreat suggests introversion; where an E most likely would have argued and defended the plan, an introvert might believe that the worth of the plan did not depend on anyone accepting it. He probably will respond favorably if you say something in the meeting such as suggested in the earlier paragraph. If you

chose to speak to him privately, you could say, "I expect Mrs. White has no idea that she caused hard feelings. She's blunt, but I think her bluntness comes from her logic, not from her feelings. She certainly isn't alert to other people's feelings the way that you are."

The Green-White episode illustrates the value of having type concepts as one of the tools of teamwork. If the members knew about type, the differences could be talked about directly in the meeting, as they arose: "I think we have some type differences getting in our way. I hear some intuitive possibilities getting discarded because the sensing specifics haven't been worked out. Can we put the type differences to work for us to get a good action plan out of this?" In this way, type is being used to address the conflict directly while steering the meeting away from behaviors that will be interpreted as a personal attack, and counter-attack. Using type concepts allows us to talk about sensitive areas of personality differences in a more objective way. When Mrs. White's behavior is seen as a natural expression of her type preferences, her team members can more easily assume that her intentions were only constructive and then move the team's work along with fewer emotional snags.

Isabel Myers' essay that follows seems especially useful for understanding situations such as the Green-White conflict.

TYPE AND HUMAN RELATIONS

By Isabel Briggs Myers

AUTHOR'S NOTE: The following section is quoted, by permission, from the 1962 (1975) Manual of the Myers-Briggs Type Indicator (Consulting Psychologists Press). Here Myers spoke about using type in understanding and improving relationships in any areas of life, and her ideas certainly apply to teacher-student and teacher-teacher relationships. As you read it, you will recognize the roots of the Green-White exercise.

The effects of type in this field do not lend themselves easily to statistical verification but can be explored by personal observation and experience. The conclusions reached from the writer's observation and experience are therefore offered as a frame of reference for the reader's own explorations. Recognition of the type differences, when carried over into the field of person-to-person relationships, may afford a useful system for understanding others whose attitudes or actions seem unreasonable. Type theory would hold that type differences yield differences in interests, values, and problem-solving techniques which may facilitate or handicap a working relationship between two or more people. Where two individuals interacting with one another are of similar type, there is a better chance of communication of ideas. Sensing types like facts; intuitives like possibilities; thinkers like logical principles; feeling types like a human angle. A good sound idea can be presented in any or all of these forms, but difficulties may be expected to occur if, say, the thinker attempts to force logical reasons upon a feeling type or possibilities upon the sensing people.

It has seemed to the writer that most people get around this difficulty by picking friends mainly from their own type column, a fact generally apparent if one enters his friends upon a Type Table. In marriage there is a significant tendency to prefer likeness to difference, especially on SN. But parents and children have no option. They are stuck with each other's types, for better or worse.

The type differences, and the resulting family conflicts, can appear very early. A six-year-old girl with feeling said in dismay after a week's visit from a five-year-old thinker, "He doesn't care about pleasing, does he?" Basically, he never will. He has to have reasons. The small feeling type will do things for the sake of "pleasing" but is quite unmoved by logic. If one expects to influence either, he must give him a motivation that means something to his type.

As individuals grow up, each type can profit by learning how to get along with the other. The thinker is by nature impersonal and critical. He likes effects to follow logically from causes, and he forgets to reckon illogical human motives and reactions among the causes. In any disagreement, therefore, he tends to state his position bluntly, without concern for the feelings of the other people involved. The effect is to stir up antagonism which makes agreement needlessly hard.

Feeling types, on the other hand, set great value upon harmony and good feelings and are very aware of the likes and dislikes of the people around them. They assume that the thinker is equally aware, and resent his tactlessness toward others as well as toward themselves. What the feeling types need to remember is that most of the time the thinker does not even know how people feel about things. He needs to be told, calmly and plainly, before trouble starts, so that he can count people's feelings among the causes to be reckoned with and act accordingly.

What the thinker needs to remember is that the feeling types prize harmony and really prefer to agree with him if given a chance. He should start every discussion by mentioning the points on which he

agrees with them. If they can feel that he is basically in the same camp with them, they are ready to make concessions to preserve that harmony and stay in the same camp. The points of difference can then be discussed rather than fought over. And the thinker's logic and the feeling type's understanding of people can both be brought to bear upon the problem.

Clashes between the types arise out of the very fact that makes opposite types mutually useful to each other; the fact that each sees the side of the problem which the other naturally overlooks. For instance, the intuitive is by nature a thinker-upper; the sensing type a getter-doner. The sensing type puts his faith in the actual; the intuitive in the possible. When an intuitive comes up with a blazing new idea, his natural course is to present it in rough and sketchy form, trusting his listener to concentrate on the main point and ignore the unworked-out details. The sensing type's natural reaction is to concentrate on what is missing, decide the idea won't work (which it won't in that form), and flatly turn it down. Result: One wasted idea and much hard feeling. Either type could avoid the collision by a little respect for his opposite. The intuitive should be realistic enough to foresee the sensing type's reaction and prepare for it, work out the details of his project, and get together the necessary facts in unescapable form. The sensing type on his part should concede the intuitive's idea a fighting chance. He can say, "It might work if —" and then bring up all the objections that experience suggests and ask, "What would you do about this and this and this?' The intuitive then spends his energies happily against the obstacles, changing his ideas as necessary, and often ends with a solution valuable to them both. When compromise between opposite types is necessary, the best compromise is that which preserves to each party the advantage he considers most important. The sensing type wants the solution to be workable, the thinker wants it systematic, the feeling type wants it humanly agreeable, and the intuitive wants a door left open for growth and improvement. People often go to the mat for a scheme as a whole, when what they really care about is one particular merit that could as well be incorporated into another plan.

Whenever people differ, a knowledge of type helps to cut out irrelevant friction. More than that, it points up the advantages of the differences. No one man has to be good at everything. He only has to be good at his own stuff and decently appreciative of the other fellow's. Together, thanks to their differences, they can do a better job than if they were just alike.

TYPE IS A FOUR-LETTER WORD: USES AND ABUSES OF THE MBTI

There is no doubt about the MBTI's practical effectiveness when it is used well. My experience tells me that competent and ethical uses of the MBTI are far more common than the misuses. In this chapter, however, I have concentrated on the misuses to help new users avoid them. Sound and ethical uses are described in Chapter 12.

In his article, "Second Thoughts About the MBTI" (Training, April 1992), Ron Zemke reported views of critics and supporters of the Myers-Briggs Type Indicator. From my 20 years of experiences using the MBTI extensively, I can confirm what he found: attitudes about it range from giddy zealousness to passionate criticism.

Why such emotional reactions to a psychological instrument? It is, after all, just an instrument. I have observed several hundred people in the helping professions use and misuse the MBTI and its underlying concepts, and I have listened to many critics and supporters. In my experience, the responses at the extremes — praising it as panacea and criticizing it as triv-ial or hurtful pop psychology — come from misuses of the MBTI, misun-derstandings and mistakes that can be avoided. This chapter is about avoiding the pitfalls and staying on an ethical path to get the most out of using the Myers-Briggs.

The MBTI has two special features of its construction not found in most other psychological instruments. These can be sources of abuse by those who use the MBTI without understanding. The first is its appearance of being simple, and the second is the unusual nature of its scales and scores.

MISUSE ARISING FROM THE MBTI'S APPEARANCE

Although the MBTI is the result of very sophisticated development, it appears simple: (1) It is self-administering; (2) the questions are concerned with everyday events; (3) scoring is a straight-forward tabulating of votes for each pole of four scales; and (4) the descriptions of the types by Isabel Myers, which portray each type at its best, can seem like horoscopes, even though they actually represent the essence of a complex theory plus the results of extensive research.

Plain Language. The non-technical language of the MBTI and the type descriptions was chosen to so that respondents would feel at ease in exploring the ideas of type. The descriptions emphasize the positive aspects of each type for the same reason. Unfortunately, the non-technical appearance also seems to invite misuses of the MBTI by those who haven't studied the user's manual.

The apparent simplicity of the MBTI leads some people into using it ill-prepared. They are usually attracted to the MBTI by first responding to the instrument and being impressed by the accuracy and usefulness of the type description that goes with their MBTI results. If a trainer involves them in some exercises that show practical implications of MBTI theory in work settings (or family relationships, learning styles, careers, etc.) they are more impressed. They know they themselves can conduct exercises like that, and they feel they could easily manage a instrument that seems so non-threatening — if they can get good quality training materials. They order the materials or borrow them and begin being an MBTI user. Unfortunately, they didn't order the essential document, the MBTI user's *Manual* (1985), that explains the complexities and subtleties, explains what the authors intended, provides appropriate language for giving interpretations, summarizes the research behind the instrument, provides cautions, and gives guidelines for dealing with ethical issues — as do all the good manuals for psychological instruments.

Who Is Qualified? Professionals such as psychologists, counselors, and some educators, who are qualified by virtue of their formal education to purchase most psychological instruments from the tests' publishers, can purchase the MBTI whether or not they have taken training in its appropriate uses or have even read the *Manual*. Publishers assume professionals will act according to the ethics of their profession, but they do not always do so.

Some practitioners who have had no formal education in using psychological instruments, but have access to the MBTI through others in their organization, begin using it without coaching or adequate self-study. Some, misled by the simple-appearing questions of the MBTI, make up their own version or borrow someone's "short version," without concern for instrument validation. In the MBTI's development, thousands of variations in items were tried before the wording that works was obtained. And while MBTI scores are tabulated simply, the construction behind the scores is very sophisticated.

Consequences of Not Being Prepared. The poorly prepared MBTI user sets off the unfortunate consequences: clients who aren't helped to distinguish between type and stereotype; who settle for and spread around quick, easy, shallow interpretations; who see type as a way to excuse their own faults; who see it as a means to try to manipulate others, to classify people for job assignments, to cater to the boss, and to use it as a pastime such as speculating about the types of celebrities. Their misuses of the MBTI also create critics who are so put off by the consequences of misuse that they dismiss the MBTI, sometimes with disgust.

Any instrument in the hands of someone not skilled in using it is a blunt instrument. And in the exhilaration of getting acquainted with a new tool we all run the risk of over-using it — like the proverbial child with a new hammer who suddenly realizes everything looks like a nail. With the MBTI, new users are tempted to see possibilities of its use that stretch beyond its range; they want type theory to explain too many things. Psychological make-up is far too complex to be reduced to one set of explanations. Type is just one template to lay on human experience.

CONFUSION ABOUT SCALES AND SCORES

There are four dimensions or indices in the MBTI, each represented as a bi-polar scale:

Extraversion/Introversion, one's orientation of energy

Sensing/Intuition, one's perception preference

Thinking/Feeling, one's judgment preference

Judging/Perceiving, one's orientation to the outer world.

In type theory, everyone uses all the eight aspects of mental processing, but has a preference for one pole or the other on each dimension; one is used most naturally, is most trusted, and is given priority. When the MBTI is scored, it produces a preference score on each of the four scales, thus providing a four-letter type designation, such as ESFP, and a numerical score for each scale, such as E21, S17, F9, and P45.

Scales

The second special feature of the MBTI that has to be understood to avoid misuse is the unusual nature of the scales and what the scale scores mean. Unlike nearly all other psychological measurements, the MBTI does not measure traits or strength of traits. True to Jung's theory, the MBTI results indicate type preferences, not trait strengths. An MBTI score that reports a person's preference for introversion over extraversion, for example, says nothing about the person's skillfulness in introverting or extraverting. The score only reports that the person's responses placed him or her in the extravert or introvert category, and shows numerically how clearly the person prefers one mode over the other. In the ESFP example just given, the scores show a much clearer preference for perceiving over judging than for feeling over thinking.

Scores

The confusion comes when respondents assume or are incorrectly told that high, middle or low scores for introversion, for example, reflect on their maturity or personality balance ("This extreme score means you overuse...or you neglect . . ." Or "A low score is good because it means balance between the opposites . . ." Or "You need to develop some balancing extraversion . . ." Or "Your introversion score means you have good powers of concentration and are good at reflecting and considering things deeply.") Another gross misunderstanding shows up in such statements as, "I need to get my extraversion score up; a lot of extraverting is expected of me in this new job." No such interpretations of MBTI scores are warranted.

There are, of course, skills of extraverting and introverting, but they are not measured by the MBTI. Someone with scores that show a clear preference for introversion would be expected to be more skillful at introverting than extraverting. But the MBTI scores say nothing about that person's introverting skills relative to another person. Someone whose MBTI scores show a very clear preference for extraversion may, by virtue of training, experience, and maturity, have better introverting skills than a less mature person whose scores show a very clear preference for introversion.

If they do not represent skillfulness or strength of character, what do the MBTI scores mean? The scores are provided as letters, such as ENTJ, and a number associated with each letter. The letter part is for designating a type description for the client to consider. Isabel Myers called her instrument an Indicator because its main function is to be a pointer, for each respondent it points to one of 16 type descriptions and says, in effect, "Try this on. This is my best estimate of the psychological type represented by your responses to the MBTI."

What the Numbers Mean

The section of the MBTI *Manual* (1985, page 58) that deals with interpretation of MBTI scores begins with this statement: "Quantitative interpretation of the MBTI scores is not recommended. Scores were designed to show the direction of a preference, not its intensity." If the respondent feels that the reported type is a good fit, there usually is no need for discussion about the numbers. When a respondent is not confident of the fit, or is uncertain about a preference, the numbers can be used in the discussion to help find the type that rings most true.

For example, if the Indicator scored a client as an ISTJ, but the person felt that the description of that type was not a close fit, the practitioner would look for a low score in that person's results to suggest an alternate type description for the client to consider. With a low score for introversion, for example, the practitioner would suggest ESTJ as an alternate type to consider for a better fit.

The numerical part of the scores is also useful in answering the client's question, "If I responded to the MBTI questions another time, perhaps in a different frame of mind, what are the chances I would come out the same type?" High scores mean a high chance of coming out the same, low scores mean more chance of another type being reported.

WRONG USES OF THE MBTI

Because the MBTI does not measure competence, its use as a screening device is usually fruitless and often harmful. Consider, for example, a situation in which the management team of a middle school decided that getting an _S_J type to fill a vacancy in an administrative assistant position was desirable. They had candidates take the MBTI to screen for that type. An internal candidate whose record of competence put her at the top of the list did not come out _S_J on the MBTI, and the job was given to an external candidate who did. There are at least two big mistakes here. Coming out one type or another on the MBTI is no assurance of skillfulness. And type should never be considered a barrier to the development of any particular skills. Secondly, because the MBTI is a self-report instrument, people taking it in a hiring situation can fake their responses in the direction of what they perceive will best fit the job description, and not report their natural tendencies.

A good use of psychological type in hiring situations would begin in a similar way, analyzing the job's tasks in light of type preferences: Which types are likely to find the tasks easy or difficult? The next step is not administering the MBTI to applicants, but planning out criteria and questions for the candidating process that will get candidates to report their experience in performing such tasks. In effect, psychological type is taken into account in the job placement by using it to sharpen the job description and the interview process.

Putting together work teams based on MBTI results is another area where misuses occur. They occur mainly because of the assumption that the MBTI measures skillfulness ("Let's put an F on that team to deal with the other members' abrasiveness"). Misuses also happen because of clumsiness of the consultants or facilitators who are assisting the team building process. Using poor entry techniques, they inadvertently cause people to be secretive or defensive about their MBTI results, or to feel manipulated. Good entry techniques are described in Chapter 12.

I saw a good example of using type concepts in selecting a team member in another middle school. After being introduced to psychological type, teachers on one team recognized they had no J type on the team, and saw a relationship between that fact and their frequent problem of getting closure on team tasks. A team member was retiring, and they asked the principal if a J could be hired in her place. He wisely said the MBTI wasn't used for screening, and asked them to help interview candidates for the job. He suggested they write some questions to put to the candidates, questions about work style that might reflect the J-related traits they were looking for. They did, and they were pleased with the way their questions worked in the interviews. Later, when the new teacher took the MBTI, she scored a J preference. Of course, many people with a P preference have well-developed skills of organizing and scheduling for deadlines. The new teacher's skills would not depend on having a J preference.

Case by case evidence of the value of the MBTI in team development is easy to find, as it is in family relationships, personal development, teaching and learning, and other areas. Getting evidence of its value through carefully constructed research studies is much harder to do, but the evidence is accumulating.

RELIABILITY, VALIDITY, AND PRACTICAL EFFECTIVENESS

MBTI practitioners are cautioned not to use the "T" word, test, when describing the MBTI to clients — so as not to raise anxieties they may carry about the kinds of tests that have right and wrong answers. Nevertheless, it is certainly a psychological test, validated by all the standards that psychometricians set for such tests. Those who critique such instruments generally regard the MBTI as meeting or exceeding expectations for reliability and validity; that is, for getting consistent results and for accomplishing what it was designed to do. When they have commented on the 1985 MBTI *Manual*, they praise it as setting a new standard by which manuals for psychological instruments can be judged.

The most-consulted reference guide for psychological instruments, the *Buros Mental Measurements Yearbook* (1989, 10th edition), a source devoted to critical reviews, gives the MBTI a favorable report. "The MBTI is an excellent example of a construct-oriented test that is inextricably linked to Jung's (1923) theory of psychological types . . . [It] is not surprising that it is held in high regard by many who subscribe to this aspect of Jungian theory. It is also not surprising that those who do not accept the tenets of the theory reject, or more typically ignore, the considerable body of evidence regarding the validity of the MBTI that now exists." The *Buros* calls the evidence of construct validity "promising." As to the evidence of reliability, the reviewer regards the "stability of type classification over time" as

"somewhat disappointing." As for the four scales viewed separately, the reviewer states that ". . . there is a wealth of external validity information presented in the extensive manual (actually a handbook) that provides a reasonably consistent picture of what the individual scales do and do not measure."

THE USER AFFECTS RELIABILITY AND VALIDITY

The practitioner's essential concern is very specific: Will the MBTI be valid and reliable *for my clients?* The answer depends on three conditions, all of them under the practitioner's control: the fit of the MBTI to the application planned for it; the skill used in introducing the MBTI into the situation; and the expectations held for outcomes from its use.

Fit

I have seen some really bad applications of the MBTI. It cannot provide valid data when it is used inappropriately. For example, when used before and after some intervention to try to show how peoples' behavior/attitudes/personalities were changed for the better by the intervention. I have read research studies in which students were being taught a set of human relations skills, and the researcher administered the MBTI before and after to see if students came out more E and F after the training. There is no basis for supposing someone's type would change even if some skills were improved or attitudes changed.

There are good applications where type is a variable being used to predict behavior or performance, but these require the skills of a researcher. They require careful attention to research design issues — sample size, control of other variables, comparison groups, etc. That is beyond the scope of practitioners not trained in research methods.

The rule of thumb for getting a good fit is to avoid using the MBTI to do something for or to employees or students, and confine its use to helping them use type concepts as a tool in their work, as part of their language of problem solving.

Skill

The validity and reliability of the MBTI for individual clients depends on the skill of the practitioner in introducing it to them. If the clients get a positive introduction to the MBTI, they will give straight answers to the MBTI questions, attend carefully to the explanation of results, remain open to type ideas, and accept help in testing out the ideas and using them well. The MBTI results and its underlying ideas will be valid and reliable for them.

When the practitioner is not skilled, there are risks. For example, many people have a tendency to treat others in stereotyped ways, to categorize them and treat them according to the category rather than as the individual people they are. When introduced to type, they are likely to see it as a new way to sort, label, and manipulate others. The practitioner who is not skillful in using type concepts is likely to present them in ways that reinforce such clients' tendency to stereotype. The conditions for validity and reliability are not there.

Expectations

Unrealistic expectations for the MBTI can cloud its usefulness and make its results invalid and unreliable: expecting a one-hour or one-time orientation to type to be an adequate introduction; expecting employees to embrace it when the boss does not; expecting type, by itself, to be highly predictive of performance; and expecting the MBTI to serve as a candidate screening device, as mentioned above.

To typify good expectations, I offer this example. A large accounting firm had a good introduction to type, with the boss making clear his support for type to be part of the way they do business. One of the accountants, on learning that his type, ENFP, was not common among accountants, and doing some self analysis, began to see type as a clue to some sources of frustration in his work life. He went to the boss to discuss the problem. The boss recognized the problem and saw an opportunity to shift the employee to a new, emerging role within the organization that would call on the natural inclinations of his type, developing new clients. The results were good in all respects.

THE ETHICS OF USING THE MBTI

Ethical guidelines for using the MBTI are essentially the same as for any psychological instrument. However, there is a special problem with the MBTI. Because of the practical insights it provides into individual and group functioning, and because its language and concepts are understandable to non-psychologists, the MBTI has attracted users who have not before had to consider the ethics of gathering and using psychological data. Their previous professional training or experience may not have taught them the essentials such as: taking the instrument

must be voluntary; results must be given only to that person; and the person must get a face-to-face explanation of the results, including what is indicated and not indicated by the results. These and other ethical guidelines I have included in Chapter 12.

The ethical problems are compounded because our clients themselves are naive about ethical pitfalls. They often get excited about using type concepts, and talk about and apply them freely without considering the ethical fallout. Obviously, we must not only model ethical behavior for them, but also explicitly teach them good ways to use type concepts and precautions to take so that their good intentions don't backfire.

This chapter has highlighted misuses of the MBTI and the bad consequences that follow the misuses. I took this approach to dramatize for new MBTI users the responsibilities that go with effective use of the MBTI and its underlying concepts. All of us want to be ethical, but sometimes in our drive to be effective and get results we run the risk of overlooking or obscuring the ethics of a situation. When we do that, we jeopardize our own credibility and the long-term effectiveness of our work. 🐾

6

TYPE AND STEREOTYPE

Stereotyping is a risk that is always with all of us. We tend to stereotype those who are most different from ourselves because we understand them less well — a rule that holds true for type differences as well as cultural, racial, etc. For example, extraverts may stereotypically project on to introverts the awkwardness they themselves would feel when stuck without having something to say or some action to be involved in. The comfort the introvert feels in reflection and silences may not occur to the extravert. The opposite projection, of course, is a risk for introverts. MBTI users have a special responsibility to examine their own stereotypes and to teach about type in ways that minimize clients' stereotypical use of type concepts.

WHY DO WE STEREOTYPE?

No one wants to be guilty of stereotyping, but all of us are. Why? Webster's definition of stereotype gives clues. When the term is used in describing ideas, the definition is: "A standard mental picture held in common by members of a group and representing an oversimplified opinion, ...or uncritical judgment ...an oversimplified generalization making it easy to dismiss divergent groups." Why do we stereotype when all we mean to do is have helpful labels for experience?

The cognitive psychologists remind us that it is human nature to categorize. We can't deal with the daily bombardment of perceptual stimuli in their raw form; the stimuli are too overwhelming in number and variety for each to be acknowledged in its uniqueness. So we sort them into categories, and deal with them in these sets. Thinking in categories simplifies the perceptual field enough for our minds to

work comfortably. The dark side of this process is that our drive for order and mental comfort leads us to form and use poorly constructed categories that are too simple and biased. And those categories are stereotypes, categories that tend to close our thought processes rather than keep them sensitive to possible bias.

TYPE AND STEREOTYPE

We who use type theory certainly want to avoid stereotyping the 16 psychological types. No doubt most of us who use type were drawn to it because it gives us categories to think with that are vast improvements over the familiar unconstructive categories by which people sort each other. Our common goal is to give people more helpful categories to put in place of less helpful ones. Carl Jung, Katharine Briggs, and Isabel Myers worked hard to select terms for psychological type that would avoid bias and minimize stereotyping. We continue that process. It surely is not a finished job.

But we are all caught with our biases showing. Being an intuitive type, my dominant intuition colors and steers my perceptions in such a way that I cannot be sure that my views of the sensing process or of sensing types aren't stereotypes, at least in some respects. Time and again my sensing friends have helped me see the stereotypes I was using. Type theory tells me that sensing is my least developed mental process or function, and the most unconscious of my four mental processes. I believe it. Sensing just doesn't get much respect in the flow of my thought processes, so how can I expect it to assert itself and show up my stereotypes for what they are? How wonderful to have some sensing friends who help me break my stereotypes about sensing. If I, who have been studying type for over 20 years, unwittingly use language that stereotypes people when I talk about the types, what happens in the minds of those I teach, who first learn about type from me? Perhaps the stereotypes get embellished and hardened as they are passed on.

Just as I am guilty of unfavorable stereotyping of people with types and type preferences different from my own, so I am guilty of favorable biases creeping into my language and thoughts about my own type preferences.

It happens to all of us.

None of us is immune from stereotyping. One person, very knowledgeable about type, and whose name we know well, wrote these descriptive phrases about thinking types. "Thinking types...are relatively unemotional people and uninterested in people's feelings . . . [They] tend to relate well only to other thinking types . . . [They] may seem hard-hearted . . ." We all know some thinking types who are accurately described by these phrases; but do you detect stereotyping here? These are Isabel Myers' words, from the 1962 MBTI *Manual* and from page 14 of the first edition of *Introduction to Type*. They are part of the section called "Effects of each preference in work situations."

Isabel Myers was a very careful writer, to say the least. It is impossible to overstate the exquisite care she took in finding the right words for describing type, clear words that would not stereotype or have misleading connotations. Her perfectionism in writing is typified in the fact that the manuscript of *Gifts Differing* was essentially complete 20 years before publication. I understand she would take it off the shelf every week or so to change a word. Isabel Myers was a dominant feeling type, an INFP. If stereotyping were to appear in her descriptions, where would it most likely be? In her description of the mental process opposite her dominant, her least conscious process — thinking. Several of us with a preference for the thinking process objected to the phrases, called them to her attention, and she changed them to read, "Thinking types...do not show emotion readily and are often uncomfortable dealing with people's feelings...(She eliminated the second phrase I quoted above)...[They] tend to be firm minded..." Allen Hammer, editing *Introduction to Type* for its 1987 version, chose to eliminate the first phrase. Its closest counterpart in the new list of phrases describing thinking types is, "... respond more to people's ideas that to their feelings." *

Are these wording changes nit-picking? Not to me. When we introduce someone to type, the credibility of type theory *for that person* is on the line. Our task is to find and use language that reduces the risk of type being distorted into stereotype.

Watching our language.

What are some signs of stereotyping, some red flags, we can watch for in our language? Phrases containing absolutes, like always and never, are suspect. "You can always count on sensing types to . . .

---

*For readers interested in examining ways that type bias persists among those of us who use and teach about type, particularly the stereotyping of sensing types, Hammer has an insightful article, "Typing or stereotyping: Unconscious bias in applications of psychological type theory." 1985. Journal of Psychological Type, Volume 10.

stuff envelopes . . . take minutes of the meeting" — an example of intuitives relegating mundane tasks no one likes. "Never trust an NF with balancing a checkbook." Another sign is excusing one's behavior on the grounds of type. "I'm allowed to be spacey; I'm an intuitive." "That's my J compulsiveness."

In dividing up jobs, some people who know about type are quick to assume that the decisions about who gets what jobs can be based on a superficial look at type preferences, without other considerations such as familiarity, desire, skillfulness, etc.

The risk of stereotypes in humor.

Watch for stereotypes in anecdotes and humor. Humor often relies on exaggeration to get its punch, and exaggerations of type character- istics may result in unwanted negative stereotypes. Some humor is grounded in stereotype, of course; for example, ethnic humor like Polish jokes and the "Jewish American Princess." This is humor at the expense of the group that is stereotyped. Jack Benny made a career out of the stereotype of himself that he created as the basis for most of his jokes. This is a benign stereotype, of course, because he invented the image and it hurt no one.

The Benny example helps us look at stereotyping in the humor we use in explaining type to people. Through the years, I have found car- toons helpful in introducing type concepts. I thought I had screened them for stereotypes, but my wife Carolyn, a feeling type, spotted some I missed in the cartoons dealing with the thinking and feeling preferences.

One is a Trudy cartoon by Jerry Marcus, a single panel, showing her confronting her husband with an exasperated look on her face. He is seated in his easy chair, his hands folded, with a smug look on his face. She is saying, "Your argument is logical, sensible, fair, perceptive and factual and I hate you."

I had been using it to show that thinking types believe an issue should be settled when they produce an objective, impersonal and log- ical argument, while feeling types don't want it settled until the reason- ing gives adequate weight to the human, personal consequences of the decision. Carolyn showed me the stereotypes. The feeling type seems to be giving in to the thinking type's argument, acknowledging logical reasoning as superior, though distasteful. Feeling gets the last word, but loses the argument. In the way I was using the cartoon, not calling attention to the stereotyping, I let pass not only the implication that feeling judgment is subordinate to thinking judgment but also that thinking is for men and feeling is for women. I still use the cartoon at times, but now I add a discussion about stereotyping.

A Frank and Ernest cartoon by Thaves is another I have used. In its single panel, the two of them are looking up at a very dark and starry night. One says, "Do you realize all the rest of our galaxy is moving away from us at one-third the speed of light?" The response is, "Do you suppose it was something we said?"

In using the cartoon, I thought I was making the point that thinking types give more attention to impersonal phenomena in looking for life's meanings, while feeling types are more likely to look to personal events as the source of understanding. Until Carolyn showed me, I had missed the stereotype: it is silly for feeling types to apply feeling criteria where they don't belong. I am now looking for a companion cartoon that shows a thinking type looking silly applying impersonal analysis where it doesn't fit.

PERSONA, SHADOW, AND STEREOTYPE

Carl Jung's concepts of persona and shadow help us understand why we are more likely to stereotype some groups that others and why we are not likely to recognize our own stereotyping when we do it. The persona is the part of myself that I show the world, the part I am comfortable enough with to allow it to represent me to other people. The shadow is the back side of the persona, the dark side away from the light of public exposure, in which are aspects of myself I tend to deny in consciousness.

How does this relate to stereotypes? First we look at the relationship of type to persona and shadow. The persona is expressed most easily through the dominant and auxiliary processes, while the third and fourth processes most often carry the contents of the unconscious shadow. In my own case, my feeling and sensing processes are mainly in the shadow; they are less mature, less conscious, less controllable and predictable when in my conscious life, and more worrisome. So when people and situations call on my feeling and sensing processes, my shadowy and immature versions of these processes color my perceptions and give me an unconscious bias that results in stereotypes. I am likely to see immaturity or threatening motives in those others who are so different from my persona, who

remind me of my shadow side, the part of me I want to keep hidden. So I project onto their behavior the dark meanings that come out of my shadow, and I have produced a stereotype.

AN ACTIVITY FOR IDENTIFYING STEREOTYPES

No doubt stereotyping is related to the attitudes of extraversion, introversion, judgment, and perception as well as to the four processes. To demonstrate to yourself the extent to which we all carry with us stereotypes of type preferences that are opposite ours, try this activity with some friends or colleagues who know type concepts. Pick one dimension of type, EI, SN, TF, or JP. I will illustrate with EI. With your group, complete three tasks.

First, each person chooses a partner whose EI preference is the same. The partners in each E pair will individually think of specific people he or she knows are introverts and write down four or five words or phrases that accurately describe the introverting characteristics of those people, taking care to use unbiased descriptors. Using the same care, the partners in each I pair will individually use the same process to identify the extraverting characteristics of their sample of extraverts. Allow three or four minutes for this step.

Next, the partners will discuss the words they wrote individually and edit them as needed to replace words that might be seen as stereotyping. Schedule five minutes for this step.

Finally, each pair of Es will get with a pair of Is to present both sets of descriptors, to discuss any stereotyping suggested in the two lists, and to find unbiased replacement words. In your discussion, you will find more stereotyping than you suppose. This discussion time is also a good opportunity for exploring the meanings of appearances, that is, for asking the group members of the opposite preference questions about their introversion or extraversion. For example, in a recent discussion an introvert asked the extraverts, "Why do you seem to need to fill every silence in a conversation?" And an extravert said, "Help me understand why introverts often seem to be aloof." You can give this discussion all the time you have available; in my experience, we always have to end it before the people feel finished with it. After the discussion, I believe you'll agree with me that stereotyping is natural and inevitable.

Sometimes when I use this activity, we take the participants' individual lists of E and I words and combine them into composite lists.

Some words appear on several people's lists. On one recent occasion, these were the extravert and introvert descriptors on two or more lists:

active	*thoughtful*
open	*quiet*
talkative	*reserved*
sociable	*shy*
out-going	*serious*
friendly	*deep*

As a whole group we examined these words and others on the lists looking for stereotypes or terms that could lead to misunderstanding. We applied three stereotype-detecting criteria to each term:

1. ***Does the*** *term raise a red flag, suggesting bias for or against?* The words listed above did not seem biased to the participants, but others on the composite lists raised red flags very quickly. For example, *superficial* and *entertaining* on the extravert list, and *loner* and *quiet assurance* on the introvert list. We all knew people for whom the words were accurate, but we all agreed the terms applied to special cases and not the general categories of extraversion and introversion.

2. ***Could the*** *term be misleading by implying a negative opposite trait for people of the other preference?* We decided this criterion eliminated most of the 12 words listed above. For example, using *active* for extraverts could imply *passive* or *inactive* as traits of introverts, *open* could imply *closed;* using *thoughtful* for introverts could imply *thoughtless* or *unthinking* as a trait of extraverts; and *quiet* could imply *loud* or *noisy* for its opposite. Each time I use this activity participants come to the conclusion that explicitly stating the opposite you intend is important to avoid misunderstanding, that is, giving the words in pairs. For example, *active and reflective* are a good pair, as are *out-going and reserved,* and *expressive and quiet.* By finding good pairs, we returned most of the 12 words to the list. But good pairs were hard to agree on, and our "good" lists never get very long.

3. ***Does it distinguish*** *between the preferences, or could it be applied also to the opposite or other preferences?* We decided that *friendly* didn't distinguish between extravert and introvert. And some extraverts regarded themselves as *shy,* so those words were eliminated. Also eliminated were *open* and *thoughtful* because they were not distinctive to extravert or introvert. Four out of five words

on the composite lists are not mentioned above; they were eliminated, mainly because they did not meet this criterion — words such as *lively, people-oriented, enthusiastic, expansive, careful, brief, self-encouraged, and discreet.* They were dropped because they could apply to more than one of the eight preferences that make up the types.

This activity always has the effect of making participants alert to the need for care in choosing descriptors for the type preferences. They uniformly speak of it as a powerful learning experience.

WHAT WE CAN DO

Stereotyping in our conceptions and language about type are natural and inevitable, but we can guard against it and head it off. And we must if we are to grow.

- We can be alert to the spots where we are most vulnerable to stereotyping, which will differ for each of us as our types differ.
- We can be aware, those of us who use and teach others about type concepts, that we have in common a very big problem. In our enthusiasm, in our desire to convince people of the value of type, we overstate and overgeneralize — a sure source of stereotyping.
- We can ask our opposites to help us spot our possible biases as we talk about type, and to suggest alternate, unbiased language.
- We can realize that improving our language about type requires an improvement in our understanding of our opposites, a deeper knowledge of type.
- And, finally, we can assume that the quest to drive out our stereotypes about type never ends.

We can help each other. On of my fondest memories of Isabel Myers is the effective way she helped people improve their understanding of type by gently offering them a non-stereotyping word to replace a biased one they had used. She'd say, "I believe they'll understand better if you say . . ." or "I used to say it that way until my ISTJ husband showed me a better wording . . ." In the same spirit, we can help each other.

7

TAKING TYPE INTO ACCOUNT IN EDUCATION

By Isabel Briggs Myers

AUTHORS NOTE: The following essay by Isabel Briggs Myers was written in October, 1971, to describe how type theory can be used to understand the learning of children from their early years in school. Isabel Myers was always very concerned with the fact that many children are taught, very early, in ways that make them lose confidence in themselves, and cause them to come to hate school. She graciously gave permission to include her thoughts here.

Schools are being told that they are accountable for educating every child. They are required to teach the basic skills, so that every child grows up able to read, write and balance a checkbook. And they are required to plant various sorts of knowledge, deeply enough so that it will germinate, take root and bear fruit.

Both demands are better met if the schools take into account the type differences among children. These are not quantitative differences that can be expressed simply as a higher or lower degree of mental ability. They are qualitative differences, differences as to the kind of perception and the kind of judgment that the child prefers to use. It is his preferences that make his type. Children of different types have a different "mix" of abilities, different needs, interests and motivations, and different degrees of success in school.

The preference that has the most conspicuous consequences in education is the choice between the two kinds of perception, the choice between sensing and intuition. Sensing focuses interest and attention upon the concrete reality that is apparent to the five senses. Sensing children are more interested in doing something, almost anything, with almost any tangible object, than in listening to what anyone is saying unless it has to do with action or adds something definite to their picture of the physical world. In contrast, intuition focuses interest and attention upon the end results of one's own unconscious processes, which include the translation of symbols-words into meaning, and meaning into words. Intuitive children thus tend to take a positive interest in language, spoken or written, and acquire a facility that is convenient in class and in verbal ability tests and also enables them to state clearly and usefully to themselves the relationships and possibilities suggested by their intuition.

It is therefore understandable that, as most schools are now run, sensing children have less use for school than intuitive children do (often no use at all), that on the average they make lower grades and score lower on intelligence tests (though not enough lower to account for their grades), and that they far more frequently drop out.

If we are to have a system of universal education that does justice to all the types, I think we must draw a sharp distinction between skills and knowledge. Knowledge spreads over a tremendous variety of subjects, each of which may be interesting and useful to certain types and a waste of time to others. But the basic skills are essential for all the types, and should be taught in such a way as to give every child what he needs.

The usual first grade has a substantial majority of sensing children and a smaller number of intuitives. The sensing children do not want to have to cope with anything unexplainable. The intuitives do not want to be bored by anything tedious and dull. Except for an occasional child who may have been let into the secret by an intuitive parent or have found it out for himself, none of the children, sensing or intuitive, know that letters stand for sounds.

In most first grades, nobody (for a long time) tells them this one crucial fact that makes sense of the process of learning to read. Reading thus consists of memorizing "sight words," recognizable only by their general shape. A new word is an insoluble mystery until teacher tells you what it is. Content is necessarily restricted to repetition of the few words thus far memorized. "Dick. See Dick. See Dick run." This method of teaching manages to frustrate both the sensing children and the intuitives. Reading, which ought to be a magical extension of one's own experience is both unexplainable and dull.

To meet the needs of the sensing children who want things to be explicit and the intuitive children who want unlimited possibilities, first grades should introduce intensive phonics at the very beginning, so that every child in the class knows that there is a perfectly good way to tell what new words are. He is going to be able to read, very soon, up to the limits of his speaking vocabulary. And removal of the artificial limits on vocabulary means that he can read vastly more interesting things. He can, in fact, attempt anything he cares to tackle.

From the standpoint of the child's success in school and his development as a person, with ambition, initiative, and confidence in himself the start of first grade marks a crucial fork in the road. That is the point at which he decides either that school makes sense or that it does not, that it is interesting or boring, that he can or cannot do these new things. If he cannot do the new things, his only defense against the humiliation of being "dumb" is to decide that such things are not worth doing.

The pitfall in the teaching of arithmetic skills is basically the same as the pitfall in teaching reading. The children who try to cope with the symbols without recognizing the realities these stand for are doomed to frustration. They never win through to the beautiful certainties in the realm of numbers. They just memorize incantations. "7 and 5 is 12." "11 minus 4 is 7." "5 times 7 is 35." When the teacher gives you the first two numbers of an incantation, you have to remember the third. If you forget that third number, there is nothing you can do about it. And if you are given a problem and can't see what kind of incantation to use, there is nothing you can do about that.

The solution is to establish the reality of numbers first. The symbols then can be understood as a way of talking about reality. There should be no operations with disembodied numerals, no incantations, no memorizing, no flash cards for "addition facts" and "subtraction facts," no verbal drill, until the children are thoroughly familiar with manual operations with quantities. To many sensing children, things you can touch and move are real but words are not.

The form in which a question is put can change the whole spirit of the proceedings. "How much is 7 and 5?" implies that the child ought to know by this time and the teacher wants to find out whether he does or not. This is wrong side to. The child is the one who should be doing the finding out. "Find out how much is 7 and 5!" is an invitation to action. Using number blocks, for instance, the child can take a block that is seven squares high and stand it against the number tower. Naturally it reaches to seven. Then he can take a block that is five squares high and stack it on top of the seven. Together they reach to twelve. Every time he does it they reach to twelve. In fact, he can see that they have to reach to twelve; the seven block is always three squares short of ten; the first three squares of the five block always get you to ten; the other two squares always stick up beyond ten and reach to twelve. A similar certainty has to exist in the case 17 and 5, 27 and 5, and so on up.

Consistent use of this approach gives the child a picture of the number system as a whole, the place of any given number in that system, and its relation to other numbers. When he starts doing operations with numerals instead of blocks, he knows the quantities they stand for and what he is doing with those quantities. And when he is given a problem, he has a decent chance of seeing what he must do to solve it.

Reading, writing and arithmetic are well-defined skills that every child needs to acquire. But knowledge, as distinguished from skills, is another matter. It has no limits. Schools must decide what tiny fraction they will try to teach. If we take it as axiomatic that a child should be taught things that are of lasting benefit to him, either by making him more effective or by otherwise enhancing his life, one brutal conclusion follows. There is no use in teaching a child things he intends to forget.

Nothing will stick in a child's mind long enough to do him any good unless it interests him, and here type plays a major role. The combination of a child's preferred kind of perception and his preferred kind of judgment tends to concentrate his interest in fields where these find scope, as shown in the comparison on page three of the *Introduction to Type*. His remaining preferences influence the kind of work he will like to do in those fields. Hence knowledge that is relevant, even illuminating, for a person with a given set of preferences can be acutely boring to a person with the opposite set. Aside from routine warnings against common dangers, like carbon monoxide and the signing of documents unread, there is probably no body of knowledge that can profitably be "taught" to every child regardless.

Time and effort spent in trying to teach a child something against his own will are worse than wasted. Real harm is done. If a child is not interested in what he is supposed to be learning, he is bored. And the habit of being bored is disastrous for children, because it destroys their native curiosity. Babies and pre-schoolers have a great urge to make sense of the world. They devote their energies happily to finding out one thing after another, whatever fixes their curiosity at the moment. They learn at a tremendous rate, and they remember what they learn, because it becomes a part of their world as they know it. Learning is high adventure, not a chore.

School should be a continuation of the adventure. Children in all the grades should be given maximum opportunity to learn the things that have meaning and interest for them in terms of their own kind of perception and their own kind of judgment. To the extent that they are given this opportunity, they gain not only in interest but in application and intelligence as well. People of any age, from six to sixty, apply themselves with greater vigor to the task in hand when they are interested. People of any age are more intelligent when they are interested than when they are bored.

A child permitted to study what interests him learns more and remembers it. The most valuable outcome, however, is the effect upon the development of his perception and judgment. A purposeful finding out about almost anything develops his perception. And a self-imposed doing of whatever is necessary to that end develops his judgment far more than would mere obedience to a teacher's authority. The lifelong importance of adequate development of perception and judgment is shown in past and current studies with the Type Indicator. Good perception and judgment are associated with achievement, which is reasonable because they make a person more effective in whatever he sets out to do. They are also associated with mental and physical health, which again is reasonable because they enable a person to cope more competently with his problems and thus lessen or eliminate strain.

Ways of making room for individual interests and study can be worked out in any school where authority will accept the idea. In fact, they can be worked out independently by any teacher. A seminar approach can be taken, in which the class is given a bird's-eye view of the different aspects of the subject and then allowed to sign up to work on whichever aspect each finds most interesting. Or a list of individual projects can be designed to appeal to widely different types. Flexibility can be achieved by framing some exam questions for sensing types, others for intuitives, everyone being permitted to leave out the two he likes least. Or it may be announced in advance that everyone may formulate and answer one question of his own, substituting it for one not in his field.

Where students are old enough to take the Type Indicator, as in 7th to 12th grades, their types can be ascertained, subject to confirmation by the students themselves. Teachers can then learn by direct observation how their subjects need to be presented in order to catch the interest of ST, SF, NF, and NT types respectively, and can share their findings with other teachers. Feedback to the students about their types can add to their understanding of themselves and others, can reassure them that it is all right to be the kind of person they are, and can relieve the strain of personal conflicts at home or elsewhere by showing how these arise from differences in type. It can even help them to develop their perception and judgment. Page four of the *Introduction to Type* has instructions how to do it, exercising each kind of perception and each kind of judgment, separately, in turn, to find out what each can contribute to the solution of a problem.

Children in lower grades can also practice using the different kinds of perception and judgment one at a time in appropriate ways. Exact observation will exercise sensing. Figuring out possible ways to solve a difficulty will exercise intuition. Thinking out all the unintended consequences that may result from an action will exercise thinking. Weighing how other people will feel about things will exercise feeling.

An early clue to a child's type may be obtainable from his response to these activities. The sensing child should find the sensing exercise easier and more fun than the intuitive exercise. The little thinker will prefer thinking about consequences to guessing about other people's feelings. And so on. An observant teacher may be able to draw useful inferences as to the way each child's mind works and what will help him most. Whether she does or not, the children will benefit directly from practice in these four different, important ways of using their minds. 🐾

8
THE DYNAMICS OF THE TYPES

A TYPE IS MORE THAN FOUR PREFERENCES

The Myers-Briggs Type Indicator provides scores on four separate scales — EI, SN, TF, and JP — and reports a preference on each scale — such as E, S, F, and J; four preferences that are apparently independent of each other. When respondents are told that the four letters taken together, ESFJ, represent one of the 16 types, it is natural for them to conclude that a type is a composite or addition of four separate qualities — E plus S plus F plus J. That natural conclusion about the four type letters is wrong. Each type is a distinctive, dynamic organization of mental energy, greater than the sum of four preferences. The name we use for the energy systems of the 16 types is *type dynamics.*

Many, perhaps most, people who learn about the psychological types through the MBTI do not learn about the theory of types as dynamic wholes, as Jung and Myers wrote about it. It is not surprising that they consider the types to be sets of four separate preferences. The confusion comes about, in part, because a self-report instrument with four separate scales is used to identify the types.

When Jung developed his theory of psychological types he foresaw it being used by professionals trained to treat emotional problems; he did not anticipate the need to identify the types with an instrument such as the MBTI. Myers and Briggs saw the need for the ideas of type to be available to people in everyday life. When they decided to develop an instrument for identifying type preferences, they faced the problem of having people self-report their tendencies and interests that would show one type as the best fit. In an instrument, they could not teach people Jung's complex theory and have them pick a type that seemed best to them. They decided the most sound way to proceed was to have people vote on the four preference pairs separately. They devised four scales, and wrote items for each scale.

The person who has scored E, S, F, and J, for example, is shown the Myers-Briggs description of the type Jung called extraverted feeling with sensing, the type to which Myers and Briggs gave the shorthand label, ESFJ. If the person reads the type description and it seems to be a good fit, the person has selected a type, not just four preferences.

If a type is more than the four preferences, what should readers of this book know about the whole patterns of the types and the dynamics of them? Some of our clients will be ready to learn about the dynamics of the types, and our job is to teach them. This chapter is about the theory of the dynamics and includes some ideas you can use in teaching your clients or students. The central feature of the dynamics is the belief that each of the types has one of the mental processes that is dominant and favored, and a second mental process that is auxiliary, a helper to the dominant. How they function in the personality and work together is the main subject of what follows.

TYPE THEORY IS ABOUT PERCEPTION AND JUDGMENT

Jung's theory of psychological types is about patterns of conscious mental activity. At the most basic level, it is about perception and judgment. In Jung's view, all conscious mental activity is either perception activity — awareness, taking in data — or judgment activity — making decisions about what has come into awareness.

Perception and judgment are truly basic in the human condition. Our troubles come from faulty perception and poor judgment, and our progress certainly comes from clear perception and sound judgment. We may not think about it often, but the quality of any human activity — caring for a child, building a house, fighting a fire, running a business, playing tennis, preparing a meal, etc. — depends on the quality of perception and judgment that goes into them. Jung saw that the ways we go about perceiving and judging differ, and the differences come in patterns.

One of the points of confusion for people learning about type is the use of the terms, perception and judgment. We who talk and write about type use the terms at three different levels of meaning. We need to try to avoid confusion by defining the three here at the beginning of the chapter. The first is the broad meaning given in the two previous paragraphs. The second and third meanings are specific meanings in the theory of types, one provided by Jung and the other devised by Myers and Briggs.

Perception, in Jung's *specific* meaning, refers to the two mental processes of sensing and intuition; in his view, all perceptions come by way of those two processes. His *specific* meaning for *judgment* is the exercise of the two ways of deciding: thinking and feeling.

The third meaning, given by Myers and Briggs, is also specific: the judgment-perception dimension of type that is represented in the JP scale of the Indicator and the last letter of the four-letter type designations. Specifically, the last letter indicates which mental process shows in a person's outer life, the preferred judging process (T or F) or the preferred perception process (S or N). Throughout the book I have tried to make clear which of the three meanings I was using in any situation. Here, discussing the dynamics of type, it is essential that meanings aren't confused.

THREE MEANINGS OF PERCEPTION AND JUDGMENT

1. Broad meanings:
> *Perception = awareness, taking in data*
> *Judgment = making decisions*

2. The mental processes:
> *Two perception processes = sensing and intuition*
> *Two judgment processes = thinking and feeling*

3. The fourth dimension of type, as represented in the **J** or **P** preference.

DYNAMIC RELATIONSHIPS OF THE MENTAL PROCESSES

What is the dominant process?

Jung said that all conscious mental activity can be sorted into four categories: the two ways of perceiving — sensing and intuition — and the two ways of judging — thinking and feeling. Everyone regularly uses all four, but not for equal amounts of time or equally well. From childhood, each of us has come to rely on one process more than the others. It seems more trustworthy, and so we trust it and use it more. And the more we use it, the more mature and reliable it becomes. Its use seems most natural and interesting, and it draws our attention more than the others. That one mental process becomes dominant, the centerpost, the core of the personality.

Why do people need a dominant mental process?

If one of the mental processes were not dominant, in charge of a person's conscious mental life, the person would not have a central theme to organize consciousness. In people with the feeling process dominant, for example, conscious mental activity is organized around keeping their lives in harmony with the values they prize most highly. They personalize their experiences, including objective events, so they can deal with them with their best skills. This approach is the polar opposite of people with thinking as the dominant process, who objectify personal events so they can use their best skills, logic and objective analysis.

There needs to be one dominant because mental processing can not be organized both ways, feeling and thinking. The contrasts between feeling and sensing, or feeling and intuition, are not so dramatic, but whichever of the four mental processes is dominant, it shows its distinctive kind of organization of mental activity. The dominant serves to unify people's lives.

How do the four different kinds of dominant differ?

People in whom sensing perception is the centerpost, the dominant mental process, are above all else practical people. Their close attention to data provided by the senses makes them well attuned to immediate experiences, the literal facts at hand, the concrete realities. People who have intuitive perception as a dominant process have their consciousness mainly focused on associations, abstractions, theories, and possibilities that do not depend directly on the senses. Above all else, they believe in intuitive insights and imagination to set life's directions.

People in whom thinking judgment is the strongest mental process are above all else logical, and have orderly, analytical minds. All experience must fit into logical mental systems, or the systems must be reworked to accommodate perceptions that don't fit. Children of this pattern may not seem logical by adult standards, but internally the drive is to test and organize all experience by logical criteria, even if the logic is still undeveloped. They naturally treat people and things (and themselves) impersonally.

Finally, people with feeling judgment as the dominant mental process direct their lives toward human values and harmony, above all else. They weigh all experience as being harmonious or dissonant with the values and priorities of their own lives and the others they care about. They are naturally more attuned to the subjective world of feelings and values, and more alert to the humane issues in any situation.

What keeps the dominant from making a person one-sided?

If people trusted and developed only one of the four mental processes their lives would be essentially one-dimensional. Unfortunately, we all know such people. There are some whose perceptions are not focused or tempered by good judgment. What they perceive from moment to moment, day to day, stirs their interest, and they flit from one interest to another without adequately weighing the value of what they are doing or the logical consequences. They are unstable like a sailboat with too much sail and not enough keel. And we know others whose judgments are locked so tightly that they remain unrenewed by fresh perception. They are like the sailboat with a keel too heavy for its small sail, keeping a steady course but not making much progress. To avoid such one-sidedness, people must develop another of the mental processes to be a major, reliable helper to the dominant. Jung called the second process the auxiliary. It is needed to balance the dominant process, as balance is needed between sail and keel.

DOMINANT PROCESS

Favorite among S, N, T or F
Governing force
Unifies one's life
Best developed and most used process
"The general"

Can any of the other three processes be the auxiliary?

In Jung's theory, the two kinds of perception — sensing and intuition — are polar opposites of each other. Similarly, thinking judgment and feeling judgment are polar opposites. In a person with intuition dominant, it follows that sensing is necessarily the least developed and least trusted (and trustworthy) of the four mental processes; it could not be the auxiliary. That is not an arbitrary feature of the theory, but rather a logical condition in human experience. In the instant that conscious attention is focused on intuitions, it cannot simultaneously be focused on sensations, and vice versa. I may shift quickly from one to the other, but not attend to both at once. Thus, I attend to my intuitive perception and develop my intuitive capacities at the expense of my sensing perception. The concentration of energy in intuition means a withholding of energy from its opposite, sensing.

Because of the polarity concepts just described, a person with intuition dominant can not have sensing as the auxiliary because sensing, being the polar opposite of intuition, will be the process that is least accessible in consciousness and least developed. The reverse is true for people with sensing dominant, and the same principle applies to the other dominant-auxiliary combinations. So the auxiliary is always formed in the dimension that the dominant is not in. That is, a person having sensing or intuition as the dominant process will develop either thinking or feeling as the auxiliary process. Similarly, a person with thinking or feeling judgment as the dominant process will have sensing or intuitive perception as the auxiliary process.

Most important is the *balance* provided by this arrangement. A dominant in the perception dimension is balanced by having the auxiliary in the judgment dimension, and vice versa. Good perception is only effective when sound judgment gives it direction and purpose. And judgments are sound only when they are informed by adequate, clear perceptions. One balances the other as it completes and complements the other with a totally different kind of mental processing.

How does the auxiliary balance the dominant?

Perception and judgment are not expected to be *evenly* balanced —whichever is dominant will always be in charge; but the auxiliary must be developed so that one-sidedness is avoided. Balance does not mean equal development or equal influence in the personality. Rather, the auxiliary complements and supplements the dominant. Continuing the sailboat analogy, the sail and keel need to be balanced. If the boat is for racing, sail is dominant and some stability is given up for the potential of speed and maneuverability. But there must be adequate keel for stability. If the boat is for cruising, stabil-

AUXILIARY PROCESS

Second favorite among S, N, T or F
A perceiving (S or N) process if the dominant is judging
(T or F)
A judging (T or F) process if the dominant is perceiving
(S or N)
Used in the outer world if the dominant is introverted
Used in the inner world if the dominant is extraverted
"The general's aide"

ity is the dominant concern, but the sail capacity has to be enough to make the trip interesting.

In the personality, a person who has a perception process (S or N) as dominant is most interested in being open to and taking in experiences. But this person needs a well-developed judgment process (T or F) as auxiliary to test the value and logical soundness of the perceptions. The person with T or F dominant needs a well-developed perception process (S or N) as auxiliary to give the judgments enough data to be sound.

What are the main differences between the dominant and auxiliary combinations?

Combining dominant and auxiliary processes, eight sets are formed:

Dominant	Auxiliary
SENSING with Thinking	INTUITION with Thinking
SENSING with Feeling	INTUITION with Feeling
THINKING with Sensing	FEELING with Sensing
THINKING with Intuition	FEELING with Intuition

The meaning of the eight sets can be illustrated by the varied emphases in the left-hand column above. The SENSING-with-thinking people focus their practical outlook on the aspects of the world that are readily subject to logical analysis — the objects, machinery, and more impersonal transactions of life. In contrast, the SENSING-with-feeling people attend primarily to the practical side of human needs. Still different in emphasis, the THINKING-with-sensing people are those who wish to put their system of logical order on the practical matters of the world. And the THINKING-with-intuition people are those who wish to put their system of logical order on the abstract and intangible matters of the world.

The differences suggested here are subtle but not superficial. The INTUITION-with-thinking people, for example, may test their intuitive inspirations with logical analysis, and the analysis may shoot down the inspiration. However, if the inspiration is compelling enough, no amount of illogic discovered in the idea will be enough to kill it. In a showdown, intuition will win because it is the dominant process in INTUITION-with-thinking people. In contrast, the THINKING-with-intuition person would likely sacrifice the intuition in such a showdown.

THE ATTITUDES: EXTRAVERSION AND INTROVERSION

How do extraversion and introversion affect the dominant?

Extraversion and introversion are called the attitudes or orientations to life, referring to the orientation of the person's *dominant* process. People who use their dominant process primarily to run their actions *in the world* outside themselves are extraverting the dominant and are referred to as extraverts. To balance their extraverted dominant, their auxiliary is used mainly introvertedly, to run their inner life. In contrast, people who *reserve* the dominant process primarily for the personal world of inner thoughts and reflections are introverting the dominant and are referred to as introverts. They use their auxiliary mainly to run their outer life.

Extraversion and introversion provide the second way that the auxiliary provides balance to the dominant: if the dominant is extraverted, the auxiliary brings balance by being mainly introverted, and if the dominant is introverted, the auxiliary brings balance by serving extravertedly.

The dominant process tells the most about a person. Extraverts, by definition, reveal their best first. Introverts, reserving their best for their inner, their favored world, reveal mainly their auxiliary process to others. Only close associates will be allowed to see the most valued process in operation. Thus we come to know introverts more slowly. It is through a well-developed extraverted auxiliary that introverts function effectively in their outer world. In contrast, it is through a well-developed introverted auxiliary that extraverts obtain reflection and depth in their inner world.

How do the eight patterns change into sixteen?
The addition of EI.

When extraversion and introversion are added to the eight dominant-auxiliary combinations they are expanded to 16. Thus there are eight extraverted sets and eight introverted sets.

Consider, for example, how the extraversion-introversion dimension expands the THINKING-with-intuition pattern. The extraverted version describes those people who direct the energy of the dominant into the world of people and things, to manage as much of it as they can. They want to extend their personal logical systems into the world around them, their favored arena for personal expression.

In contrast, introverted THINKERS-with-intuition want to exercise their dominant process mainly in the inner realm of ideas, of private mental activity, and they strive above all else to have orderly, logical minds. They direct the energy of their auxiliary process (intuition) mainly outward to run their outer (extraverted) lives, and this gives them *the appearance* of having intuition as the dominant process. When we meet an introvert, we first see the auxiliary.

The General and the Aide

In *Gifts Differing*, Myers used the analogy of the general (the dominant process) and the aide (the auxiliary) to show the relationship of the process that is introverted and the one that is extraverted. The general who is extraverted leaves the tent to take care of outside business directly, leaving the aide in the tent to continue working there. The general who is introverted sends the aide to deal with the outside business while remaining in the tent working there and awaiting a report from the aide. Anyone who deals with the aide of the introvert will benefit from knowing that the one in command is in the tent and can be only somewhat represented by the aide. Of course, our mental processes do not wear the insignia of rank, and it is not so easy for someone to know if the mental process they are meeting is the one in charge.

Simple symbols can show these ideas. Capital letters are used to represent the dominant process and small letters are used to represent the auxiliary process. Using Myers' general-aide-tent analogy, a triangle is used to represent the tent walls, the dividing line between the inner and outer worlds that people live in. Here are two examples, the first for ESFJ and the second for ISFP. Both are FEELING-with-sensing types, but differ as to which process is extraverted and introverted.

ESFJ

Feeling judgment is **dominant** *and* **extraverted**
Sensing perception is **auxiliary** *and* **introverted**

ISFP

Sensing perception is **auxiliary** *and* **extraverted**
Feeling judgment is **dominant** *and* **introverted**

The people represented by the first symbol make their feelings public, naturally and frequently. Their antennae are out to pick up feeling signals, and they are the practical harmonizers and weavers of compromises. The general is there to do the public business.

The people represented by the second symbol have no less wealth of feeling, but it is reserved as a private process, revealed only to family and close friends, and it is more often seen in deeds than in words. The aide does the public business, and the aide's work is the practical usefulness of the sensing process. Of course, the general knows what the aide is doing, and will come out to do business with us if the general sees it as important enough. Loyal and devoted, ISFPs harmonize matters through a receptive, quiet-helper role, in contrast to the activist and often warmly-aggressive stance of those who have feeling dominant and extraverted.

Why are extraversion and introversion called "attitudes" or "orientations" rather than mental processes?

It may be helpful to recall here Jung's statement that all conscious mental activity can be sorted into the four functions or processes: sensing, intuition, thinking, and feeling. In that view, where do extraversion and introversion fit? Aren't they conscious mental processes? The terms function and process are interchangeable and are used to refer only to sensing, intuition, thinking, and feeling. Extraversion and introversion are attitudes or orientations, not processes. That is, they tell the direction of a process, outward or inward. Each process is oriented, and mostly used, inwardly or outwardly.

Thus for people who have the INTUITION-with-thinking pattern the intuition may be extraverted or introverted, and the auxiliary thinking needs to be in the opposite attitude to provide balance. So the fuller name for the extraverted INTUITION-with-thinking type is: extraverted intuition dominant with introverted thinking auxiliary. If the INTUITION-with-thinking person preferred introversion, the name for that type is: introverted intuition dominant with extraverted thinking auxiliary.

In subsequent paragraphs, we will see how to recognize ENTP as the shorthand for the former and INTJ as the shorthand for the latter — and all of the other type designations as well. If you want to skip over to those paragraphs and learn the rule for recognizing the dominant and auxiliary in any type, please come back here to the theory explanation afterwards.

KEEPING TYPE LANGUAGE CLEAR

FUNCTIONS:
Four basic mental processes — sensing, intuition, thinking, and feeling

PERCEPTION:
The two functions or processes for perceiving — sensing and intuition

JUDGMENT:
The two functions or processes for decision making — thinking and feeling

ATTITUDES:
*Two directions for the flow of energy — extraversion (outward)
and introversion (inward)*

How do E and I provide balance?

For each of the 16 types, Jung's dynamics show the dominant and auxiliary in different attitudes — if one is extraverted the other is introverted. Why didn't Jung let the general and the aide both be outside the tent? or both be inside the tent?

The answer is not hard to find. Jung and other professionals who use his theory of types have observed and written about people who seemed to be so dominated by events outside themselves that they did not see their own part in what happened to themselves, or seemed unable to reflect on the consequences and learn from them. In type terms, they extraverted not only their dominant but their auxiliary as well. They did not have a good means for introverting, the role their auxiliary should have been playing. Conversely, there are people who use both dominant and auxiliary introvertedly and have no good way of functioning in the world outside themselves. Engrossed deeply in their inner lives, they pay insufficient attention to what is going on around themselves, and do not take effective action. In Myers' view, personal effectiveness requires that the introvert have a well-developed auxiliary process for extraverting and the extravert a well-developed auxiliary process for introverting. In her words, "The extraverts' auxiliary gives them access to their own inner life and to the world of ideas; the introverts' auxiliary gives them a means to adapt to the world of action and to deal with it effectively."

In summary, the auxiliary process provides balance to the dominant in two essential ways: (1) a dominant from the perceiving dimension, sensing or intuition, is balanced by an auxiliary from the judging dimension, and vice versa; and (2) when the dominant is mainly extraverted, the auxiliary is mainly introverted, and vice versa.

THE DOMINANT AND AUXILIARY PROVIDE BALANCE

Between Perception (S or N) and Judgment (T or F)
Between the outer world (E) and the inner world (I)

J AND P REVEAL THE DYNAMICS

How does the judging-perceiving dimension fit into the sixteen patterns?

The *patterns* in type theory are complete when extraversion and introversion are added into the eight sets of dominant-auxiliary combinations. Using just the letters of the preferences, and lower case letters for the auxiliary, we can see the 16 types. Notice that the J and P letters do not appear in these shorthand descriptors.

ST Combinations	SF Combinations	NF Combinations	NT Combinations
IS+t	IS+f	IN+f	IN+t
IT+s	IF+s	IF+n	IT+n
ES+t	ES+f	EN+f	EN+t
ET+s	EF+s	EF+n	ET+n

If the 16 types can be designated this way, why are J and P needed? As explained in Chapter 1, the JP dimension refers to the preferred way of conducting one's outer life, in a planful or spontaneous way. Briggs and Myers devised this fourth dimension for two reasons: to provide a pair of descriptive categories for the planful (J) or spontaneous (P) behaviors people *show in their outer lives;* and to provide *a way of identifying the dominant process* in each type. The first purpose is obvious, and the JP descriptions are very useful. The second purpose, to be a pointer to the dominant, needs explanation. Consider the problem of a self-report type indicator instrument that has no JP dimension. Suppose a person scores ESF on the indicator. How can anyone know from the results whether sensing or feeling is dominant? One possibility is to regard the one with the higher preference score as the dominant, with the lower score being the auxiliary. In this instance, ES+f could be used as a shorthand designation to show that sensing had the higher score, and EF+s to show feeling having the higher score.

That solution was not acceptable to Myers and Briggs. They wanted an instrument fully consistent with Jung's theory. Following the theory, an extravert with sensing dominant will be sensing dominant no matter how high the score for sensing or whether the score for the auxiliary, in this instance feeling, is higher. In my own case, if the ENTP type description is the best fit for me, it should not matter whether my N score was higher than my T score. If one's type were reported by designating the dominant according to the higher score between N and T, and if my T score were higher, I would be directed to the ENT profile with thinking dominant, which is ENTJ. But when I read the ENTJ description, I know it is not describing me.

The JP preference points to the extraverted mental process

Myers and Briggs found that they could identify the dominant by means of the JP preference. Here is the basic rule: the JP points to the mental process that is *extraverted*; for extraverts, that is the dominant; for introverts, that is the auxiliary.

Let's see some examples. It helps to keep in mind the order of the four preferences reported by the MBTI, such as ENTP; the two mental processes are in the middle, N and T, and the attitudes (orientations) are on either end, E and P.

1	2	3	4
	Perceiving	Judging	
EI	SN	TF	JP
E	N	T	P

On the MBTI, my type comes out ENTP. The four letters direct me to the type description for ENTP, which is short for extraverted INTUITION with thinking auxiliary. Just by seeing the four letters, you can tell that intuition is the dominant — by using the JP rule. My last letter,

P, says that my **p**erceiving process (the letter in position 2) is *extraverted,* showing in my outer life. Because extraverts show their dominant outwardly, the P points to my *dominant.*

Contrast this with the other ENT_ type, ENTJ. The last letter, J, says that the judging process (the letter in position 3) is extraverted, used in the outer life. Because extraverts show their dominant outwardly, the J points to the dominant. So the dominant is thinking, and ENTJ stands for Extraverted THINKING with intuition auxiliary.

Let's contrast these with the introverted NT types, INTP and INTJ. In INTP the P says that the perceiving preference (N), in position 2, is extraverted, used outwardly. For introverts, we know that the process that is extraverted is the *auxiliary,* so intuition is the auxiliary and thinking is the dominant. INTP thus stands for introverted THINKING dominant with intuition auxiliary.

In the case of INTJ, we know the J means that the judging preference is extraverted. We also know that introverts use their auxiliary for their extraverting. So thinking is the auxiliary, leaving intuition as the dominant. INTJ thus stands for introverted INTUITION dominant with thinking auxiliary.

Here is a formula you can use for finding the dominant in any of the four-letter type designations:

Step 1: JP points to the letter of the mental process that is extraverted; J points to position 3, T or F; P points to position 2, S or N. Mark that letter with an E, as the extraverted process.

Step 2: If the first letter is E, then the marked letter is the dominant. If the first letter is I, then the marked letter is the auxiliary.

Use the formula to identify the dominant on several types and check your results on page A19 of the Appendix, and by using the following table. It is just like the table presented earlier, but with the Myers-Briggs terms added.

ST Combinations	SF Combinations	NF Combinations	NT Combinations
IS+t	IS+f	IN+f	IN+t
ISTJ	ISFJ	INFJ	INTJ
IT+s	IF+s	IF+n	IT+n
ISTP	ISFP	INFP	INTP

ST Combinations	SF Combinations	NF Combinations	NT Combinations
ES+t	ES+f	EN+f	EN+t
ESTP	ESFP	ENFP	ENTP
ET+s	EF+s	EF+n	ET+n
ESTJ	ESFJ	ENFJ	ENTJ

Here is still another way to check your results:

For E__Js, the third letter is the dominant
For I__Js, the second letter is the dominant
For E__Ps, the second letter is the dominant
For I__Ps, the third letter is the dominant

Knowing the dominant of each type, without having to stop and apply the rule, does not come quickly. I used the type concepts in my work for several years before I could quickly bring to mind the dynamics of each of the types. The knowledge of this deeper layer dramatically extended my effective uses of type, as it will for you. But it does take time.

THE THIRD AND FOURTH MENTAL PROCESSES

What are the third and fourth mental processes called, and how do they work in the dynamics?

Jung saw that a person's conscious mental life consists mainly of the activity of the dominant process. The auxiliary is also often in consciousness, but it plays a secondary, helping role. What about the less preferred mental processes? Using again the example of my own type, ENTP, N is dominant and T is auxiliary. The mental processes that do not appear in my type letters are S and F. How do S and F work in the dynamics of my type? In each type, the mental processes that are not represented in the four letters are what Jung called the third, or *tertiary*, and the *inferior* processes. They can serve the dominant process also, but they are much less available than the auxiliary. The third process is more accessible than the inferior, but less than the auxiliary.

Jung called the opposite of the dominant process the inferior process because it is at the bottom of the hierarchy of the four processes for that type. Some others refer to it as the "shadow." Jung used the term shadow to cover more than the inferior process, so I do not use it in relation to the type preferences. The inferior process is the most childish of the processes when it does appear. It is the process we have the least control of, and is the one that has taken over when we say "I wasn't being myself just then." *Beside Ourselves: The Hidden Personality in Everyday Life* is the title of a book by Naomi Quenk (Consulting Psycholgists Press, 1993). I recommend it for further reading on the dynamics of the inferior process.

Being in one's dominant process just happens, it is automatic. A well-developed auxiliary is easily accessible. But it takes conscious effort to stay in one's third process, and even more effort to keep the fourth process working in consciousness. We are mostly unaware of their functioning in our personalities, except when we deliberately call on them to help out. For example, when I am writing I try to lock into my sensing when I am proofreading, and call on my feeling process when trying to personalize my NT abstract reasoning that tends to get too heavy.

In Chapter 10 you will find a "zig-zag" method for problem solving that may be helpful to you in engaging all the four mental processes when working through a problem.

Through conscious effort, over the course of a lifetime, some people do become quite aware of the functioning of the third and fourth processes, and as awareness increases control increases. To the extent that they remain out of our awareness and control, they represent blindspots that can get us into trouble.

TERTIARY PROCESS

Third favorite among S, N, T, and F
The opposite of the auxiliary (as S is opposite N, and T is opposite F)
Less developed and less accessible than the auxiliary
Later in developing than the auxiliary

INFERIOR PROCESS

The opposite of the dominant (as S is opposite N, and T is opposite F)
The least developed process
Our relatively childish and primitive perception or judgment
An escape from the conscious personality
Is in charge when "You don't act yourself"
A source of much undiscovered personal energy

In what ways are the third and fourth processes our blindspots?

For each type, it is important to remember which mental process is the least used and least trusted. The inferior process is always the polar opposite of the dominant process, as sensing is the opposite of intuition, and as thinking is the opposite of feeling. A previous paragraph explained the polarity concept. The third and fourth processes are one's blindspots; they represent areas that are most neglected. Whenever I am working with someone to solve a problem, I try to keep in mind not only the person's dominant but also the inferior — seeing the dominant as the best avenue to good communication and the inferior as the probable roadblock. To explore for yourself the nature of the blindspots, now that you know about the dominant and inferior, I suggest your turn back to the page in Chapter 1 entitled "Brief Descriptions of the Sixteen Types" and the related paragraphs. The material there takes on a deeper meaning when the concepts of the dominant and inferior are applied to it.

It is also important to remember that the tertiary and inferior processes are not what get us into the most trouble. The neglect of the auxiliary brings the most serious problems. A dominant not supported by an adequate auxiliary means one-sidedness not only in the perception-judgment balance but also neglect of either the inner life or outer life. The problems of an unsupported dominant were described earlier in the chapter. All 16 of Myers' descriptions of the types (see Appendix A) include an "If . . ." paragraph in which she identifies the major source of possible trouble. In each case the "if" statement refers to the problems that follow from an underdeveloped auxiliary process.

How can the third and fourth mental processes be developed?

In *Gifts Differing*, Isabel Myers argued for helping the inferior process to develop by letting it play, but not by pressing it into service. When working with a sensing dominant student, for example, the teacher is not helping, and is probably harming, the student by requiring learning activities that depend mainly on intuition for a sustained time. And with intuition dominant students, the surest way to bring out their worst behavior is to keep them on tasks that require them to follow uninspiring routines, step by step, with careful attention to details.

The inferior process can be developed in two ways, according to Myers. First, the inferior process can be developed by letting it play — giving it outlets that are recreational. Some examples are intuitives who enjoy hobbies that are essentially sensory such as gardening and woodworking; and people with sensing dominant who let intuition play in recreational reading. A feeling dominant person I know gets genuine pleasure in keeping a ledger, and another who is thinking dominant finds recreational enjoyment in caring for animals.

Second, the inferior process can be developed by letting it serve the dominant process in some way that is very important to the dominant. An illustration of this second method can be found in the work of Isabel Myers herself. She was an INFP, an introvert with dominant feeling, and her heart's desire was the perfection of the Type Indicator. To accomplish this goal, prompted by her dominant feeling, she mastered statistics and research design — fields that are totally grounded in the thinking process, and would spend weeks of mathematical work to discover one fact that might improve the Indicator.

Here are other examples of the inferior being developed as it serves the dominant. An excellent elementary school teacher I know, an ESTJ, uses her inferior feeling process every day to gauge the effect of her lessons on her inner-city students. She works hard to remain sensitive to them individually because she knows her carefully crafted instruction plans will not succeed with these at-risk students without fine tuning that comes by taking their feelings into account. An ISTJ department manager I know, who supervises 30+ people, mostly intuitives, daily uses her inferior intuition process to keep the big picture in mind, to map out long-term plans, and to stay in tune with her people. They are grateful for her dominant sensing process keeping everyone focused on the immediate targets and the means to reach them. Finally, I can use myself as an example of dominant intuition, inferior sensing. Knowing that many of this book's readers are sensing types, I regularly edit with my sensing eye as I go along, asking myself: Is this practical, explicit enough, giving enough concrete examples, moving from specific experience toward abstract generalization? How well I succeeded in making it readable for sensing types is hard for me to know, but what you are reading did get a sensing critique as best as I could provide it (with the help also of some sensing people who read all or parts of the manuscript).

The approach to developing one's third mental process is the same as just described for the inferior. As with the inferior, it is best treated with invitations and not demands, and certainly not with the same standard of quality performance as we apply to our dominant.

THE PRACTICAL BENEFITS OF KNOWING TYPE DYNAMICS

When we study type dynamics, the main benefit is a better understanding of our own tendencies — our basic mind-set and our blindspots. My dominant process tunes me in automatically to some viewpoints and life experiences and tunes out others. Knowing about that, I can be more alert to the side of things I will naturally neglect and will need to attend to through careful discipline. When we experience the most uncertainty, confusion, and distress, when we feel off-balance and out of control, we can be fairly sure that our inferior is active. Because the inferior stays almost hidden from consciousness, it is hard to understand. But the off-balance experiences can alert us to the fact that the inferior is afoot. We then can look for its effects and better see how to compensate for our blindspots.

Knowing the dominant and inferior processes of people close to us, family and friends, we can begin to see the reality of the differences in type dynamics in their types. Staying tuned in to them becomes easier, and cooperative problem solving works better when we can anticipate how their dominant or inferior will react in given situations. Having one of them as a confidant who knows and can talk about type dynamics in our everyday relationships sharpens skills and gives insights we can use in other parts of our lives.

Being aware of the dominant and inferior mental process is especially important when working with students or employees whose types are most different from our own. The teacher who effectively engages students' attention and interest does so by finding some common mental ground. in type theory, the common ground includes shared perceptual data and/or shared judgments. These usually are easy to anticipate in students who are like us in type, but they are hard to find in students whose types are unlike our own. Fortunately, the study of type gives us ways to understand and work with the mental patterns of different types, even when we cannot "be there" and know existentially what they are experiencing.

Now that you are aware of the dynamics of the types, you can read Myers' type descriptions more deeply. In Appendix A, *Introduction to Type*, you will see that the opening paragraphs in all the descriptions

are about the dominant in its favored attitude, extraverted or introverted, and the interests and skills associated with it. The paragraphs at the bottom of each page are about the auxiliary and how it modifies the dominant. As I mentioned previously, she also included some sentences about the problems that arise if the auxiliary is not well developed. And some of the descriptions include statements about the least developed process, the blindspots it represents, and ways to keep it from being disruptive.

To close the chapter I have included a type concepts test like that in Chapter 1. Before going on in this second section of the book, you may want use it to check your grasp of the main concepts of the dynamics of the types.

Record your multiple choice answers on a separate sheet and check your responses with the key that follows the test. Some of the items have *more than one* correct answer.

1. The term "dominant process" in type theory means
   a. either extraversion or introversion
   b. either a judging or perceiving attitude
   c. the favorite process, the one used most

2. The auxiliary process is
   a. the opposite of the dominant
   b. the least used process
   c. the second favorite

3. If the favorite process is a judging one, the second favorite is
   a. also a judging one
   b. a perceiving one
   c. any of the other processes

4. If the second favorite process is a judging one, the favorite will be
   a. a perceiving one
   b. also a judging one
   c. any of the other processes

5. One's attitude or orientation to life is either
   a. judgment or perception
   b. extraversion or introversion
   c. the dominant or the auxiliary process

6. One's attitude toward the outer world is
   a. either judging or perceiving
   b. governed by the favorite process
   c. governed by the second favorite process

7. The effects of the combinations of perception and judgment
   a. are arbitrary and unpredictable
   b. produce the different types of personalities
   c. produce different sets of interests, values, needs, habits of mind and surface traits

8. The last letter in the four-letter type designation indicates the mental process you use in the outer world
   a. if you are an extravert
   b. if you are an introvert
   c. for both extraverts and introverts

9. The introverts rely on their auxiliary process
   a. for dealing with the outer world
   b. for dealing with the inner world of ideas
   c. in the same way as the extraverts
10. The introverted judging types (with I__J in their type designa tion) have as their favorite process
    a. a judging process, either thinking or feeling
    b. a perceiving process, either intuition or sensing
    c. any of the four mental processes named above
11. The extraverted judging types (with E__J in their type designa tion) have as their favorite process
    a. a judging process, either thinking or feeling
    b. a perceiving process, either sensing or intuition
    c. any of the four mental processes named above
12. A well-developed auxiliary process is necessary
    a. to prevent superficiality in the introvert
    b. to help the extraverts put their best foot forward
    c. to help both extravert and introvert achieve balance, and keep them from ignoring either world
13. In types whose favorite process is a judging one, the perceiv ing auxiliary provides
    a. help in making quick decisions
    b. the raw material needed as a basis for judgment
    c. a second line of attack when the favorite process does not work
14. In types whose favorite process is a perceiving one, the judg ing auxiliary provides
    a. a steadiness of purpose
    b. a means of evaluating the worth of their perceptions and the uses to be made of them
    c. help in suspending judgment when data are insufficient
15. The remaining processes, after taking into account the dominant and auxiliary
    a. should be suppressed
    b. are not necessary, and can be ignored
    c. can make contributions toward greater effectiveness

1. c. the favorite process, the one used most. (Sensing, intuition, thinking and feeling are mental processes, one of which will be the favorite or dominant.)

   a. *Extraversion and introversion are defined as attitudes, not mental processes.*

   b. *A judging or perceiving attitude refers to how one runs one's outer life, and the dominant may or may not show itself in one's outer life.*

2. c. the second favorite

   a. *The opposite of the dominant conflicts with it and therefore is the least developed of the four processes. The auxiliary, to be helpful, must serve the dominant process, not compete with it.*

   b. *The opposite of the dominant is the least used, least trusted process.*

3. b. a perceiving one (Its responsibility is to supply facts and understanding as a basis for judgment.)

   a. *If both dominant and auxiliary were judging processes, there would be no balance. Also, the auxiliary would be opposite the dominant.*

   c. *The opposite of the dominant is excluded as a candidate for the auxiliary. The opposite is the least developed process and the slowest to develop because the energy that flows to the dominant is denied to its polar opposite.*

4. a. a perceiving one (When the second favorite process or auxiliary is a judging process, it is because the favorite or dominant process is perceiving and needs a judging assistant for balance.)

   b. *If both dominant and auxiliary were judging processes, there would be no balancing perception.*

   c. *One of the other processes would be the inferior process, which cannot be the favorite.*

5. b. extraversion or introversion (This is called attitude or orientation to life because extraversion means "to be focused outwardly" and introversion means "to be focused inwardly." Orientation means the attitude (direction) of the dominant process; in extraverts, the attitude of the dominant is outward, and in introverts the attitude of the dominant is inward.)

   a. *The JP preference indicates whether a person shows a judging or perceiving process to the outer world. Stated another way, it shows which function preference is extraverted. And still* *another way, JP show whether the person takes a judging or perceiving attitude toward the outer world. While EI shows one's orientation to life, JP shows the orientation or attitude toward one's outer life.*

    c. *The dominant and auxiliary are mental processes which are used in the extraverted or introverted orientations (or attitudes).*

6. a. judging or perceiving

    b. *Only the extravert's attitude toward the outer world is governed by the favorite process.*

    c. *Only the introvert's attitude toward the outer world is governed by the second favorite process.*

7. c. produce different sets of interests, values, needs, habits of mind, and surface traits

    a. *The combinations of perception and judgment, when understood in type theory, give us a way to increase our ability to predict people's behavior.*

    b. *The "types" are produced by more than the combination of preferences of perception and judgment. Types result from the combinations of the EI preference, the dominant and auxiliary mental processes, and the JP preference.*

8. c. for both extraverts and introverts

    a. *and* **b.** *It is important to keep in mind that, by definition in the theory, JP points to the process used in the outer world by all types.*

9. a. for dealing with the outer world

    b. *Introverts use their favorite or dominant process for dealing with the inner world of ideas. Consequently, the "best side" of introverts is not seen by the casual observer, who mainly witnesses the less-developed auxiliary (second favorite) process.*

    c. *Extraverts, on the other hand, use their favorite process in the outer world, and the observer sees the best of them at once.*

10. b. a perceiving process, either sensing or intuition. (The J in the four type letters indicates that the outer process will be thinking or feeling. For an introvert, the outer process is the auxiliary, so the dominant process must be sensing or intuition).

    a. *An introverted type with a P in the four type letters has a perceiving outer process (either sensing or intuition). For introverts, the outer process is auxiliary; therefore the dominant process would have to be thinking or feeling.*

c. *Introverts with a J in their four letters could not have judging processes (thinking or feeling) as their dominant, because these functions would be used in their outer world and the introvert's dominant is used in the inner world.*

11. a. a judging process, either thinking or feeling (The JP preference points directly to the dominant for extraverts.)

    b. *For extraverts to have sensing or intuition as their dominant, they would have to have a P in their type formula, because JP points directly to the dominant for extraverts, and both S and N are P processes.*

    c. *Extraverts with J in their formula could not have a P process (sensing or intuition) as their dominant function.*

12. c. to help both extravert and introvert achieve balance, and to keep them from ignoring the less preferred world

    a. *The introverts are less subject to superficiality than are extraverts.*

    b. *Extraverts have fewer problems in putting their best foot forward than do introverts.*

13. b. the raw material needed as a basis for judgment (When the favorite process is a judging one, perceptions provide the information on which to make choices; sound decisions cannot be made without adequate information.)

    a. *Whether decisions are made quickly or slowly depends on other factors. For example, extraverts are more likely to act quickly or impulsively, and introverts after thoughtful consideration.*

    c. *Although it is true that the auxiliary provides a second line of attack when the dominant does not work, the statement would not be restricted to the types with a dominant judging process described in this question.*

14. a. steadiness of purpose

    b. *a means of evaluating the worth of their perceptions and the uses to be made of them. (Both answers are correct. Perceiving types with insufficient judgment may spend too much time simply enjoying perceptions and too little time in using the information their perceptions provide).*

    c. *is incorrect. Judging processes are more likely to speed judgment, not suspend it.*

15. c. can make contributions toward greater effectiveness (Not only must the less-developed processes be heard, but they can be a source of richness and growth.)

a. *If the less-developed processes are suppressed, they are very likely to express themselves in embarrassing and detrimental ways.*

b. *The four mental processes are needed and used every day, for effective functioning. None can be ignored.*

TYPE AND CURRICULUM REFORM

In this chapter we shift from the use of type in one-to-one and small group relationships to more global applications. Specifically, the problem of introducing type into curriculum planning. I am writing here to those who want to use type in curriculum work, to influence curriculum policy beyond the individual classroom, and to help more people bring their constructive energies into the process of reforming education through curriculum improvement.

The big curriculum question is, what should be taught? Among all the limitless information and skills available to be put in the curriculum, what should we choose? And out of those chosen things, what should be required of all students — and at what stages of their schooling? These are huge questions. And our question to ourselves is, how can a knowledge of type help us take initiatives in improving the quality of curriculum decisions?

TAKING TYPE PREFERENCES INTO ACCOUNT IN CURRICULUM WORK

Most of the chapter will be devoted to aspects of type not yet covered. But first we will revisit some ideas from previous chapters that have a bearing on curriculum work. There we looked at the four dimensions of type — EI, SN, TF, and JP — and considered their value in improving instruction. Their role in improving the curriculum is no less important but is much less obvious.

THE EXTRAVERSION AND INTROVERSION PREFERENCES

Of all the psychological concepts that have a place in curriculum making, none probably is more important or more neglected that the one represented in Jung's terms extraversion and introversion. Consider them in their largest meanings. It is only through introverting that we gain depth, and it is only through extraverting that we gain breadth. In reflection we construct the meanings of our experiences. In our extraverting we test our mental constructions outwardly and become open to new experiences stimulated by the world outside ourselves. Our world is just as wide as our encounters with it; our understanding of it is just as deep as the quality of our reflection on the encounters.

Of course we want every student to develop breadth and depth. For that truly to happen, we must be aware that young people who prefer extraversion are likely to neglect the skills of introverting unless their environment prompts them to learn and use the skills. In schools, the curriculum must specifically include them. Young extraverts may also settle for immature development of extraverting skills unless the curriculum leads them to higher development. They may settle for breadth that is ineffective because it is shallow. The reverse, of course, is true for young introverts: a neglect of the skills of extraverting, and settling for depth that is ineffective because of its narrowness.

The goals within the curriculum would be unrealistic if they expected the extraverts to be as reflective and as concerned with depth as the introverts. Likewise they would be unrealistic if they expected extraverts to develop fewer but deeper interests, in imitation of introverts. Development of the skills of the less preferred mode provides needed balance, but the balance scale would never be level. For extraverts the curriculum goals should include skills of introverting sufficient at least to avoid shallowness. For introverts the curriculum goals should include skills of extraverting they will need to connect effectively with the world outside themselves.

Skills of Extraverting, Skills of Introverting.

What kinds of skills should curriculum planners consider to help students develop both breadth and depth? First of all, planners would not suppose that extraverts should learn the skills used in introverting by imitating introverts, nor introverts learn the skills associated with extraversion by following the extravert's path. For example, the skills of social interaction, of presenting oneself or one's ideas in public, develop slowly and incrementally in the introvert, with plenty of time given to planning, preparation, and rehearsal. The skills will form best when the topic of the extraverting is one the introvert feels fluent in, keenly interested in, and well prepared to present.

As another example, the capacity to concentrate quietly for a long time that comes easily to the introvert is hard work for the extravert. Always scanning the outside world for stimulation, the extravert breaks away into sustained reflection only with discipline that takes real effort to develop. The skills of reflection are best developed when the extravert has a topic of strong interest that requires reflection to pursue it well. Strong interest is the springboard to skill development in both cases.

Curriculum Assumptions.

The curriculum structure we have inherited, I believe, favors the introverted way of experiencing life. It puts more emphasis on the skills of reflection than the skills of action. It is built on the assumption that young people get their connection to the world of action outside the school or college. The curriculum structure is built on book learning, on reflective, vicarious experience rather than direct, active experience. When a particular curriculum departs from this pattern, it is because the curriculum developers consciously made the effort to depart.

The prevailing curriculum structure more nearly fits the introvert's way of learning than the extravert's. The extravert's natural way to learn is first of all to plunge into new opportunities; then pause briefly to reflect on the experience to sort out its meaning and usefulness; then get back into action. If the curriculum were designed to honor the extraverted way, then it would be framed by action. Books would be resources for the reflection part of the cycles of learning; they would not be mainly for initiating the learning cycle as textbooks are now used.

How might the curriculum be changed to accommodate extraversion and introversion differences? Whatever the skill, in whatever curriculum — mathematics, composition, social studies, etc. — the curriculum planner should aim for designing themes and units that have both action and reflection throughout the entire study sequence. I am using "action" to mean the learners physically engage the world outside themselves, the people and objects that become part of their learning. The curriculums I have seen that do this best are ones that

carry the classroom into the community, and bring the community events and resources into the classroom. The curriculum designer then checks the plans to be sure that the skills associated with introverting and extraverting are specifically provided with activities and guidelines that can be used in the coaching and practicing of them.

Everyone who develops a curriculum works from assumptions about human nature. The basic realities of type differences need to be part of their view of what is important in human nature, important enough to get conscious attention in curriculum making. A curriculum developed without attention to all four dimensions of type will certainly disadvantage some students while favoring others.

THE SENSING AND INTUITION PREFERENCES

The ideal curriculum for sensing types puts them in direct personal contact with the physical realities of what is being studied — contacts that make use of all their senses. The ideal curriculum for intuitive types intrigues and inspires them to pursue the curriculum's content; it engages their intuition to explore the meanings and possibilities that seem to lie just ahead.

The best curriculums accomplish both at the same time. Some very elaborate curriculums, such as Man — A Course of Study, and some much more focused ones, such as a manipulative lab approach to mathematics, engage sensing and intuitive students equally well, with the same materials. They accomplish this because the curriculum developers gave first priority to engaging students in *direct inquiry*. Curriculums that emphasize direct inquiry are beginning to appear in schools and colleges. Several dental and medical schools in the United States are getting very good results from programs in which classroom book-driven instruction is paralleled with hands-on clinic or lab inquiry from the beginning. If the developers (including teachers, of course) knew how to use the concepts of psychological type, I believe they would have still more success.

When I taught high school social studies, long before I knew about psychological type, I knew that some of us in the department emphasized facts and some emphasized general concepts — all using the same textbooks. I taught the facts of American history only to illustrate the general concepts I thought were important. That seemed to me the much better way, and I felt superior to those who "just taught facts," not knowing, of course, that I was merely exercising my intuitive bias.

As I look back now it seems to me that this group of bright and conscientious teachers were only moderately successful because we relied too much on the textbooks to initiate and guide the studies. Sensing type students had to settle for the "facts" provided, most of them just statements or pictures in the book, because three-dimensional facts were not available in the classroom. Intuitive type students had abstract concepts to work with, but too few new direct experiences to inspire them, to spark their idealism and interest in life's possibilities. Had the teacher's guides helped us see the importance of keeping our students' senses and intuitions fully engaged, I believe we could have been much more effective. Now, when I see teachers launch units of study with concrete, direct activities and materials that provide personal experiences for their students, I see students light up, and I see the way I would like to have taught back then.

THE THINKING AND FEELING PREFERENCES

With the exception of some college programs that teach counseling skills, and a few others, our curriculums favor the side of life experienced by thinking types. Jung's view that both thinking and feeling judgment are *rational* processes is not generally accepted among educators. Most of us see thinking as rational and feeling as irrational. We want our curriculums to be rational, to encourage sound reasoning, so we design them to fit our idea of what is objective, analytical and logical. The subjective approach that is central to feeling judgment is seen as secondary, perhaps inferior. Type theory shows us that feeling judgment is neither secondary nor inferior to thinking judgment. It is an equal partner providing the other face of rationality, the personal side.

What would a curriculum look like if it gave an equal place to a subjective approach? Perhaps the evolution of human knowledge could be seen through the subjective experiences of men and women who have pushed our understanding forward. Their biographies and autobiographies would be important tools for learning, as would videotapes and films that provide subjective insights. The scientist as an inquiring person would be studied as well as the scientific understanding he or she gave us.

Still more important in the curriculum would be opportunities for direct personal inquiry, as mentioned in the previous section. Inquiry that starts with strong personal interest, that reflects what individual students care about deeply, will automatically call on feeling judgment, the mode of judging preferred by half of our students. As we construct our curriculums and sort out the curriculum materials available to us now, we can use this criterion to select the ones most likely to energize students of all type preferences: Do they emphasize direct personal inquiry based on strong personal interest?

THE JUDGMENT AND PERCEPTION PREFERENCES

All curriculums need to provide structure for student learning activities. What kind of structure and how much structure are decisions that can be better made with a knowledge of type preferences.

As shown in Chapter 2, students who prefer to run their outer lives with a judging process, the J types, learn best when they have a clear goal in mind and a definite plan that leads to the goal. They need a curriculum structure that lets them see a learning pathway at the beginning of each inquiry or plan — where to go and how to get there.

The J types differ in how they want the learning pathway to be planned. The _S_J types tend to believe that the world they are learning about is a definite reality. It is a reality requiring them to have a command of facts and skills that go with each responsibility they must take on as adults. They believe that the authors and teachers who plan and guide their learning should know what facts and skills are needed and should plan the learning pathway for them to get them to the goals by the most direct means. Pathways they see as indirect or open-ended seem inefficient to the _S_Js, and make them suspect their teachers don't know everything they are supposed to know. They want a structure decided in advance by competent authorities.

The _N_J types, in contrast, tend to be suspicious of a "cut and dried" learning pathway, where their intuition feels cramped. It is the nature of intuition to see appealing possibilities and new ways of doing things. The _N_J types would prefer to have a hand in choosing their own specific goal and in making the plan that will get them there. They want to build in some fresh approach or possibility that intrigues their intuition.

Students who run their outer lives mainly with their perception preference, the P types, learn best when they can spontaneously follow an inquiry wherever it takes them. The perceptions that come to them, however they come, will tell them they are on a learning path that will pay off; they don't need a pre-set plan to tell them that. A general learning plan is fine for them so long as they can remain receptive and not feel bound into a path that seems to stifle the flow of perceptions. The process of finding out is just as satisfying for them as having whatever is found.

The _S_P types seem to need a curriculum that encourages them to go step by step in exploring a hands-on, sensory-rich learning environment — for example, a hands-on science or natural history museum, or lab work with tangible materials and a learning guidebook in which to record observations. A curriculum well suited to _S_P types will reward them for doing what they thrive on: being *keen observers of the details of the sensory world.* Their interest in that kind of observation is a natural starting point for instruction through the whole of schooling, from beginning to read and write to the most advanced studies.

The _N_P types seem to do well in a curriculum that is structured to allow open-ended exploration, not requiring step by step processes, but allowing spontaneous, inductive means of solving problems. That kind of structure will ignite what they thrive on: the *surge of energy from insights* that intuition gives them. The curriculum also must help them learn to check and evaluate their intuitive solutions carefully, and also help them recognize that they live in a J world that values schedules, completions, and products.

USING THE TYPE PREFERENCES IN CURRICULUM MAKING

How can any one curriculum accommodate all these differences in type preference that will show up in any classroom? There are teachers I have observed who seemed to do well teaching to all or most of the type preferences — whether or not they knew about the theory of psychological types. They provided their students with the structure and experiences suggested in the paragraphs above. The teachers of the early grades generally had the same basic structure for all children, but were notable by the variety of activities in their rooms, many ways of learning besides the printed page, and paper and pencil. They regularly provided for physical, whole-body activity, in and outside the classroom. They made clear the curriculum goals, and made use of students' individual natural interests as means of reaching the goals. In most other aspects of their teaching they were often quite different from each other.

The middle school teachers generally followed the same pattern, except that they gave students more choices in ways of doing their work. Three examples from the middle grades are reported in Chapter

3: the greenhouse project, the inner-city housing project, and the aluminum can project.

At the high school, college and adult education levels the successful teachers also provided action, variety and concrete experiences. But they differed from teachers of the lower grades in their expectations that students would take initiatives in bringing their own personal interests and goals into their individual learning plans that were negotiated with the teacher. For students who didn't take the initiative, they prompted them. Generally speaking, the older the students, the more responsibility they would take to see that the classroom learning fit their needs in their lives outside the classroom.

My recommendation is that curriculum makers take these teachers successes as clues to bringing type differences into their work. They will need to find for themselves other teachers to observe who are successful with all or most types of students, and learn from them the specifics of how they accomplished the things described here in general terms.

CURRICULUM ASSUMPTIONS THAT NEED TO BE CHANGED

There are structural assumptions that underlie our American curriculum, what some call the hidden curriculum. I start this section with a look at some of the assumptions to show why they hinder efforts to integrate the concepts of psychological type into the curriculum.

Structural Assumptions Underlying Curriculum Making

Behind the familiar curriculum work of formal education is a set of givens that are not often examined, but must be if we are to have real reform, and if type ideas are to be an integral part of curriculum making. We have inherited these structural assumptions that have remained essentially the same for over a century. Some key features of the structure are:
- Students are separated by age and by "achievement level"
- Teachers are separated from each other
- Curriculum is separated into subjects
- Subjects remain separate and are sequenced into time slots
- A predetermined schedule regulates movement from subject to subject
- A predetermined curriculum regulates what should be studied and in what order

- Curriculum and instruction are geared to achievement of predetermined goals, and not to children's developmental processes or sequences
- Instruction emphasizes right answers to predetermined problems and tasks
- Achievement is measured by predetermined paper and pencil tests
- The tests compare individual students' achievement to norms of other students in the same grade level
- Results on standardized achievement tests are used to provide accountability, student by student, school by school, district by district, and state by state
- Predetermined rules, procedures, and behavior norms are the teacher's responsibility to monitor and maintain
- Almost all classroom activity is verbal, in oral or written form
- Inside the classroom, the natural, informal social structure of students is discouraged.

You may detect some biases of mine in the description of the structural assumptions. But these features of schools are truly the norm. They are not true of all schools and classrooms; but when departures are made from this structure, it is because someone made an intentional decision to follow a different drummer.

The structure fails much of the time, and for many students. It fails because it works against respect for individual differences in students and teachers. I truly believe our work with type theory will make only superficial improvements in schools so long as schools adhere to this structure. So when we want to help a school, we need to help the faculty evaluate and change some features of the structure before or at the same time that we introduce type.

ACHIEVEMENT VS. DEVELOPMENT

I am also convinced that the main reason this threadbare structure still stands is because our culture still sees achievement as more important than development. It was not the first item on the list of structural features, but I believe the primacy of achievement is a pivotal feature. If development were given the priority, I believe a new structure would emerge.

First, we have to be clear about the distinction between development and achievement. The focus of formal education is almost totally on

achievement. Children are supposed to know their ABC's by the end of kindergarten, and be ready to start reading. Their achievement of this and everything else is compared to the achievement of all the other children. A child should be able to do certain things in kindergarten or else experience the negative comparisons that are likely to make him or her feel shame and humiliation. Needless to say, these are not good motivators. The reason the system tolerates such consequences is its concern for holding children, teachers, and parents accountable. The system applies this pressure because it doesn't want any children to fall through the cracks; it wants everyone to move along. How ironic. A child's development *and achievement* are set back because the system doesn't adequately attend to developmental differences.

The structure I have described downplays the importance of developmental differences. Never mind that this child knew how to read before kindergarten, or this other child had almost no exposure to printed material. Or this child does not know how to act in a group of peers, and this other child is already socially adept. I believe most readers who have come this far in the book will agree that children's achievement should be measured in the context of their own development stages and sequences. All who affirm that conviction reject certain features of the existing curriculum structure. I argue that we should reject all the structural features I named because they are all logically unsound when development is given priority.

Development-based curriculum has had its advocates throughout the century, but they have not changed the structure. When the testing movement gained credibility, the concern for achievement became paramount and has gained increasing emphasis until now. But today there is hope for a shift in emphasis. Many Americans are disillusioned with schooling as it is today, and many of them point to the achievement and testing treadmill as a major culprit. When achievement is viewed in the context of development, when curriculum and teaching both promote students' development, achievement follows naturally.

This fact presented itself to me vividly as an outcome of some data I obtained several years ago from 240 adults, mostly teachers. I asked each person: "Describe a learning experience you have had, as an adult or as a child, in school or anywhere else, that you regard as a potent learning experience — where the ingredients for learning came together in an especially effective way for you. It need not be a big event in your life, small is fine, but it should be an example of what you experienced as effective and efficient learning." I had them write a paragraph describing the episode, and a few sentences telling what they thought were the ingredients that made the learning potent. Their responses ranged over all ages and diverse situations, from the impact of a second grade teacher who enlisted the respondent to be a reading helper, to the flying instructor who let go of all the controls and said, "You've learned what to do. Now do it; get us back on the ground in one piece."

I analyzed their statements of ingredients to look for patterns, to see what common ingredients emerged. I found 15 common factors that appeared in a majority of the statements. I put them into a list, showed it to over 100 of the respondents, and asked them to mark the items that accurately represented for them the nature of the potent learning experience they had described. Most people marked 10 or more of the items, and all 15 were clearly supported. In discussions, we added two more to the list.

Here is the list. Before you read it, you may want to pause and think back to a potent learning experience of your own, and then see how many of the items you find to fit your experience.

The potent learning environment is one in which:

- the learner is moving toward a goal he or she strongly desires
- a dramatic emphasis is given to needs
- there is a social context that supports the learning
- the learner feels a sense of community
- the learner's personality strengths are engaged
- self-reflection is sponsored
- discovery, the aha! experience is sponsored
- the learner's patterns of thought are respected
- there is a clear and present desire for learning
- immediate and practical application is encouraged
- sustained success occurs
- the learner is aware of the interest and expectations of others
- feedback is clear, appropriate and quick
- the learner can synthesize prior experience
- the learner's capacity to deal with his or her world is enhanced
- the learner sees desired behaviors modeled
- the learner as a person is respected.

Looking back over all those responses, I have recognized one other ingredient that encompasses them all: the learning episodes the respondents chose to report were experiences that were *developmentally* right for them. What made them potent was the developmental fit. Perhaps the obverse is true: learning experiences that don't match the person's developmental situation aren't potent.

The message in the responses seems clear to me. If curriculum workers took these features as criteria for planning learning environments, the result would be curriculums that had student development in the center of the planning, with achievement seen as a natural by-product of development. What they need to guide their planning are sound theories of development. There are various good theories of development available. Type development theory is to me one of the most promising.

TYPE DEVELOPMENT

Let's review some key features of type development. In the theory of type development, individuals grow and flourish as they first build strength in their dominant process. Once the dominant is secure enough, trustworthy enough, they then have energy freed up to develop strength in the other processes, starting with the auxiliary process. If we act on these principles, young people should be given continuous opportunities to specialize in activities that call on and strengthen their dominant process. The curriculum that leads teachers to teach a little bit of everything is unlikely to support the needed specializing.

A recurring theme in this book, the importance of using a personality strength to strengthen a weakness, is based on the crucial role of the dominant mental process in a person's development. The conventional belief that teachers should identify students' deficits and teach directly to the deficits may often violate the principle of strengthening the student's dominant process. The teacher's question should always be "How can this student's dominant be engaged to energize the learning needed to meet the curriculum objectives?" And the curriculum should be planned to give teachers ideas and resources for addressing that question.

Teachers need to know how to recognize the expression of type preferences in students' behavior. Teachers who do can tell when students are using their dominant process confidently and effectively. Those students may then be ready to take on responsibilities that put their auxiliary process in the foreground. Some young people become ready for that in the elementary school years, some not until later. Recognizing and working with students' dominant and auxiliary processes is the subject of the next chapter, Chapter 10.

It is time to insert another of Carl Jung's ideas: one's type implies a developmental pathway through life. The 16 paths differ in just the ways that the types themselves differ. When a child is allowed and encouraged to stay on the path, the development that results is strong and healthy. If circumstances, including school life, push the child off the path, development is hindered; the child's energy goes into non-integrated skills and defenses; the process of becoming one's own person is slowed or stalled; and in adult life this person will have neuroses that absorb much energy and require still more energy to overcome.

I believe this. I believe it as strongly as I believe that psychological types are a fact. Believing that the types are developmental pathways, I have no choice but to work as hard as I can to convince education leaders that curriculum decisions must take type development into account.

TAKING TYPE DEVELOPMENT INTO ACCOUNT IN CURRICULUM WORK

If the curriculum took type development into account, what would it look like? Let's take for example an ESFJ boy. With extraverted feeling as his dominant process, he will thrive on opportunities to be a harmonizer, to do things for people that they value, and to take leadership in social situations. If school can provide him with situations that draw on his extraverted feeling, he will achieve — not just in categories his type favors, but across the wide spectrum of curriculum objectives. But his *sequence* of achievements, the order and timing of what he knows and can do, will be an ESFJ sequence and be different in many respects from that of other types.

How Many Pathways?

Taking 16 types into account is an enormous job. Would we need 16 different pathways? Where would we start? First we have to remind ourselves that curriculums are not built around individuals. By their nature, they are designed for students in general, not for particular students. They are abstract road maps, plans designed to get educators and students to the goals the society wants met. To make the maps, the curriculum makers must base their work on theories of how to get from one educational point to another. So, consciously or unconsciously, they use theories and beliefs about human nature and how to structure and sequence learning experiences to best fit their view of human nature.

In the *ideal* world, we would have all curriculum makers be enthusiastic about type theory. They would know that psychological types are realities that can't be ignored. So they would make up 16 different structure and sequence plans, taking into account the developmental pathway of each type. And they would write evaluation plans that do not expect all types to reach certain achievement goals in the same year of school. Of course, they would take into account other good theories of development too.

INFLUENCING THE SYSTEM

Now back to the real world. Having no magic wand to use on the curriculum makers, we have to work out a strategy for influencing the existing system, taking into account the realities we face. I offer a plan I believe can work. It is a global plan that will play out over a number of years. It will take time, but I think it points us in the right direction. It has four main steps.

Step one is to support all movements aimed at decentralizing the curriculum process. I am not making a case for decentralizing everything, just the curriculum process. State agencies should not be making curriculum decisions. Of course, they must be responsive to the public and carry out their mandate to set up goals for which schools must be accountable. But the *means* for reaching the goals should be decided locally, with the state agency providing assistance, but not mandates. The forces for decentralization are out there, and we can align ourselves with them. Our state legislators will listen to intelligent arguments from citizen groups such as school advisory committees. Nearly all of us can get on our local committees.

How does this first step fit our goal of promoting uses of type? We can influence individual schools to use type, perhaps even whole school districts. But state agency people mostly rely on top-down regulation, and mandates from the top about using type would surely set up resistance and work against our purposes. So long as schools are free to use whatever means they wish in reaching the state's mandated goals, we have the opportunity to influence curriculum decisions.

Step two is to get entry into the culture of individual schools. The problem of making major changes in curriculum and instruction is, as the phrase goes, like redesigning a bicycle while riding it. Schools have to keep going. They don't have many stopping points at which new designs can be put in place and tried out. Users of type have all learned about the problems of introducing type to people who aren't ready for it. As another phrase goes, help that isn't perceived as help isn't helpful. So we learn to be more sensitive to the culture of a school, and we try to match our entry techniques to it. Chapter 12 deals with this topic in some detail. Whether we move directly or indirectly, our ultimate objective is to have the majority of the staff convinced that types are real and need to be part of the means for reaching mandated goals.

Step three is to convince the school staff that student *development*, and not just achievement, should drive the curriculum. The more sensitive they are to the idea of types as developmental pathways, the easier this job will be. Our best ally in the job is each teacher's own experience of his or her own type pathway. They know the surge of energy and satisfaction that comes from working on tasks that call on their type strengths, and they know the depression that comes from being denied access to the path.

In introducing people to type in workshop settings, many of us who teach about type put participants in eight or sixteen type alike groups, and have them talk about characteristics they have in common. The insights from this activity are often powerful. And when the type groups report out to the whole workshop, most participants say the reality of the types became strikingly clear to them. If your lead such an activity, consider next time having them do a second part: to describe their type's developmental pathway. They won't know what you mean by developmental pathway, but try such language as, "When you were a child, what kinds of responsibilities energized you? What can teachers do to promote such roles for children?"

If student development is driving the curriculum, a new view of accountability will emerge. Students won't be expected to reach the common goals at the same time or in the same sequence. Achievement testing based on one sequencing of achievement for everyone will likely be replaced by student portfolios, and competency testing will be done in many ways besides paper and pencil tests.

In the 1930s a large-scale experiment demonstrated the feasibility of such a change in student evaluation. Called the Eight-Year Study, it involved 30 high schools and 300 colleges. The college admissions people knew the reputations of the high schools in the study, and they agreed to accept any student from those schools just on the recommendation of the school principal. No records of courses taken or grades were needed. This gave the schools freedom to experiment with their programs. Many of the schools continued to use fairly conventional courses and evaluation procedures. Others experimented in many ways, including the use of student portfolios instead of grades and standardized achievement tests. Data on all these students were taken during their four years at the participating colleges. Their academic results were as good or better than their college classmates who had come through conventional college-prep curriculums. Their leadership in college activities was distinctly superior. When a sub-group of students from just the high schools that had the most experimental programs was considered separately, those students outperformed their college classmates in all categories. Unfortunately, the arrival of World War II brought an end to the cooperative experiment, and it was not revived after the war.

Step four is to help the school staff put type theory into the curriculum process. Let me make an aside here. As most of us using type have found, the term "type theory" puts off many people. They take it to mean that type is just a theory, not a fact. Jung, Briggs, and Myers had absolutely no doubts about the existence of psychological types. Nor do I. Types are a fact. They used the term "type theory" to mean a way of explaining the nature of types. They did not use the term theory to mean a speculation, as we might use it in saying, "I have a theory about the conspiracy to kill John Kennedy." I often try to bypass the problem by substituting "type concepts."

KINDS OF MIND

For curriculum decision makers to be convinced that type theory should be used in the curriculum process, they must first believe that the theory describes fundamentally different kinds of mind. To convince people of that, I believe we should begin to talk about the types with a little different language.

As I explain in Chapter 11, we have inherited a centuries-old view of what mind is. In this view is the assumption that all humans, except perhaps those regarded as mentally defective, have the same basic mental equipment; we just differ in the amounts we possess of different traits — traits such as self-confidence, IQ, motor skills, social awareness, etc. Some people even put type preferences such as extraversion and intuition on the list. This could be called a unitary view of mind. Everyone has the same "hard wiring," as an engineer I know has called it, but we differ in our software.

What Jung has given us is a different view of mind. The theory of psychological types suggests that even our hard wiring is different, probably in 16 different ways. To communicate to others the significance of Jung's view, I believe we should begin to talk about the types as 16 kinds of mind, as 16 different ways of processing human experience. Types should not be viewed as 16 minor variations on a unitary model of mind, along with other variations, but as 16 distinct ways of being in the world, 16 ways of deciding what is important to know and to do.

I no longer like the term "cognitive styles" as applied to type. It suggests surface variations, not fundamental differences. Type differences are fundamental. I believe the types can be constructively proposed as 16 forms of cognition. The practical effect of the proposition should be to help us explore and better define 16 developmental pathways. In situations where 16 is too many to handle, the types can be sorted into groups. The groupings will differ depending on the learning situation. The function combinations — ST, SF, NF, and NT — should often work well as a stand-in when considering patterns of mental processing. Even better, but bringing the number to eight, is grouping by "cousin types," the type pairings as shown in Appendix A, pages A-9 to A-16. The two types on each page have the same dominant process in the same attitude; such as, the two extraverted dominant thinkers, ESTJ and ENTJ.

ENGAGING ALL THE TYPES THROUGH THEIR STRENGTHS

The theory of type development and other good theories of development need to be given priority. When that is done, curriculum decisions will be driven by the progress of *individuals*, in their own developmental pathways, and their own time frames. Curriculums are, of course, for groups and not individuals; but the curriculum can give the teacher recipes for learning activities in which all students can participate successfully irrespective of their own achievement levels.

When school faculties are free to make the decisions, we can help them use type to design programs with activities in them geared to all the types. All of us, from time to time, have seen learning activities that were engaging to all types of students. What we are aiming for is more and more of them until they fill the curriculum — activities that span the whole range of *responsibilities* that motivate the types: responsibilities in investigating, producing, trouble-shooting, caretaking; responsibilities in creating, organizing, harmonizing, analyzing, managing, and more. As you read Myers' descriptions of the 16 types, you will see that the kinds of activity in this list are associated with particular types. Some types, especially ESFJ and ENFJ, instinctively take on harmonizing responsibilities. Others, particularly ISTJ and ISFJ, take on caretaking; and so on.

We will start from where we are and, little by little, will fill the curriculum with such activities. I close the chapter with a story that suggests the kind of small step I mean. It comes from a visit I made to a special school for students who had been designated learning disabled or emotionally handicapped. After I had given a type explanation and MBTI results to the whole faculty, I met with small groups of teachers to help them see the uses for type in their work. Each teacher stayed with her students all day, except when they were in "special area" activities. They were sophisticated teachers who had worked hard to find good instruction techniques. As they talked about the difficulties of teaching their students, ages nine to 14, I realized that some, perhaps many, of them were not responding to the good instruction techniques because the techniques were not addressing the developmental needs.

I asked the first group of teachers to choose three or four students they all knew, who were the most enigmatic and frustrating . After they selected them, one at a time we guessed their types, based on clues in their behavior. One they guessed to be I N T P. His teacher said he didn't take his work seriously at all, was withdrawn, and could seldom be pulled into classroom activities. They asked what might help his situation. I thought about the INTP's dominant introverted thinking preference, and while not trying to teach them about the dominant, I told them that all the INTP boys I knew loved computers. Had they tried to reach him through the computer? Well, they said, he has one at home, apparently knows a lot about them, but here at school he never earns enough points to go to the computer lab. I suggested they try to start his engines by getting him assigned as assistant to the computer lab director. Their lack of response told me I hadn't sold them on the idea or hadn't made the point clear to them. Structure one, Gordon zero.

So we discussed another child, a boy they guessed to be an E N T J. They said his classroom behavior mostly alternated between bullying and sulking; he did not do his assignments. I had them read a brief description of the ENTJ type. Then I explained that the extraverted thinking types want, above all else, to put logical order into their environment. I highlighted the statement that said ENTJs thrive on being in charge. When I asked what opportunities this ENTJ student had to be in charge of anything, his teacher said, "None. He can't even manage his own behavior, so how could he be made responsible for anything else?" I suggested she find something she could put him in charge of, and let me know the result.

At the close of the day that teacher found me and excitedly told me, "You are not going to believe what happened with Duane! On the way back to my room this morning I thought of something for him to be in charge of. We have a classroom library that students check out books from, and I don't do a very good job of managing it. I asked Duane if he would manage it, and he almost instantly became a different child. No bullying, no pouting, just cooperation and doing his work. And he figured out how to run the library."

Of course this small change was just an opening into the complex task of helping Duane get onto his path. But I believe the results convinced the teacher that understanding type was a worthwhile investment of her time and energy. Also that some instructional problems are really *developmental* problems. And I believe the teacher began to get a glimmer of a key principle of type development theory: to get a responsible behavior from someone acting irresponsibly, entice their dominant into something constructive. Look again at the type descriptions. They clearly suggest responsibilities each type will *want* to undertake, will need to undertake to find psychological nourishment.

The changes I have proposed are big ones, but they are possible. Many small steps like the one taken by Duane's teacher can accumulate into big change. People who care about and use type concepts have seen major changes happen in their personal lives because of their understanding of type theory. Those personal events give them the conviction and energy to promote the uses of type in the world beyond themselves. People who care about type *can* begin to improve the curriculum structure; *can* affect curriculum policy, locally and state-wide; *can* promote the priority of development over achievement; *can* help people see that the types are 16 kinds of mind; *can* make concrete the idea of the developmental pathway; *can* demonstrate the leverage of the dominant process in influencing young people's lives; and in all these ways can help schools move toward genuine reform.

DEVELOPMENTAL NEEDS AND TYPE CONCEPTS

Promoting achievement of skills and knowledge is the first goal of American schools. Helping students develop as integrated persons is another goal. The realities of schooling are such that achievement gets virtually all the attention and development gets almost none. One reason for the imbalance is that teachers have many practical models to follow for promoting achievement, but very few models for helping students with development needs. Type concepts, as yet unknown to most educators, are a practical resource that teachers can use to help individual students in their development.

LOOKING AT DEVELOPMENT THROUGH THE LENSES OF TYPE

This chapter is about helping students individually. Teachers have very little time for working with students singly. When they do make time for it, their attention is usually on achievement matters, not development. When a student's achievement seems to be blocked, and usual academic assistance doesn't help, the student may be developmentally stuck. Type theory often can shed light on the development problem. Teachers and others in helping roles who know type well usually find that thinking through the type dynamics of the student is an effective way to use their limited time.

Strengths and weaknesses in peoples' development, as shown by type theory, come in patterns. By analyzing students in terms of type concepts, you can get some insights into their strengths and weaknesses and get clues to use in planning ways to help them develop.

OBSERVING AND ANALYZING DEVELOPMENT PROBLEMS

Type preferences appear in some people when they are very young. And in those early years evidence of development problems can also be seen in their behavior. A knowledge of type preferences can help us understand what the behavior may mean. Also, type can often point to ways to help the development along.

Observing type in young students

Let me illustrate with some things I observed in a Kindergarten class. It was a few days before Thanksgiving and the teacher had put on the tables in front of each child a box of crayons and a piece of paper with a fanciful design of a turkey on it. The turkey had big loopy feathers, and in each feather was a color name. The assignment was to color the turkey using the right color for each feather. The teacher said, "If you don't know your color words yet, it's OK. See up here? We have these color charts on the wall with their names on them. Look at one of the feathers and see the word in it. That same word will be on one of the charts and on one of your crayons. You can find the right crayon by looking on the side of the crayon. You see the word there? Look at different crayons until you find the one with the same word on it as the feather. The shape of the word will be the same. Then color that feather. Remember to color carefully and stay inside the lines. Then do the same thing for the next feather. And so on, until you finish."

In the next few minutes I watched several children, three in particular. The first was a boy. He didn't know the color names, so he began to compare the words on the crayons to the Blue he saw in the lower left feather on his sheet. When he found the matching crayon, he started to color the feather briskly. Before he finished the feather, his eye fell on another "Blue" three feathers away. He then spotted another. He stopped coloring the first feather, scanned the whole sheet, and put a blue mark on each feather that needed that crayon. After finishing the first feather, he quickly went to the second, and the next, each done a little faster and less neatly.

By the time he had finished all the blues, and started on the orange feathers, the girl next to him was just finishing her first feather. She had laid down just as much crayon on the paper, just as many strokes, but all inside one feather. She was clearly getting a lot of sensual satisfaction from the smooth, careful strokes and the dense, neat layer of wax she had created.

I turned then to a third child, a girl, who had not yet touched crayon to paper. She sat with the blue crayon poised over a blue feather, looking distressed. I got down on her level and said, "Got a problem?" She nodded. "What's the problem?" "They're not the same," she said, pointing first to the feather, then to the crayon. "What's not the same?" "They're not the same." I looked more carefully to her pointing. She touched the front of each word, and I saw what she meant. On the feather was "Blue," and the crayon and wall chart both said "blue." "Ah, I see the problem. They are the same word; only sometimes the very first part of the word is shaped differently. If the rest of the word shape matches, go ahead and use that crayon." "OK?" "OK."

Moving around the room, I noticed that the boy had all but finished his bird, was getting real enjoyment out of his speed and his system, and neatness didn't interest him at all. The first girl was on her fourth feather, the first three looking like enamel ware.

Then I returned to the second girl. Just one feather was colored. She had the red crayon poised over the right feather, but had not touched crayon to paper. "Same problem?," I said. "Same problem." "OK. Each time the problem comes up, it is alright to use the crayon if the rest of the word matches."

The boy, with his eye drawn to the repetitive pattern of color names in the turkey and his desire to move through the task quickly, was showing an intuitive way of handling this assignment. The sensory aspects of it did not much interest him. He may need some help to appreciate the sensing experience of using crayon, but there was nothing in his behavior to suggest a development problem. If the teacher wants him to learn neatness, a different strategy is needed.

The first girl, surely showing a sensing preference, was also doing what came naturally, with no development problem evident. The second girl, however, stuck on the shape of the words, was showing another aspect of the sensing preference. Her concern over the exact physical appearance of the words is evidence of the sensing preference for being grounded in physical realities. Her problem seemed to me to be a distrust of her intuition. Her intuition showed her the pattern similarities of the *Blue* and the *blue*. But even after my explanation, she didn't trust her intuition enough to make the small leap from the Blue-blue solution to using my instructions for all cases. Perhaps she was inordinately afraid of making mistakes, and needed the teacher to show the importance of taking mental risks like this, and assure her that asking for help is a good thing.

In itself, this small incident doesn't give much evidence of a development problem. But it raises a red flag. If the child continues not to ask for help from the teacher when confused (she did not ask), and if the teacher does not see the situation as potentially serious, the problem may grow into something very serious. The teacher who knows type can add this bit of data to his or her picture of the child, and consider ways to help her and others in the class who may have a similar need.

Analyzing an adolescent's development problems

Let's turn to an adolescent. Consider Lisa, for example, who was described in the Introduction to the book. Reread the two paragraphs about Lisa. Now that you know about type concepts, could you form a hypothesis about Lisa's type preferences? Extraversion seems obvious (talkative, gregarious). The friendliness and the desire to be helpful and popular strongly suggest a feeling process at work. The other preferences are harder to detect in this brief description.

Here is a speculation. The easy rapport with others suggests a sensing-feeling combination. A preference for S and F is further suggested by her choosing to avoid complexities and her difficulty in getting an objective view of herself. Because she wants very much to be helpful and be accepted, but then misses the mark and annoys her friends, she may be a judging type — so intent on ends that she neglects the means. Since her own motives seem to her to be so pure, the hurt and resentment she experiences from criticism further support the feeling-judging choice. So we can hypothesize Lisa's type to be ESFJ.

The first step in using type theory to help Lisa is to analyze her behavior, looking for clues to type preferences. Analysis of this kind draws on an understanding of the dynamics of a specific type, in this case ESFJ, and is a skill that people new to type theory should not expect of themselves. I present the process in this chapter because I want the book to be a useful resource for future reference as well as an introduction to type. I believe you'll find many ideas here you can put to use now no matter your degree of familiarity with type theory. But however well we understand type theory, it pays to always treat a guess about someone's type as a hypothesis to be tested and revised as needed.

Looking at opposites

If Lisa is indeed an ESFJ, how does that identification help us think about her personal development needs? There are two fairly easy techniques for starting the process. First consider the type that is opposite hers, INTP. In general INTP's strengths are ESFJ's weaknesses, and vice versa. What INTP does well naturally, ESFJ probably does least well. In *Introduction to Type* read the description of INTP (Appendix page 10) and see if you think Lisa's weaknesses seem to be INTP strengths. When you examine the profile of the opposite type you can better see the pattern and range of the strengths and weaknesses of the type you are trying to help.

THE ZIG-ZAG ANALYSIS

The second technique for analyzing strengths and weaknesses is to look at the person's "zig-zag" process. Zig-zag refers to a sequence in using the four processes — S, N, T, and F — in solving a problem. When the two kinds of perception are placed at the poles of one line, and the two kinds of judgment are placed on a second line, with arrows connecting all four, the problemsolving sequence looks like a "Z" or zig-zag.

Isabel Myers believed that good problem solving could be viewed as a sequential use of the four processes — from S to N to T to F. When faced with a problem, we start constructively with sensing to identify the facts, the given realities of the situation. The raw data by themselves do not settle the problem.

The meaning of the data, their relationships to prior experience, are given by intuition — so the arrow goes from S to N. Intuition also asks: What are new ways to look at the problem and new possibilities in these data for finding a solution?

The arrow moves from N to T when we engage thinking judgment to analyze and decide the logical consequences of acting upon each of the possibilities. And finally the possibilities are also weighed by feeling judgment (F) to assess how deeply we care about the effects of each option; we test the human consequences, the harmony with basic personal values, or the values of others we care about and trust.

A mature settling of the problem will have involved the four processes in a balanced way. But, of course, each type plays favorites with the four processes, and balance is difficult to achieve.

In Lisa's situation, if she is an ESFJ, the imbalance favors feeling, her dominant process, and sensing, her auxiliary process (Remember? An E__J's favorite process is one of the two kinds of judgment — F in Lisa's case — and the extravert uses the favorite process in the outside world.) So an ESFJ gives most attention to feeling, second most attention to sensing, and less to the other two processes. With these preferences added to the diagram, Lisa's zig-zag would look like this:

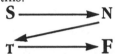

Let's test the ESFJ hypothesis with the zig-zag analysis. A person with F dominant, developmentally stuck as Lisa seems to be, would have the unbalancing power of her F pulling her mental processes too quickly through S and N, zipping past T and coming to rest in a comfortable feeling judgment; but the judgment, unfortunately, is based on too few raw data (S), consideration of too few possibilities (N) inadequately analyzed (T). That seems to be happening in Lisa's situation; she is regarded as flighty and her work is described as trite and shallow. A mature ESFJ, on the other hand, has learned to use all four processes appropriately, even though the F will always exert the most influence in the zig-zag.

Using a strength to strengthen a weakness

Let's consider a helping plan for Lisa. Lisa needs especially to give more time to sensing, to gather better data, and then develop her intuition and thinking. What can be done to help her? The first principle in a helping strategy is: use a strength to strengthen a weakness. The message or action of a teacher that will have the most influence with Lisa is one that will appeal to her feeling process, her strongest process. Her E_F_ combination means she has a very strong need to be accepted, to maintain harmonious relations with her friends. The need impels her to be very good at friendly talk and maintaining easy rapport. How can she use this strength to strengthen her weaknesses? Here are a few ideas:

1. Next time she is rebuffed by a friend, the teacher can ask her,

"What was your friend feeling when she criticized you? What happened just before? What were you feeling just before?"

The objective is for her to tune more precisely into clues about her friends' feelings, to sharpen her sensing perception and to stay longer in the perceiving mode. The place to show her the value of improved perception is in an area of great importance to her — her status with her friends.

2 . She is likely to do much better schoolwork when teamed with a classmate friend whose perception is better developed than her own, perhaps an ES_P, a dominant S type. The guidelines for two-person teams in Chapter 3 should be helpful. Schoolwork that permits extraverting seems more likely to help Lisa develop her sensing more fully; she probably needs dialogue to help her see what she is missing. And if the assignments she is given require objective judgment (T) and reflection (I), the teamwork dialogue should also stimulate her to do both thinking and reflecting better than she would when working silently by herself.

3. Some exercises for listening skills — such as perception checking and paraphrasing — would appeal to her ESF_ nature and would strengthen her S.

4. She needs and will respond to honest praise much better than to criticism. She probably would receive and give attention to positive suggestions when they follow praise but not when they are couched in criticism.

5. Lisa probably would respond to values clarification activities that ask her to recognize values implicit in her behavior, prompt her to make value choices, and have her affirm her values to her schoolmates. To match Lisa's _S_J preferences, the teacher should select valuing activities that are fairly concrete and not too vague and open-ended.

6. The teacher could assign tasks to Lisa that progressively require and reward greater amounts of commitment and risk-taking. The natural step beyond value clarification is commitment and action on the priority values that have become clear.

TYPE DEVELOPMENT ANALYSIS

The process used for analyzing Lisa's situation can be applied to anyone. A good way to begin using the zig-zag is to reread page A-4 of the Appendix at this point and then apply it to other cases.

Also look at page A-19. It is a type table showing the dominant and auxiliary processes of the 16 types. Each type's dominant and auxiliary suggest the bias you can expect to find in the zig-zag of that type.

Let's examine what type theory tells us about the natural bias in problem solving by considering three examples, ENFP, ISFJ, and ENTJ.

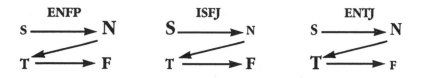

| ENFP | ISFJ | ENTJ |

ENFP Natural Bias: Brainstorming and exploring possibilities are what ENFP sees as problem solving. The dominant extraverted N works like a radar screen, picking up all sorts of possibilities without regard to their relative merit. In the zig-zag the tiny S is likely to be consulted just enough to show ENFP something about the present situation that might need changing. Insights provided by N may be built on very few facts except the fact of the personal excitement found in creating something new. The third process, T, is not seriously consulted, except perhaps to consider the language needed to persuade thinking types who may otherwise be roadblocks. The auxiliary F is a cheerleader, picking the favorites among possibilities and strengthening commitment to them. The natural bias of ENFP is to let the possibilities and dreams of intuition govern, with a little checking from feeling. The less preferred thinking and sensing may be overlooked or used solely to "sell" what intuition wants, not to check it out.

ENFP Effective Zig-zag: The ENFP's effective zig-zag probably begins when the auxiliary F reminds the dominant N about what's at stake: "What do you care about deeply in this situation? Sort out the important values in your dream from the trivial likes and dislikes. Now stop long enough to find out all the relevant facts (S) and the logical flaws (T) that will wreck your dream (N) if you neglect them."

ISFJ Natural Bias: An ISFJ sees problem solving as adjusting day-to-day events to make life and work more satisfying — for oneself and others. The dominant introverted S carefully collects all the facts one should need to run one's life. In the zig-zag the facts of the situation provided by the dominant S loom so large and seem so solid that N shows few or no possibilities for constructive change in the status quo. T is not seriously consulted, except to consider the gloomy logical consequences of acting on N's "ill-founded" possibilities. F closes the zig-zag with the value judgment that things will be worse than they are now if one tinkers too much.

ISFJ Effective Zig-zag probably begins when the auxiliary F recognizes a threat to basic values and prompts S into a partnership to sort out the facts that mean the most from those less important, and to consider unpleasant facts that may disrupt life if they are not paid attention to. As sensing and feeling begin to work together to establish the need to fix something, T is called on to look at unpleasant consequences if the problem is not solved and N is asked to suggest new possibilities for sensing and feeling to take into account. The zig-zag can then work effectively and S can see the facts that will help make the change.

ENTJ Natural Bias: The natural, central features of problem solving for an ENTJ are to see problems and make decisions. The dominant extraverted T drives toward having things decided, organized, and settled in logical systems. Problems appear to the ENTJ as confusions that need logical analysis (T) to clear them up. ENTJ thinking applies a cause-and-effect formula to the situation. As the zig-zag suggests, ENTJ attends to S and N only long enough to see a possible solution that stands the test of logic, and then is ready to act on it. F is not likely to be consulted for human consequences or value implications. The desire for closure tends to block consideration of other appropriate facts and options for the fast-moving ENTJ.

ENTJ Effective Zig-zag probably begins when the auxiliary N recognizes the complexities of a situation, highlights possibilities that can't be ignored, and thus slows down the decision process to allow S and N to provide more data. N also provides hunches about how the decision might affect people and values that ENTJ wants to protect and support. T closes the problem solving with the conviction that a more logically-sound conclusion has been reached.

Effective use of the zig-zag for any type

Each type has its own type bias and its own effective way of using the zig-zag. The rule of thumb for finding the effective path for each type is to expect the auxiliary process to play a pivotal part. The dominant process must lead the problem solving, but the auxiliary determines whether the problem solving has a balance of perception and judgment. The types with a dominant perceiving process (the I__J and E__P types) need the judgment of their auxiliary to provide balance. The types with a dominant judging process (the I__P and E__J types) need the perceiving auxiliary to keep the dominant from closing the inquiry too soon, and to supply the facts and possibilities for a more considered judgment.

The Role of EI in Problem Solving. Extraversion and introversion also affect problem solving. I puts emphasis on having the concepts and ideas clearly understood. E puts emphasis on finding out the influence of the environment on the problem, and on making sure there is an action plan after the decision has been reached.

The Role of JP in Problem Solving. The judging attitude provides energy toward closing options and making the decision. The perceiving attitude provides energy toward gathering more information and finding new possibilities. If J moves without enough P, the decision may come too quickly, without adequate consideration of the necessary information. If P collects information and options past the time when these are useful in the situation, the decision may be delayed to the point that it is no longer timely.

CASE STUDIES IN TYPE DEVELOPMENT ANALYSIS

Here are brief descriptions* of four more situations of students with problems that you can use to test your ability to recognize type and to prescribe actions to help the students' development.

Instructions: Read each of the descriptions (enclosed in a box), form a hypothesis as to what four type letters best fit the student, and circle the appropriate letters. Then on a separate sheet, write a brief analysis of the kind that was done for Lisa, and identify several activities or teaching techniques you can recommend for helping the student. You can compare your analysis and recommendations with those that follow each box.

Jan: A conscientious student who gets off target

Jan's remoteness suggests introversion and thinking. Her conscientiousness and focus on work suggest sensing and judging. Her judgment seems poorly developed: she plods along without analyzing her work (thinking judgment) or putting it in perspective (intuition); and

Adapted from descriptions and analysis prepared by Anna Nuernberger

E I	Jan is conscientious and hard working, seems to take her work very seriously, but sometimes accomplishes surprisingly little. At times her work is totally off-target. She often is silent and seems remote, and doesn't even try to make others understand what she's doing, or why. Most people have given up trying to understand her and leave her alone.
S N	
T F	
J P	

she does not tune in to other people's values, and may be unclear about her own priorities (feeling judgment). Based on this limited data, we can guess Jan to be an ISTJ who especially needs help in making better judgments.

Planning to help Jan: With the hypothesis that Jan's type is ISTJ, here is her zig-zag, followed by some suggestions the teacher could try.

1. If she is an S, she will be impressed only by specific, detailed suggestions. Advice not carefully worked out will seem like meddlesome interference to this independent type.

2. Her perseverance can lend stability to her work group. If she can see that the group may need her to help them keep on track, she may be more motivated to become an active group member.

3. Whenever possible, put her in charge of important routines, and arrange for her to work out the policies with others. If she is an
   S   J, this responsibility will help her use her natural inclinations to strengthen weak areas. Within the division of labor, help her obtain jobs that are clearly defined.

4. Peers should be encouraged to explain their motives as clearly as possible to her, and expect that she do the same.

5. Role-playing simulations of how a communication should transpire might be helpful. She can play the part of the person trying to understand Jan — perhaps she can even interview the person who is playing "Jan."

6. Jan should be encouraged by small victories. Any small progress she makes in the developmental tasks described above should be given prompt recognition.

Dean: The class clown who doesn't pay attention

Fun-loving, easy-going, and adaptable describe a sensing, feeling, perceiving extravert. Dean is probably an extraverted sensing type, ESFP, the type that has more trouble with academics than any other. Of all the types, ESFPs are most attuned to the present moment. Dean probably does his off-task socializing because academic work seems too remote and abstract to him, and it fails to hold his attention.

E I	Dean loves to entertain, and can and does keep the group amused and distracted. Consequently, his own basic skills are poorly developed, because he's usually on stage instead of at work. He seems to take nothing seriously, including himself. With no apparent effort he can read people and situations, and instantly find fun in them.	
S N		
T F		
J P		

Planning to help Dean: With the hypothesis that Dean is an ESFP, here is his zig-zag, followed by suggestions for working with him.

1. He may be cutting-up to avoid having to read. If reading is troubling him, check him out on phonics. Because of the sensing types' literal approach to reading printed symbols, Dean may need special help to get the symbol-meaning connections right. Getting to feel comfortable and competent in reading, especially in reading aloud, may be a turnaround for him.

2. ESFPs learn best by doing. The more sensory input they have, the greater chance they will learn. Whenever possible, lessons should be multisensory. If he is an ESFP, he may especially like a variety of media. Demonstrations and pictures would mean far more to him than words or writing.

3. He is not likely to listen to a lot of talk. When giving him assignments, keep instructions to him simple and to the point. Don't expect him to read between the lines or come to conclusions without help.

4. Whenever possible, give him the responsibility of acting as arbitrator for conflicting factions. In that role he can direct his knack for easy rapport with people into the serious business of resolving real problems, and improve his judgment skills in the process.

5. Planning and follow-through may be weak spots; team him with people (probably E_ _J students) who will show him those skills in action.

6. Glasser's Reality Therapy may help him clarify his goals and plan alternative behaviors.

7. Of ESFPs it is especially true: "I hear, and I forget. I see, and I remember. I do, and I learn." Dean probably needs activities that engage him and are satisfying to him in the present moment and that are not just skills "needed in the future."

John: The tactless bulldozer

E I **S N** **T F** **J P**	John is hasty in voicing conclusions and he hurries on to new tasks before old ones are completed. Action for the sake of action seems to be his approach to everything. Although he often shows a lack of concern for the rights of others, he seems sincerely sorry when reproached about his transgressions. However, he seems to make the same blunders over and over, and his teacher wonders if there is any hope for him.

Because he is described as active, quick to voice conclusions, he is probably an extravert. His rush to reach conclusions shows that he is probably a judging type, but Js are more likely to finish what they begin. If his haste is due to an intolerance of complexity, he may be a sensing type, but if his hurry to new activities is due to having more ideas and inspirations than he can control, he is probably an intuitive. Neither his thinking or his feeling judgments seem adequately developed, a real handicap for a judging type. Because he has a positive attitude toward work in general, a lot of energy and a desire to accomplish things, John has a lot of good things going for himself. His "life-field" lists, forces in him that work for and against his personal effectiveness, would look like this:

John's Life Field

Forces for his effectiveness	**Forces against his effectiveness**
1. Energy	1. Jumps to conclusions
2. Interest in activity	2. Leaves work incomplete
3. Quickness	3. Behaves "blindly"
4. Desire for accomplishments	4. Seems purposeless
5. Sympathy for others	5. Behaves inconsiderately

With these data, it is hard to see John's type. His forces against (1, 3 and 5) suggest a lack of perception, and (2 and 4) a lack of judgment. It is quite likely that his teachers' inability to understand him is due to their being very different types. It is apparent that his education has not been effective for him. His teachers don't understand him because he himself is confused and sending out contradictory signals.

Planning to help John. John's teacher probably should begin with a plan that takes into consideration the possibility that he is an E__J type, and attempt to gather more data about his preferred processes. In the meantime, he will benefit from:

1. Learning activities that allow action and free movement.
2. Activities that have as their aim specific standards, criteria, consequences and products, all made clear to him in the beginning. If he is a J, he is likely to take learning as serious business, and his bulldozing may be coming from frustration that others, perhaps including the teacher, are not taking a business-like attitude toward classroom work. E__Js generally thrive on having certain leadership responsibilities, and John may modulate his behavior so as to merit having leadership is some classroom function(s).
3. Learning to state his own behavioral objectives when undertaking new learnings.
4. Being teamed with students who easily see the need for rational planning to reach goals.
5. Learning listening techniques, such as paraphrasing and summarizing what has been said.
6. Carefully outlining and planning each project in detailed sequence.

While trying out these ideas with John, the teacher should be watching for evidence of S, N, T, and F preferences. The four E__J types are different in the kinds of responsibilities they like to carry, and John's preferences may show themselves in his working with others.

Bob: Trying hard but fearing failure

E I	
	Bob has little self-confidence. He almost never volunteers a response in class, except privately to the teacher, after class is over, because he isn't sure he's right. He often undertakes projects of such complexity that failure is almost certain, even though he is willing to work long and hard. It almost seems as though he were his own worst enemy and critic.
S N	
T F	
J P	

Shyness and a preference for complexity suggest introversion and intuition, and the long devotion to undertaken projects is characteristic of the feeling types. Working long and hard without closure may indicate a perceiving type. With the hypothesis that John is an Introverted Feeling type, INFP, here is Bob's zig-zag, followed by suggestions for helping him.

Planning to help Bob. For an INFP who is trying hard but fearing failure, self-confidence will come best from successful work on projects he deeply cares about.

1. Busywork is not for INFPs. If that is his type, Bob must feel there is an important purpose in which be believes behind the work he does. He should do well with a contract plan in which he can choose some materials and activities for himself.

2. His confidence will be bolstered if he is shown the evidence of real benefits to others that are the results of his own efforts, even though the results fall short of his own expectations.

3. Teach him goal clarification techniques, and show him how to break his large over-all goals into small, component, sequential goals that can be evaluated independently of each other.

4. Teach him evaluation techniques so that he can objectively assess his own work.

5. Teach him to check his plans with a dissimilar type who will tactfully question him about details and sequences.

6. He is likely to benefit from uninterrupted periods of intense work on a single project, and from frequent and sincere statements of appreciation and support.

EXERCISE: ANALYZING STUDENT DIFFICULTIES

Lisa, Jan, Dean, John, and Bob had at least one thing in common: their achievement of school objectives was being blocked by difficulties in their development — what teachers in earlier times called character development. If you now have some students who need help as these did, you can follow the process shown in the analysis of Lisa's situation. Try the process with at least two students.

Steps in Analysis:
1. Write a paragraph or two describing their basic traits;
2. Hypothesize a type for each, keeping in mind that you know them only in a small part of their lives, and their behavior in the classroom may not present their true types;
3. Analyze their strengths and weaknesses based on type descriptions;
4. Analyze their zig-zags;
5. Make a list of things that could be done to help them in their development. *Introduction to Type*, in Appendix A, is a good resource for this task, particularly pages 4, 5, 17, 18, and 19.

6. Reconsider your hypotheses of their types as you try the ideas. Continue to observe the students. If the intervention doesn't work well enough, see if other type preferences might be a better match to their behavior. If you can, talk about them with someone knowledgeable about type.

Activities that teach use of perception and judgment

Many teachers have found that ideas for activities come to them when they scan a list of judgment and perception terms such as this one:

Judgment	Perception
goal clarification	communicating
values clarification	observing
managing time	listening
choosing	smelling
deciding	touching
organizing	summarizing
criticizing	imagining
analyzing	collecting (data)
empathizing	investigating

Both perception and judgment

classifying	applying (concepts)
finding relationships	designing (projects)
interpreting	evaluating
hypothesizing	taking risks

Examples of lessons that promote perception and judgment can be found in many sources. Two important sources are:

1. *Teaching for Thinking*, Raths and others, and
2. *Values and Teaching*, Raths, Harmin, and Simon (both published by Charles Merrill Co.)

THE CONTRIBUTION OF TYPE DEVELOPMENT
TO THE TEACHING OF CHARACTER DEVELOPMENT

The task of helping our young people to become integrated and worthwhile persons is infinitely complex. Type theory illuminates only a part of the task. But it is not a narrow viewpoint. At the heart of the theory is the fundamental concern for two of education's broadest goals: the development of keen perception and sound judgment. If people differ significantly in the mental processes by which they perceive and make judgments, educators need to recognize, honor, and use those differences. While the overall task may be infinitely complex, one part of it — the problem of getting in tune with students' different ways of processing experience — is made much more clear and tangible by type theory.

In type theory, one's type is a developmental pathway for that person. As one moves through childhood and young adulthood, the path that offers most constructive growth is the path that permits active use of the type preferences. The life energy, however defined, goes into mastering the preferred perceiving and judging processes. If life circumstances block the normal expression of type preferences, the energy must go mostly into faking one's type to comply with the demands of one's environment, making the energy unavailable for the development of the dominant mental process, the foundation of the personality. In Jung's view, the person who in childhood is pushed off the developmental path that type provides is the person who in adult life must expend much energy and suffer much pain to find personal integration. This view is a major piece of his theory of mental health.

A teacher who wants to help young people in their personal development has precious little time and opportunity to give the help. There are too many students and there is not enough time to learn about their individual development needs. This problem highlights the usefulness of type concepts. The teacher who can recognize type being expressed in a student's behavior has a tool for quickly seeing developmental needs in the student without having to probe more deeply into the student's personal life. That is, type gives the teacher a framework from which to hypothesize helping techniques that will fit the student.

I recommend that teachers begin using this approach with just a few students — the ones who seem clearly to have their academic progress blocked by development problems, like Lisa and the others we looked at in this chapter. Taking them one at a time, we can consider the dynamics of their types. As a simple example, read the student's type description and highlight with a marker the words and phrases most revealing of that type's natural motivations and strengths. Then, once a day anyway, find something to say or do that acknowledges the student's strengths. It is through a sense of security in one's strengths that a person finds the energy and confidence to work on development needs and problems. With practice, this approach becomes less and less time-consuming, almost second nature, and easy as well as rewarding.

EXERCISE: TYPE STRENGTHS AND TROUBLE SPOTS

An important resource for helping such students is a colleague of the same type as the student. Here is a group discussion activity that works for me to demonstrate to teachers the value of using another teacher to help diagnose the problem of a student whose development is blocking achievement. The activity requires a group of 20 or more teachers of various types. I form them into eight groups rather than 16, combining the "cousin" types; having all 16 types represented among the participants is very unlikely except in a large group, while having the eight sets present is more likely. Cousin types are the two that appear on the same page of Appendix A, pages A9-A16. (If you use the expanded edition of *Introduction to Type*, the version now being published, it shows the cousin types on facing pages.) In their groups I have them record on chart paper the key features of their types they agree on, and at the bottom of the sheet report the contrasts that make them different types. I show them a sample sheet with sections marked on the bottom for the contrasts; for example, ESTJ/ENTJ written at the top, and sections for S and N contrasts marked at the bottom eight or so inches of the chart. Of course, if only ESTJ is represented in the group, or only ENTJ, there will be no contrasting report at the bottom on the sheet.

Group Activity

Objective: Getting acquainted with key characteristics of the 16 types, the strengths and potential trouble spots.

Instructions:

1. We are arranged in groups by "cousin" types. Do this activity with them. If you have no partner(s), do it on your own.
2. Use as a reference the page from *Introduction to Type* containing the description of your types.
3. Answer these two questions:
   a. If we could use only a few words and phrases to tell the rest of the world about our two types, which ones would we choose? Take 10 minutes. List only the features you agree on.
   b. If students of our type were performing below expectation in

school, what reasons for the poor performance can we hypothe size out of our own experience? Take 10 minutes, and list only the reasons you agree on.

4. Each group chooses a recorder who records on chart paper the key words and phrases the group agrees on, and the answers to part b. Put part a. and part b. reports on two separate sheets of chart paper. If you are by yourself, you get the job of recorder, of course.

5. We will reconvene in 20 minutes to discuss what is on the chart papers.

Your type description can be found in Introduction to Type on the following page of Appendix A of this book:

ESTJ and ENTJ — A9	**ESTP and ESFP — A13**
ISTP and INTP — A10	**ISTJ and ISFJ — A14**
ESFJ and ENFJ — A11	**ENTP and ENFP — A15**
ISFP and INFP — A12	**INTJ and INFJ — A16**

Debriefing/discussing the group activity

1. Give the groups 20 minutes to agree and produce their charts.
2. Have recorders, one at a time, give their charts to the leader, who puts them on the wall, with the recorder reading/reporting the group's work. Allow about 2 minutes for each report.
3. Call attention to interesting contrasts on charts as they are posted.
4. When all charts are posted, ask these questions:
   — Was talking in your group a comfortable process? Why? Was understanding each other easy?
   — As you listened to other groups' reports, what went through your mind?
   — Are the differences between the groups real and important differences?
   — The potential trouble spots noted by each group suggest the value of diagnosing the problems of a student by consulting a faculty member of the same type. Does that seem sensible to you?

OBSERVATION AS A WAY TO IDENTIFY CHARACTERISTICS*

On the next eight pages are checklists you can use to infer students' types from their overt behavior. If the students you choose to analyze are not able to read the MMTIC or MBTI, or if you decide not to use them, the checklists are a useful substitute. Teachers who know type concepts and who know their students well can make reasonable guesses about their types. Even if your guesses are not entirely correct, you will still understand your students better, after using this exercise. The checklists reflect the work of Isabel Myers and other students of type. However, only the Extravert-Introvert lists have been field tested as an observation instrument, in a somewhat different form. The lists do not constitute a type indicator instrument.

Directions: Put student's name at top and put a check mark in each box opposite a phrase that describes him or her. Comparing tallies of E and I, S and N, T and F, J and P can give you an estimation of the person's type.

---

*The author acknowledges with appreciation the contributions that Anna Nuernberger and Carolyn Mamchur made to this section.

If your student is an **EXTRAVERT**, it is likely that he or she:

				chooses to work with others, with large groups
				plunges into new experiences
				is relaxed and confident
				readily talks over events and ideas with others
				is interested in other people and their doings
				readily offers opinions
				shares personal experiences
				wants to experience things so as to understand them
				is enthusiastic about activities involving action
				asks questions to check on the expectations of the group or teacher
				has a relatively short attention span
				dislikes complicated procedures and gets impatient with slow jobs
				is interested in the results of the job, in getting it done and in how other people do it
				eagerly attends to interruptions
				acts quickly, sometimes without thinking
				likes to work by trial and error
				communicates well and greets people easily

If your student is an **INTROVERT**, it is likely that he or she:

				chooses to work alone or with one person
				holds back from new experiences
				chooses written assignments over oral presentations
				performs better in written work than in oral presentations
				pauses before answering, and shows discomfort with spontaneous questioning
				asks questions to allow understanding something before attempting to do it
				is hard to understand, quiet and shy; seems "deep"
				is intense, bottling up emotions
				prefers setting his/her own standards when possible
				spends time in thought, before and after actions
				has a small number of carefully selected friends
				likes quiet space to work
				works intently on the task at hand
				works on one thing for a long time
				prefers jobs that can be done "inside the head"
				dislikes interruptions
				may spend too much time in thought and neglect to get into action

STUDENT NAME

If your student prefers **SENSING**, it is likely that he or she:

				Is realistic and practical
				is more observant than imaginative
				wants to have senses fully engaged and satisfied
				enjoys owning things and making them work
				prefers memorizing to finding reasons
				is aware of environment and changes moods as physical surroundings change
				learns best from an orderly sequence of details
				is interested in facts and what is really true
				keeps accurate track of details, makes lists
				is patient
				is good at checking, inspecting, and precise work
				likes to know the "right way" to solve problems
				likes an established routine
				enjoys using skills already learned more than learning new ones
				works steadily, not in fits and starts
				is impatient or frustrated with complicated situations
				seldom uses imagination or has inspirations

If your student prefers **INTUITION,** it is likely that he or she:

				seems to like something new all the time
				is more imaginative than observant
				attends more to the whole concept than to details
				is aware only of events that relate to current interests
				becomes restless, impatient with routines
				is an initiator, promoter, inventor of ideas
				sees possibilities that others miss
				is quick with finding solutions
				doesn't always hear you out; anticipates your words
				likes to have and do things differently from others
				likes problems that require new ways of being solved
				dislikes precise work with many details
				enjoys learning a new skill more than using it
				works in bursts of energy, with slack periods in between
				jumps to conclusions; makes factual errors
				finds reading easy
				readily grasps meanings of words and symbols

If your student prefers **THINKING**,
it is likely that he or she

				wants logical reasons before accepting new ideas
				tries to be fair; is impersonal, impartial
				finds ideas and things more interesting than people
				is more truthful than tactful, if forced to choose
				is brief and businesslike
				takes very seriously facts, theories, and the discovery of truth
				takes seriously the solution of objective problems
				treats emotional relationships and ideals quite casually
				contributes intellectual criticism
				exposes wrongs in the habits and beliefs of others
				is offended by illogic in others
				holds firmly to a policy or conviction
				hurts other people's feelings without knowing it
				has a low need for harmony
				is upset by injustice
				seems not to know how his or her own actions affect other people's feelings

If your student prefers **FEELING**,
it is likely that he or she:

				is personal, likes warm personal relationships
				is more interested in people than things or ideas
				is more tactful than truthful, if forced to choose
				is likely to agree with others in the group
				thinks as others think, believing them probably right
				finds it difficult to be brief and businesslike
				takes emotional relationships and ideals very seriously
				is offended by a lack of personal consideration in others
				is motivated by others
				may comply or conform to avoid disharmony
				permits feelings to override logic
				forecasts how others will feel
				arouses enthusiasm
				is upset by conflicts; values harmony
				dislikes telling people unpleasant things
				relates well to most people
				is sympathetic

If your student is a **JUDGING** type, it is likely that he or she:

				likes to have things decided and settled
				is more decisive than curious
				lives according to plans
				lives according to standards and customs not easly or lightly set aside
				tries to make situations conform to his or her standards, "the way they ought to be"
				makes definite choices from among the possibilities
				is uneasy with unplanned happenings
				bases friendship upon beliefs, standards and tastes which are assumed to be shared
				has enduring friendships
				sets up "shoulds" and "oughts" and regularly judges self against these
				aims to be right
				is self-regimented, purposeful and exacting
				is orderly, organized and systematic
				likes assignments to be clear and definite
				has settled opinions; may be tolerant of routine procedures

If your student is a **PERCEIVING** type, it is likely that he or she:

				is more curious than decisive
				lives according to the situation of the moment
				may not plan things, acts spontaneously
				is comfortable in handling the unplanned, unexpected, or incidental
				looks for new experiences, expects to be interested
				samples many more experiences than can be digested or used
				takes a "live and let live" attitude
				bases friendships on propinquity and shared experience
				takes on friendships easily; may also neglect, drop, and resume them easily
				aims to miss nothing
				is flexible, adaptable and tolerant
				wants to understand things more than manage them
				leaves things open
				has trouble making decisions
				starts too many projects and has difficulty in finishing them
				postpones unpleasant jobs
				welcomes new light on a thing, situation or person

KINDS OF MIND

ARE THE 16 TYPES 16 KINDS OF MIND?

The centuries-old view of mind we have inherited is that all humans, except perhaps mentally "defective" people, have the same basic mental equipment; we just differ in the *amounts* we possess of different *traits*: I.Q., abstract reasoning, social sensitivity, artistic gifts, attention span, assertiveness, curiosity, etc. Even intuition, extraversion, feeling judgment, etc., are often put on the list. This could be called a unitary model of mind. Everyone has the same "hard wiring," as one engineer I know has called it, but we differ in our software. Jung's theory of psychological types seems to be at odds with the unitary view. Trait theory fits with the unitary view of mind; type theory appears to suggest something else. It suggests that even our hard wiring is different, probably in 16 different ways. Perhaps we should begin seriously to regard the 16 types as 16 kinds of mind.

The types described by Jung and Myers are patterns they found in people's observable behaviors. Because the patterns were persistent, predictable, and meaningful in human interactions, and because they helped to explain large sets of behavior, Jung called the patterns types and distinguished types from traits. The trait/type distinction is explained in Chapter 2. Let's revisit it for a moment, using extraversion and introversion as examples.

Types not traits. Jung invented the terms introversion and extraversion to designate two basic orientations in life. Everyone prefers one or other, and the preferred one is our automatic, instinctual orientation. We are all capable of being in the other orientation, but it is not our automatic, initial response. He did not mean these type

preferences to be treated as traits, as most people have done. Extraversion as a *trait* means extraversion as a strength or weakness. As a strength, it refers mainly to social skills; as a weakness, it refers mainly to the inability to move out of extraverting into introverting when appropriate. If extraversion and introversion *were* trait-strengths, we could talk about how much of each one a person possessed. We might expect a mature, well developed person to be highly skilled in both. Clearly, this use of the terms is not what Jung intended, and it is not what Myers intended to identify with the MBTI. As type terms, they are opposite orientations and not strengths or weaknesses. The MBTI sorts people into types; it does not measure skills.

If extraversion and introversion are not traits or skills possessed in some quantity, then they do not fit well into the view of mind I referred to as the unitary model. As type preferences they represent two different kinds of mind — the one tending to plunge into new experiences, and the other hesitating to reflect beforehand.

The same can be said for each of the other dimensions of type — SN, TF, and JP; they do not represent traits, but are different ways we process our experiences. We can expect certain traits to be more associated with one type preference than with its opposite; for example, among people who consider themselves shy, we can expect to find more introverts than extraverts. But we should not treat introversion as another trait alongside of shyness.

MIND AS VERB

In effect, type theory gives us 16 distinct behavior patterns that can be considered as 16 kinds of mind. The Myers-Briggs descriptions show us 16 minds-in-action, or stated more accurately, 16 kinds of mind-as-action. While the latter term sounds clumsy, I like it better because it emphasizes mind as verb rather than noun.

Mind as thing vs mind as process. The common assumption behind the unitary view of mind is that mind is a thing — a noun, a part of the human organism, an entity that causes us to attend, observe, reason, make judgments, and take action. Some regard mind as synonymous with brain. Expressions such as "Use your mind" and "A mind is a terrible thing to waste" reflect this view. If we regard mind as some kind of moving force or controller behind behavior, then mind is a mystery behind the scenes that can only be inferred from observed behaviors, but can't be studied by *direct* observation.

If, in contrast, mind is a verb, and the terms we use to talk about mind are process or action words, then people's behaviors show us mind-as-action. Using mind as verb is a way of talking about the person in mindful, purposive action — the person attending, observing, reflecting, caring, reasoning, etc. Mind is then a quality of the whole person, not a thing prompting the person to act in certain ways.

Jung's functions as observable qualities. I emphasize the noun-verb distinction because it bears directly on how we treat the idea of types. If we accept type preferences as real factors in our lives, then we have the choice of treating Jung's "functions" as entities, as components of the mind (as noun) that prompt our behavior and can only be inferred but never directly observed; or treating the functions as qualities (actions, verbs) that can be directly observed and described. I can only support the latter attitude, because it keeps us more open to growing in our understanding of type by reminding us to observe, observe, observe. It disciplines us to always try to treat type theory as a hypothesis that continually needs testing and validation.

It disciplines us to avoid treating the type preferences as forces assumed to be *causing* behaviors. In practical terms, treating mind as verb is the difference between saying such things as, "You're a thinking type and that's keeping you from seeing when to show appreciation" (the unitary/trait/noun viewpoint) versus "Your difficulty in showing appreciation is certainly consistent with a preference of thinking over feeling" (the mind-as-action viewpoint). Another example: "Your intuition is causing you to overlook some details" versus "You've overlooked some details; intuitives often do."

The mind-as-verb approach also helps us see and treat persons as persons, not just as types. Consider this contrast: "We need an ISTJ for this job. Pat's an ISTJ; let's bring him in" versus "This job seems to need ISTJ skills and interests. Who's got those skills...Pat?"

THE TYPES AS KINDS OF MIND

So, accepting mind as verb, can we say the types are kinds of mind? If we say that "mind" is a term for the processing of experience — in all the many ways there are available — then it seems to me very important that we hypothesize the types as kinds of mind.

Those of us who use type concepts know that the types as Myers described them are ways of processing experience that are *essentially* different from each other. To me that makes them a worthy alternative

to the prevailing view of mind. To emphasize that type is fundamental and not superficial in our psychological constitutions, I propose that type theory be sponsored as a challenge to the unitary model of mind.

Some people, apparently accepting the unitary model, refer to the types or Jung's function combinations as "cognitive styles." To me that term suggests stylistic variations on a common, unitary mind, and is not an adequate alternative to "kinds of mind."

What Jung and Myers have given us is, among other things, a pioneering theory in the field of cognitive psychology. Today, when some cognitive psychologists and educators are beginning to attack the unitary model of mind, the time is right for Jung's types to be proposed as a more constructive model. The challenge can be launched in all arenas, by the practitioner as well as the theorist.

HOW CAN WE KEEP TRACK OF 16 DIFFERENT KINDS?

Being able to call to mind the main characteristics of each of the 16 types is a skill that takes a long time to develop. For me it took several years. Now, after 20 years of having type concepts in my daily life, the process of improving my understanding of the types is just as active as it ever was.

Don't be discouraged by the fact that learning about the types is a long, slow process. Fortunately, there are ways to put type concepts to work bit by bit as we learn them. Long before the complexities of all the types emerge in our understanding, we can use the concepts without distorting them or making them trivial. Any of the type dimensions — EI, SN, TF and JP — can be considered separately. If you have a basic grasp, say, of E and I, you can put it to work. For example, in a brief exchange with someone, guessing E or I may be useful as you decide whether you want to help the person process a thought aloud or allow time for the person to process the thought quietly inside.

In this EI example, all the 16 types are sorted into just two categories. That is the simplest way of using type ideas. Often, however, it is far more revealing and useful to sort the types into four categories, as I did in Chapter 3 in presenting IS, ES, IN, and EN groupings as a practical way of looking at classroom instruction. In this chapter we will concentrate on one other four-way sort: ST, SF, NT, and NF.

Focusing on Jung's four functions. In Carl Jung's view of our psychological make-up, *all* conscious mental activity can be sorted into four categories: sensing, intuition, thinking, and feeling. Jung called these the four mental functions. Myers referred to them as the mental processes, as I have in this book. The other type preferences — E, I, J, and P — are *orientations* of the processes, not the processes themselves. E and I show a person's preferred way of being in the world, oriented toward outer events and people, or toward the inner world of ideas. J and P show the preference for orienting one's outer life in a planful or spontaneous way.

The previous chapters have shown that everyone uses all four mental processes or functions, but we have favorites. Each of us favors one of the perceiving processes and one of the judging processes, making four combinations of preferred processes: ST, SF, NT and NF. To help us with the problem of keeping track of 16 types we can use the four process combinations as four kinds of mind. Treating them as four kinds of mind is not inconsistent with Jung's theory. There is a strong practical reason for it as well: four patterns are much easier to remember and to manage than 16.

When we say that four types have a common mind-set, for example, the NF types, we know we are bundling together a lot of differences. Those of us who have been using type concepts in our daily work know we can expect an INFP to react to something differently from an ENFJ. Some differences can be accounted for by their orientation preferences: E, I, J, and P. We also know that a lot of differences can't be accounted for by type. But it is clear that we can expect a lot of commonality among people of the four NF types. I believe there is real practical value in searching it out.

The idea of four kinds of mind was given an important boost by the work of Humphry Osmond, Miriam Siegler, and Richard Smoke, reported in their 1977 article, "Typology revisited: A new perspective," in the journal *Psychological Perspectives*. I have used, with gratitude, their terms for the ST, NF, NT, and SF combinations. They called the ST combination Structural, the NF Oceanic, the NT Etherial, and the SF Experial. As explained in the next section, they invented the term experial to contrast with etherial. They developed their insights without knowing of the work of Isabel Myers and the extensive research done with the MBTI. My presentation here differs somewhat from theirs because mine is based on Myers' work.

FOUR KINDS OF MIND

ST: The Structural Mind. Four types have the ST combination: ISTJ, ISTP, ESTP, and ESTJ. Similarly, four types have NF in common, four have NT, and four have SF. What the ST types have in common is their S way of experiencing life and their T way of organizing their experience. They value what their senses experience that their T can turn directly into objective reality. The best analogy for the structural mind is the computer as an elaborate filing system. STs want clean data that will file exactly where they want it, so it can be easily retrieved in the same form that they filed it. The ST process works best with unambiguous facts and specifics that can be clearly and correctly sorted into mental files. Of course, life doesn't present just unambiguous experiences that can be neatly classified. The ST solution to that problem is to simplify experience by reducing it to what will fit the filing categories. Mature STs recognize that this solution may oversimplify things, but they believe the reality they hold onto is the part most needed for future use; they will have the essential things ready for use when they are needed.

NF: The Oceanic Mind. NFs process experience in an entirely different way. To NFs, the unique, subtle, personal and "ambiguous" features of experiences are what make them most valuable and interesting. In their view everything is ultimately connected to everything else; life is a seamless whole. To objectively sort and file experiences is to lose the subtle features that make possible the rich connections and relationships between things and people. NFs see the ST way of reducing experiences to distinct, objective categories as destroying the essentials rather than saving them.

Rather than being a filing system, the NF mind is like an ocean. Swimming around the edge of the ocean, just over the rim of consciousness, are all the bits of distinctive experiences that the NFs want to save for quick reference. When the conscious mind is through with the bits, they are allowed to swim away, over the rim, to find their own place. When a new problem is faced that requires recalling those bits of experience, they become available — not from a systematic file, but from a process of letting associated memories come into consciousness, one pulling in another and another. Some that come are the exact ones sought, some are different. The NFs have faith that this process will preserve the best of experiences for future use; if the exact ones sought aren't found, others perhaps more interesting and just as useful will be retrieved and provide a creative solution to the new problem at hand.

NT: The Etherial Mind. NTs have in common with NFs the global approach provided by intuition. In common with STs they have the concern for objectivity that thinking gives them. Ideas in the form of mental models are the central feature of the NT mind. Before they launch themselves into the hurly-burly of life events, the NTs want to have mental blueprints or maps to guide them, to provide an advance system of meanings by which they can stay oriented in daily life. Some NTs are bothered by the term etherial as implying insubstantial. One suggested the term conceptual mind. Osmond and his colleagues chose the term etherial for the NTs to suggest their reliance on abstract constructs and principles, the ether-like material that is primary in their mental functioning. They also see NTs as tending to process every-thing, with ". . . everything being grist for the mental mill." Directly experiencing life, without first conceptualizing it, takes effort and feels awkward. NTs are keenly interested in objective data, not just facts as facts, but as evidence to support one of their mental models.

As you read this material, you are witnessing my **NT** mind: doing what is most natural to me — presenting a mental model.

SF: The Experial Mind. The SFs have in common with STs the concreteness and matter-of-fact qualities that the sensing function pro-vides. With the NFs they share the personal, subjective approach of the feeling function. "Experial" is a term coined by Osmond and his colleagues to contrast with etherial and to convey the central feature of SF mind: everything is validated in personal, practical, daily experi-ence. Like the NTs, SFs believe in conducting their lives according to principles. But while the NTs seek out abstract principles first and then test them in life experiences, the SFs reverse the process. They take life events matter-of-factly; then when their experiences show them what works and what doesn't work, rules-of-thumb emerge — per-sonal, practical guidelines that are credible as guiding principles because their own experience produced them. SFs are immediately in touch with the tangible qualities of events and they know directly the literal, personal meanings of what happens. In contrast, STs turn events into objects before they react to them personally, and the intu-itive function of the NFs and NTs probes behind the literal experience before it settles on the meaning and value of it.

In these four descriptions I have tried to use language that reaches

beyond my own NT mind-set. My long range goals for my own self-improvement include a big, never-ending task: finding phrases, anecdotes, and ways of framing ideas that bridge across type differences. Of course, none of us can ever leave our type behind and experience life through the mind-set of another type. I hope readers will write to me with suggestions for improvements of the language I have used to describe their type.

ST, SF, NF, NT MENTAL PRIORITIES

While each of the 16 types has a distinctive pattern of priorities and values associated with it, the four **STs** have some priorities in common, as do **SFs**, **NFs**, and **NTs**.

ST Priorities
- conserving valued resources and protecting practices that work
- finding situations where they can use and enjoy their technical skills
- minimizing or eliminating ambiguity and uncertainty
- getting roles defined in specific, objective ways
- knowing exactly what output is expected of them
- having or making objective rules
- dealing with concrete, objective problems that are uncluttered with emotional issues

NF Priorities
- finding situations where they can pursue their deep concern for broad, human value issues
- finding situations that allow them freedom for creative expression
- exploring the possibilities in relationships
- finding situations that value their insights into complex interpersonal problems
- making institutions responsive to people
- promoting the ideals of harmonious relationships

NT Priorities
- finding situations that need their objective curiosity and lead to intriguing possibilities
- working at the abstract level of broad concepts and general ideas
- analyzing complex, objective situations

- working on problems that respond to their own new techniques and solutions
- pursuing their own idealistic images of how things should be
- having opportunities to independently produce innovative, ingenious solutions

SF Priorities
- working in harmonious, familiar, predictable situations
- maintaining the practical contacts that keep personal relationships warm and free from conflicts
- enjoying the present moment, making the best of life's conditions
- attending to the tangible needs of individuals
- making a distinctly personal physical environment in which to live and work
- being in situations where their keen attention to the here and now is useful and appreciated

ST, SF, NF, NT INTERACTIONS

I believe everyone who uses type ideas daily begins to collect anecdotes and examples of type characteristics in action. Here are a few that to me typify the mind-set of the four function combinations and the results of their interactions with each other.

Three women, two NFs and an ST, were appointed to be a management team. Before they became managers, each was recognized as highly competent, and they had high regard for each other. One of the NFs headed the team. In their team meetings, the NFs talked effortlessly with each other, brainstorming various means of solving problems. The ST felt left out of the whirlwind style of dialogue, seldom talked, and often was unsure of exactly what was decided. She concluded that she had previously misjudged the two NFs and now saw them as condescending toward her and fickle. Over the weeks she came to doubt her own ability to be a manager. The quantity and quality of her work declined, and she finally asked to be relieved of management responsibility — even though the team as a whole was regarded as very effective. If we read this problem as one of NF oceanic work style predominating to the point of handicapping the ST structural partner, we get some insight into what happened.

An SF, a single woman, received Valentine letters from two male admirers — one an NF, the other she believed to be an ST. She

showed the letters to an ST woman friend and asked her reaction. The friend said the NF's letter was insincere and flaky, and the ST's letter showed genuine caring.

An NF, an assistant principal, enthusiastically presented to her principal a plan for hosting representatives from each of the district's elementary schools so they could see the innovative program the fourth and fifth grade teams had developed. Expecting encouraging comments, she asked the ST principal what he thought. His response: "That's maybe 50 people. Where do we park the cars?"

Obviously, it is hard to anticipate the viewpoint that is natural and automatic to a mind-set different from one's own. I believe the place for us to begin in bridging the differences is to first examine our own instinctual frame of mind.

DISCOVERING THE BIASES OF ONE'S MIND-SET

Probably the main value of viewing the types through the four function combinations is the opportunity it gives for discovering one's own biases. I do not mean bias in a negative sense, such as prejudice, but rather as a slant of mind, one's angle of seeing things. Whenever I have trouble understanding another person's point of view on something, or when my own perfectly clear ideas draw blank stares from people, I often turn to type differences for an explanation. Many times, the ST, NF, NT, SF differences give me insights I can use to clear up the problem. When you know people's types or can make a good guess about them, you will begin to see the four kinds of mind in their language and actions. Here are examples I have observed.

Mind-sets in organizational problem solving.

Working with the school superintendent and the senior staff of a large school system, while teaching them about type, I sat in on a senior staff meeting. At this point they knew each other's types, and I was observing to help them see type differences in action. The four kinds of mind were on display. When the superintendent turned the meeting to a discussion of a new performance appraisal plan for administrators, an ST began to identify specific ambiguities and misunderstandings her school principals were concerned about. She was describing flaws in the details of the plan. The man in charge of the new plan, an NT, responded that there could be no ambiguities because he drafted it carefully and he *himself* had explained it in detail at meetings attended by every administrator in the district. He said the flaws had already been found and the plan was crystal clear. The ST began again to explain a particular complaint. Two other STs nodded and suggested refinements to the plan. The sole NF in the meeting said this seemed to be a communication problem that could be worked out better in another meeting specifically for that purpose. Two members had not yet spoken, an NT and an SF. When the superintendent asked for their views, the NT said he thought the plan was "conceptually sound, and ought to be workable." When the SF was asked about the plan, she said, "What plan? Until it's in place and running smoothly, there is no plan."

Later, going over this exchange with them, I tried to show them the examples of type in action: the NT with his blueprint that was "conceptually sound;" the STs with their concern for the small but crucial problems in the implementation; the NF with the suggestion for harmonizing the differences before going further; and the SF pointing out that the plan and its implementation are not separate and are nothing of importance until people use the performance appraisal system to their satisfaction in their daily work. Each person's slant on the problem, when seen as a natural contribution of his or her type, could be taken as constructive, and all were needed to arrive at a workable solution.

Here is another, less complex example. NF and ST are partners in consulting work; NF is the senior partner. They freely exchanged ideas with each other and planned their work carefully. After they had worked together for several months, ST revealed that she had strongly considered breaking the partnership until she realized NF really meant to act on only about 10% of the possibilities proposed in their meetings. The structural ST wanted to ground their planning in given facts and move step by step. The NF needed her imagination to explore widely until one possibility jumped out and gave the inspiration for action. Both were grateful for their knowledge of type in helping them to have the patience needed for understanding each other.

Whichever aspects of type are prominent in a meeting or relationship, groups whose members know about and use type differences constructively have a very big advantage. When type terms are part of the group's language, there is usually better listening, more good-natured humor, and a smoother flow of problem solving toward outcomes that all members can support.

An exercise highlighting mind-set differences in an organization.

How members view the priorities of their organization can be very much influenced by their kinds of mind. In their article, "Stories managers tell: A new tool for organizational problem solving" (*Management Review*, July 1975), I. I. Mitroff and R. H. Kilmann reported very successful uses of an exercise that shows the importance of the mind-set differences. To teach problem-solving techniques to managers in large business organizations, they obtained the managers type preferences and guided them through a three-step activity.

Step one was to have each person individually write a short story about his or her idea of an ideal organization. The story could take any form they liked. Step two was to put the participants into four groups — ST, NT, NF, and SF — and ask each group "to come up with a story that best expresses the group's concept of an ideal organization." There were no other instruction and no constraints. The conclusion of step two was each group reporting to the others the story its members agreed on.

People who know type theory will find no surprises in the outcomes; the groups gave stories fully consistent with type theory. But participants were always startled by the striking contrasts. Here is a brief version of the patterns of stories reported by the authors. "The ideal organization of the STs is characterized by complete control, certainty, and specificity." Work roles are defined in detail, with clear hierarchical lines of authority, and are monitored with impartial, impersonal rules. The heroes of the ST stories are leaders who brought order and stability out of chaos and gave the organization a specific sense of direction.

The NT stories are centered on broad, global issues, with little if any attention to roles, rules, and lines of authority. Their ideal organization is guided by intellectual and theoretical concepts of good organization, and is impersonally idealistic. They focus on big-picture economic issues, and on new products and new horizons. The heroes of NT stories are broad conceptualizers who turn around a narrowly-focused organization and steer it successfully toward new goals.

The NF stories also emphasize global, idealistic themes, but focus on the personal and human goals of the organization. The ideal organization is organic and adaptive, serving the needs of humanity and its own members. If the NF groups draw a visual representation of the ideal organization, the diagram shows a circular or wheel-like structure in which there is no hierarchy, no clear lines of authority. The heroes in the NF stories give the organization "a new sense of direction in the human or personal sense."

The SF stories focus on "the detailed human relations in their particular organization," the details of the interpersonal environment of the workplace, and not on theory or broad conceptual issues. Their attention is on "the human qualities of the specific people" in the organization and not on work roles or rules. The stories are realistic rather than idealistic. The heroes of the SF stories are people who "create a highly personal, warm human climate," who make you want to come to work to be with your work family.

The third step in the Mitroff-Kilmann exercise is coaching the participants in using the four points of view in solving problems of their own organization. Agreeing on a particular problem or issue to work on, the participants individually write their own view of the problem — objectives, issues, value assumptions, what an ideal resolution would look like, etc. They are then formed into the four groups to develop a group statement incorporating their individual statements. The actual problems look strikingly different from the four perspectives, each of which has its special contribution to make to satisfactory solutions: ST, attention to day-to-day operational issues; NT, long-range strategic planning, NF, long-range human goals; and SF, day-by-day human relationships. The authors argue that failure to take into account all four viewpoints "can be disastrous to an organization."

The three-step exercise works with any kind of organization, highlights the reality of the differences among the types, and demonstrates the value of the different viewpoints to the welfare of the whole group.

Mind-set influencing teaching.

Looking at teaching and learning through the lenses of the four mind-sets is often more effective in highlighting issues than is the use of whole types or the EI, SN, TF, and JP dimensions separately. Here is an example of bias in our mind-sets that comes from conversations with a student of mine in a graduate seminar in education called Instruction: Theory and Research. He was a biology instructor at a community college. After the seminar members had taken the MBTI and had learned the basics about type in education, he came to talk after class about an insight he had and to ask my advice. He had been

having trouble with one class. The trouble baffled him because he was highly regarded as a teacher and knew he was good. The students were conscientious and seemed bright enough to handle the material of the course, but "their eyes glaze over when I get about five minutes into my presentations." His insight was triggered by a transparency I had shown in class. It showed the percentage of several thousand nursing students in each of the 16 type categories. Seeing that SFs dominated the type table, and knowing that most of the students in his problem class were in a nursing program, he came to talk with me about how type differences might be part of the problem. His type is INTP. He wanted to see how his effectiveness with them might stem from the NT-SF differences.

I asked him to demonstrate a sample of a recent presentation that didn't work for them. He sketched on the chalkboard a simple abstract model he used to start a lecture on the nervous system, to demonstrate how synapses work. Part way into it he said, "This is where they glazed over." I reminded him of the contrast between NT etherial and SF experial, and he quickly realized how remote his model was from his students' personal experience. I asked him what kinds of direct experiences of the nervous system the nursing students were likely to have in their training. He said they had practicum work in hospitals, so they must be encountering patients with atrophied muscles, bed sores, cramps, etc. I asked him if he could begin a lecture on the nervous system using those as a starting point. He said he wanted to work on the suggestion, and we planned to meet the next week. He came in a week later grinning with excitement and announced, "I've just invented a new kind of instruction for them. It works like a charm. I call it backwards teaching."

In the reasoning of this NT instructor, teaching is backwards when it goes from concrete, personal experience toward the abstract and impersonal principles underlying experience. What he was saying, of course, is that the sequence of learning that makes sense to him and is most helpful to him is turned around in the approach he devised for his SF students.

Guarding against mind-set bias in teaching.

This instance and others I have encountered brought me to a general rule for planning instruction. When preparing a lesson, we need not only to plan for ways to engage the EI, SN, TF, and JP differences.

We also must consider how our own mind-set bias is likely to intrude in the planning and cause us to want to teach as we prefer to be taught. To emphasize the point, consider the opposite of the NT-SF example above: an SF teacher and an NT student. The student is likely to be put off by the instruction unless he or she sees where the lesson fits in the abstract, impersonal scheme of things. The teacher will feel most natural in grounding the lesson in personal and concrete experience, and would think the heart of the material is left out if he or she didn't start there.

Consider the ST-NF difference. ST teachers are going against their instincts if they don't begin the lesson by telling students exactly what is going to be learned and the sequence that will be followed. NF students may see the teacher's efforts as lifeless, too cut and dried, and then feel they must steel themselves to handle the imposition. Similar problems can be seen with the other combinations of mind-set differences.

To guard against one's mind-set bias affecting planning and teaching in unwanted ways, the teacher needs to consciously raise the issue at the beginning of planning and again as a double check when finishing the plan. I have framed the checking process as a set of questions.

1. Have I provided some kind of brief orientation to the new material, an advance organizer, that helps students see how it relates to their prior experience? Intuitive students will be looking for a familiar *conceptual organizer*, something that calls up the abstract frame of reference they need for processing the new material. Sensing students will want a familiar *concrete organizer*, they will want an anecdote, specific example or sample that shows them the topic of the new material and alerts them to the category(ies) of their memory bank to bring into awareness.
2. Have I planned for or allowed students to have choices in the way they study? Keeping in mind the range of natural interests of the types, have I provided access to diverse materials and experiences from which they can choose?
3. Do they have some leeway in deciding the kind of product of their study they will present for evaluation?

Giving students choices

What kinds of choices? Here are some examples.

Technical school example. Two ST instructors at a technical

school, who taught their courses with linear, self-checking, programmed materials, were concerned about the number of students who dropped their courses after the first week or so. Because psychological type was a regular feature of the school, the two instructors were able to find out that nearly all the students who dropped were intuitives. By making a simple change in their instructional plan, they eliminated the problem. On the first day of classes, they told the students to work with the programmed material for two or three days and decide if that style of study suited them. Those who decided it didn't fit them were then free to choose or invent any means to learn the material, including working in small groups. All students were given the course objectives and shown the evaluation process all would go through; how they reached the objectives and prepared for the evaluation was for them to decide. As you might suppose, some students chose to invent other ways to study, and nearly all were intuitives. The rate of dropping out of these courses was reduced, and achievement levels remained the same — irrespective of the methods students chose.

A college example. NT college instructor of physics, keenly interested in teaching and learning processes, spent many hours preparing a course format that offered more approaches to learning than the standard lecture and lab. He spent the most time preparing instructional modules, packets that guided students through various resources, including printed material, computer and lab work. After trials of the new system, he was disappointed to find that student achievement did not improve; some achieved very well, as before, but the new approach still left many students at levels lower than he wanted. With the help of an instructional resource person at his campus he concluded that he had written the modules to fit his NT way of working and they did not fit students of other types well enough. He tackled the problem by enlisting graduate students who were sensing types to help him write a parallel set of modules designed for a sensing approach. He said it was painfully hard for him to conceptualize. At the beginning of the next term, he has two parallel sets of modules for students to select from, the original with the intuitive slant and the new one with a sensing approach. Students were told to sample the two sets by working through the first module of each and then decide which set suited them better. He made lecture sessions optional, and set up small group work with graduate student mentors. Test scores went up.

A high school example. After learning about type differences, an SF business education teacher decided to teach her students how to build a portfolio to present samples of their work and other evidence of their skills to a prospective employer. The contents and style of the portfolios varied dramatically, reflecting student differences in type, achievement, and tastes; but by starting this at the beginning of her course, it provided her with an evaluation system as well as giving students a practical introduction to employer expectations.

Mind-set in family relationships.

Nearly every household has a mix of kinds of mind among its members. Most of Erma Bombeck's stories document that fact and show us the funny side of the mix. It isn't just the generation gap that interferes with communication. Messages are often not received with the meaning intended, and decisions made by one member may mystify the others. Understanding type differences helps demystify the miscommunications. Here are some examples in which knowing the ST, SF, NF, and NT differences makes a problem more manageable.

A. An NF and NT mother and father, both professionals, have an SF daughter, an only child, now middle school age. While she gets good grades, she doesn't show nearly enough seriousness about her studies to suit her parents. When she was four, her parents thought they saw in her an interest in being a doctor, and have firmly in mind for her an academic path that will get her to medical school. The parents, in effect, want her to devote her present life to achieving a future life they can clearly visualize. The SF's instincts are to live fully in the present and let the future happen as it unfolds. The parents give her plenty of reasons, both logical and personal, why she should be more future-oriented.

   These conditions have set up a tension in the family that type concepts can help explain, can help alleviate — but cannot remove, because the mind-set differences are a fact of life that will not change. When all three recognize the mind-set bias they bring to the family's life, and try to help each other on their separate pathways, their present lives and futures should be more satisfactory for all.

B. In a similar case I know of, the parents, both NFs, have had the advantage of knowing about type for many years. Their SF son has just entered college. They recognized during his elementary

school days that his sensing mind saw the world differently and had different priorities from theirs. While he was bright, it was clear to them that he would not approach academic work as they had. They helped him be involved in many sensory-rich activities through the years that showed him how to manage academic work. He chose college, and his parents helped him find one where residential groups form close relationships; and his best friend has enrolled with him.

C. I offer an example from my own childhood. My ST father, a bank officer, wanted me to learn about budgeting and being responsible about money. Each Friday when I got my allowance, I was to give him an itemized account of how I spent the previous week's allowance. He said he didn't care how I spent it, just that I kept track. I told him I didn't think that keeping the record would help me be responsible about money. The requirement did not appeal to my NT mind at all. My SF mother, wanting no disharmony, persuaded me to accept my father's plan. So I agreed, and five minutes before suppertime each Friday, when I got my allowance, I sat down and made up a list of expenditures that I probably had made that week. I see now that both of them felt they were conveying to me some values that were high priorities in their mind-sets, and I was exercising my NT autonomy.

D. Mind-set differences can, of course, strongly affect relationships between siblings. Three daughters, four years apart in age, were NT, NF, and NT, from oldest to youngest. As reported by the NF, now an adult, she felt squeezed into an NT sandwich. Day after day, her sisters talked NT — all sorts of abstract, impersonal subjects she felt were structured in a way that would annoy her. Their talk seemed intellectual to her, and she decided she was not so bright as they. Now a highly successful professional, who has learned about type, NF has come to see herself as the intellectual equal of her sisters, but with a different kind of intelligence.

Thoughts in summary.

A case can be made that the traditional concept of mind has practical limitations for us as we try to find useful ways to deal with the human mental diversity we are all aware of. Treating the 16 types as 16 kinds of mind gives us an hypothesis to test. If the types represent truly *fundamental* differences in mind-set, then using the lenses of type to examine and deal with our human problems will yield better results that using the unitary model of mind as our basic assumption. If we are dissatisfied with our progress in solving our problems of human understanding, perhaps some of our root assumptions about human nature need changing.

In this chapter I have argued for considering type differences not as style variations, but as distinctly different ways of processing our experiences, different kinds of mind. That means we accept the type differences not as strengths or weaknesses to be shaped or improved but as given structures within which anyone can be helped to improve — in his or her type's own distinctive way.

When there are situations in which the 16 types are too many variables to deal with, there are good reasons to sort them into four categories, the four mental process combinations, and deal with them as four kinds of mind. I hope the examples given in the chapter provide ideas you can develop and test in your own situation. I invite you to send me your reactions to my characterizations of the four kinds of mind, to help improve and extend the descriptions.

Finally, I propose that each of us look at his or her own mind-set bias to see how our preferred processes affect our interactions with people of other mind-sets. Once we first see and understand our own slant on things, the door is opened to seeing the other person's mind-set and then learning how to engage it for mutual benefit.

INTRODUCING TYPE
INTO AN ORGANIZATION

Many of us who use the Myers-Briggs Type Indicator have introduced type into organizations with the intention of having type become part of the organizational culture. Sometimes we are successful, but too often we are disappointed in the results; some individuals in the organization benefit, but we see no wide-spread effect.

We know the value of type in our own lives and expect through our teaching skills and enthusiasm to energize an essential core of fellow enthusiasts in the organization who will also see the value and spread the benefits of type throughout the organization. We expect a kind of chain reaction. We expect type concepts to become a part of the language the members use in working with each other, because they recognize the constructive qualities of type theory.

This is not realistic. Some organizations are ready to be influenced by just our teaching skills and enthusiasm, but most situations require more. What does it take to successfully influence an organization — beyond what is needed to teach individuals effectively?

The question is at the heart of the career of those who specialize in organizational development. Some of them have added the MBTI and a sound knowledge of type theory to their other skills and are sharing what they know with others, through the Association for Psychological Type and various publications.

In this chapter I present the approach I use. Most of my experience has been with educational organizations, so most of my examples come from them. Some of the techniques I use are adaptations of ideas I learned from Bill Drummond and Lee Bolman, and I am grateful to them.

In the chapter are suggestions for:

- analyzing the organizational situations you want to deal with,
- identifying the factors supporting and factors that would resist uses of type concepts,
- planning possible points and means of entry,
- using type theory to help you plan, and
- making a specific plan that has a good chance of success.

OURSELVES AND OUR SITUATIONS

The readers I had in mind in writing this chapter are those who want to introduce type into their own organizations. I hope the readers who would be introducing type as an outside consultant or trainer will find the chapter helpful, but it does not deal directly with their situation.

As a teacher of graduate students in education, I found it easy to introduce type to my students. I decided the specific content of my courses, I saw type as relevant, and I taught it. Most students appreciated learning about it, and some made it part of themselves and their work. But they faced quite a different situation if they wanted their schools or colleges or other organizations to adopt type as part of the institutional culture. They found resistance just as I had found it in my efforts to get wider use of type in my college and university.

We all know it is the nature of organizations to resist change. The more hierarchical they are, the more bureaucratic; and the more bureaucratic they are, the more invested they are in existing systems and thus resistant to changes. Public education institutions are among the hardest to change.

I and others undertook many varied means to introduce type directly to the faculty and administrators of our university. We had some positive results from these direct efforts, but they were considerably more modest than we had hoped. After several years, I found myself shifting mostly into indirect approaches to influence the system — to reach the faculty and leadership through the students. Students who were residence hall advisors, members of student leadership groups, and undergraduates in specific academic programs took type into the culture of their groups. Faculty and administrators began to be influenced by the student leaders. The academic credibility of type began to grow as highly regarded graduate students chose to do research projects and doctoral dissertations involving the MBTI. In my own college, individual faculty members became interested, and all students in the educational leadership program were introduced to type. But type did not become part of the curriculum of the teacher preparation program.

This gradual introduction of type was truly gradual, spanning 17 years. As you might suppose, I envisioned and advocated many applications of type that did not materialize.

I mention all of this to make the point that those of us who want to influence other peoples' use of type have widely varying situations, different ingredients, that have to become part of our plan. I have helped many of my students plan ways to introduce type into their organizations, and every situation is different, requiring a plan designed to fit it specifically. What I have written here is a general strategy for devising situation-specific plans.

DESCRIBING AND ANALYZING THE SITUATION

As you start thinking seriously about how to introduce type into your organization, begin by writing a description of your situation. Whether you put it in good prose form or just phrases, it pays to write it in detail. My suggestion is that you write it in the form of answers to some key questions.

What goal or on-going effort of the organization can type be linked with?

This is the first issue to address in your analysis of the situation. Unless the leaders of the organization, or of a unit within the organization, are open to and looking for tools to help them deal with problems or pursue particular goals, they are not ready for you to introduce type. Are they seriously committing resources to improving individual effectiveness, teamwork, mission clarity, the quality of products and services, and other such goals that can be enhanced by uses of type? Even if you know that type knowledge is what the organization needs, your attempts at teaching type will probably not influence organizational behavior to any extent unless the leaders are actively inquiring into means of improvement and will themselves see type as a possible means to help their situation. In most cases, learning about type and using the ideas will not be accepted as a goal of the organization just on the merits of type theory. The time it takes to learn and develop the skills of type can be justified in the members' minds to the extent that they are committed to the goal that type is supposed to help them reach.

How can you judge the readiness of the organization to use type?

Even when you know there are leaders and others who are committed to improving organizational processes, that is no assurance they are ready for type. Do they seriously believe that people's individual differences need to be used more constructively? Are they committed to giving people time, training, and resources to work on developing their individual effectiveness? Are they ready to use a tool like type ethically, or is there a real risk that they may use it as a weapon? If it is hard for you to find positive answers to these questions, a direct introduction of type into the organization is not realistic. Perhaps a small scale introduction is feasible; some means for that are given in the paragraphs that follow.

What happens when type is introduced in situations where people are not ready for it? Consider two contrasting cases, out of my experience. In the first situation, the faculty of a large community college, after a long and hard struggle, had decided on a new constitution for the faculty senate. It moved the senate from being a low-profile and advisory body into a role of proactive leadership in the college's instructional program. The senate's leadership team had to begin to function as a team, to deal with power struggles and personality clashes in the senate, and to build new relationships with the college administration, including the president who was hired just the year before. One of the team knew about type, saw its potential usefulness, oriented the others to it, and they invited me to conduct a two-day retreat for the team on uses of type in their situation. The members were highly committed, had a very clear purpose for using type, and the results were very positive in the long run as well as at the retreat.

In a contrasting situation, the superintendent of a large school district invited me to introduce type to his senior staff and to the school board members. The superintendent said their purpose was to better understand each other so as to accomplish more collaborative decision making. Because he was very interested in type and quite comfortable in openly discussing his type with the cabinet and board members, I made the mistake of assuming that he and the others were open to the conditions of collaboration: trusting relationships, straight talk, respect for differences, etc. That turned out to be a poor assumption. There were three meetings: first the superintendent and his cabinet; then he and the board members; then a combined group. All meetings seemed to go well, but I learned in debriefing the third meeting that there was no consensus about a purpose for this work, that there was suspicion about hidden agendas, and that learning about type was not seen as being a means to a common goal or in service to a commitment. In that situation, some months later, I learned that their understanding of type did not affect their work or radiate beyond them into the organization.

An important step in introducing type into an organization is to find out the goal that the knowledge of type is intended to serve; the members' clarity about the goal; and their commitment to achieving it. In the absence of these, type knowledge is likely to be just a curiosity that some will appreciate and others will forget. And the organization will not be broadly affected.

What is my position of influence in the organization?

Who listens to me and regards my ideas as credible enough to be given serious consideration? Who is in my circle of influence, and are they people who have credibility with others outside my circle?

Your answers, carefully thought out, will suggest the pathways for spreading type ideas. The circle is your base for introducing type. In many kinds of organizations, psychological theories, including type, are suspect and negated. Your credibility will have to carry type through the initial stages of introduction until the base group members see for themselves the value of type and are willing to commit to supporting the next step of its extension into the organization.

If you are the top administrator or a high-level resource person who is expected to bring new ideas into the organization, you have a different set of opportunities and constraints than do teachers or other employees who may not have those expectations attached to their jobs. All of the questions that follow apply to people lower in the organization; some will apply to the top leaders as well.

What are my purposes and motives in this situation?

It pays to examine carefully your motives in introducing a change into the organization. Do I have purposes other than the obvious ones of using type to improve the ways we work? Do I have other motives I may not have acknowledged to myself? Am I hoping that by taking the lead in introducing type I will become more visible as a leader or potential leader? What other agendas do I have that may ride on the coattails of the change I hope to introduce?

The answers to these questions are just for your own consideration, to clarify what is energizing you in your plan for introducing type. Being clear about your purposes will help you make better judgments about the plan and the situations that come up as you act on the plan. *If your personal reasons do not mesh with the organization's objectives and active commitments, do not try introducing type.* Once you have tried it and type is not received well, the organization is likely to turn off to other attempts; reintroducing type may be impossible once the door has been closed.

Do I have a client or am I my own client?

One way of looking at your role in introducing type into your organization is to consider yourself as a change agent. In introducing type you are proposing that people change some aspects of their ways of thinking and relating to each other, and that is what a change agent does. I am using the term change agent in a way that is somewhat different from general usage. I do not mean that you are necessarily someone who orchestrates and directs a change process. With respect to type, you are the bringer of a resource, and in doing that you may be simply a helper to the designated change agent.

Whatever your role in the change process, you have to have a client, a person or group that, in effect, authorizes you to bring a proposal for a change into the organization. Tacitly or explicitly, you negotiate with the client to find out what the client wants. If you introduce type to co-workers without considering their client relationship with you, you may have no client, no support, and what you are trying to do may seem to them an unwanted intrusion into "the way things are done around here." If you bring in something the client doesn't anticipate, or objects to when you bring it, it will be ignored or rejected. If the client does not see type as helpful to the situation, your work with type will not be accepted as help. In other words, you need to be sure a welcome mat is laid out for type ideas by the people who will be responsible for nurturing a change in the organization.

Sometimes the welcome mat doesn't go out until after they have had an initial orientation to type, such as taking the MBTI and getting a face-to-face explanation of the ideas. In any case, your first client needs to be in your circle of influence. From that base you can build the next base that includes the next client or set of clients.

The caution I am recommending may feel like a wet blanket, an attempt to stifle your enthusiasm. That's not my intent. I am urging careful planning so that your first effort to introduce type is successful, and the success will sustain your enthusiasm.

If you do not have a client in the sense described here, then you start out as your own client. That is, you do with type ideas what you can do in your own work, and invite others to observe you using type. Invite those who believe you to be competent and credible in other respects. Invite those who themselves are credible, are informal status leaders among co-workers. I am suggesting that your invitations to them be informal, casual opportunities to see how you use type. If you are a teacher, show them specific ways type helps you in your teaching — for example, in better understanding and working with problematic students. These people can then become a client group and help you plan the next steps in introducing type. If you learned about type from a co-worker, you and that person most likely would be part of each other's client group, part of the base for next steps.

Can I find members who share the values implicit in type theory?

What has attracted many of us to type theory is the way of viewing human differences it represents. By showing the complementary strengths and blindspots of the types, and showing that all types are valuable, Myers provided basic guidelines for the constructive use of the differences. Implied in the theory are values such as the worthiness and dignity of individuals despite their differences; the importance of collaboration for best results; and the necessity of trust, mutual support, and openness that allow the collaboration to happen. People who hold these values and try to practice them are the ones most likely to be ready for learning about and using type. They will see type as a practical tool for advancing the values. As you decide which people make up your base for introducing type into the organization, consider whom you know that appear to share these values and try to act on them. If most members of your organization pay lip service to the values but actually are steeped in habits of distrust of differences, the task of selecting the base is more difficult.

When and how should I involve the organization's leadership?

Whether you have a client or are your own client to begin with, you will be aiming to involve the top person of the organization as soon as you feel quite sure he or she will see type as a credible and feasible set of ideas for the organization to use. It is a truism that people are likely to support a change they help to design. The reverse is true too: the chances of their resisting a change go up to the extent they were not involved in planning the change. These rules of thumb certainly apply to the top people, who see facilitating or resisting changes as a major part of their leadership.

They also want to know that you are loyal to them, and that the introducing of type into the organization will contribute to their success. They know that most innovations fizzle out, so they will be skeptical until they can see clearly the likelihood of success. No leader wants to be advocating an idea that gets rejected or ignored by others in the organization.

This may seem a very slow process. If type ideas took you by storm, you may be hoping they will surge through the organization as well. Organizations resist and slow down changes for a lot of reasons. The resisting forces won't be bulldozed or bandwagoned away. They exist for reasons that can be understood. They can be anticipated, and, with careful planning, can often be converted into supporting forces.

The process will move more slowly than you want for another reason. As I said in the Introduction to Chapter 2, there is a natural progression in the absorption of type concepts that takes time. This may be a good place to reread it.

How does type fit into the organizational culture?

Some organizations are open to new ideas, with leaders actively looking for them. Some are quick to attend to new ideas, but resist using them. That is, the leaders enjoy playing with the idea of an innovation while most members of the organization do not want to make changes in their practices. Some leaders are slow to consider new ways, but, when convinced of their value, will give solid support for change.

One way of looking at these organizational differences was developed by Earle Page and published by CAPT as a training handout called "Organizational Tendencies." Page saw that the organization's culture was strongly influenced by the type preferences of its leaders, either the current or founding leaders, or both. The organization tends to attract and hold members who fit well in that culture. He saw the energy of an organization being distributed into four categories corresponding to the type preference combinations of extraversion or introversion, and sensing or intuition: IS, IN, EN, and ES. An organization needs the perspective of all four tendencies. But usually it is steered by one of them.

 IS energy, reflective and always practical, is directed toward conserving what has proven itself to work well enough. Drawing strength from continuity, from protecting and enjoying the proven, it resists novel and unproven ideas, expecting them to be more disruptive than beneficial.

 IN energy, reflective and engrossed in possibilities, is directing the organization to question the tried and true, take the long view, and imagine new ideas. Focused on anticipating the future, it assumes that a better way can be found, and must.

EN energy, pushing toward action on fresh ideas, is focused on vitalizing the organization to take risks in trying new ways. Drawing strength from surges of enthusiasm for the new ways, the EN viewpoint assumes organizations are at their best when caught up in pursuing important changes.

ES energy, directed toward action on life's practical realities, steers the organization to get on with its obvious responsibilities. The emphasis is on staying on track, doing what is needed, and getting results.

All four perspectives or energies may be active in the organization. If they are recognized and valued for their positive characteristics, and used in appropriate ways, the tension between them will be constructive. Otherwise, the tension will be seen as negative, and adherents of each viewpoint will see the others as having "excessive" influence and squandering the organization's resources.

One of the four is likely to be a major shaper of your organization's culture, with the others playing a lesser role. Whichever is dominant will have a bearing on your approach to introducing type. The credibility of type will be an issue with all four, but for different reasons. If IS is dominant, and the organization is perceived as working well, you will need to show at the beginning that type helps to continue and protect well-accepted values and ways of working. That is quite a challenge, considering that uses of type are usually promoted as *new* ways of communicating and working, meant to replace the familiar. But if the IS organization is experiencing pain in areas where type could be helpful, it may well be open to considering *practical* new tools. In either case, in the IS organization, as you plan out your credibility base, you will need to draw into it some status leaders who are IS stalwarts, and let them help you pace the introduction of type.

If your organization is energized around IN or EN values, change and newness are not unwelcome, but the credibility of type is an issue in another way. IN and EN leaders are likely to have given considerable thought to the ideas they see as the guiding principles of the organization. For type to become one of those ideas, the leaders will need to see type as consistent with their vision for the organization. In contrast, if ES leaders are to see type as credible, they must believe that it is clearly practical and will help the organization get better results on its accepted objectives.

The best of the values and skills of IS, IN, EN, or ES may not be steering the organization. The blindspots associated with each are important to consider. The leaders of most organizations can recite what the research shows that makes organizations effective, but most of them don't use the knowledge. Earle Page also saw the negative side of the four tendencies. *If not balanced* by other perspectives, the IS influence "may dry up the organization, narrowing leadership and productivity;" the IN influence may weaken the organization by pulling too much energy into "irrelevant ideas and alternatives;" the EN efforts for change may fail to see practical limits and exhaust the organization's resources; and the ES view may keep the leaders from seeing the necessity of change, and keep the organization stuck in a rut. If you see some of the negative tendencies in your organization, they may help you size up the situation for introducing type.

It is also useful to consider the organization's culture in terms of the type preferences that seem to be most emphasized in the day to day work of the organization. Does the work mostly call upon and reward introverted or extraverted behavior? Does the work attract and hold introverts more than extraverts, or vice versa?

Similarly, consider SN, TF, and JP. Combining the four preferences gives you an hypothesis of the modal type of the organization. Read the type description of that type and you will get some clues about the approach to introducing type that will be most appealing.

What are my assumptions about the specific influential people in this situation?

At this point in your analysis, you have a fairly clear idea about which people are most influential in the situation, those who most affect the plan you are forming for introducing type. As you begin to see the roles you expect them to play in the plan, it is time to examine your assumptions about the ways they will act and why they will act that way. If you are assuming a key person will act in a certain way and he or she doesn't, your plan may be upset. Try to test your assumptions ahead of time. Often you can ask people directly about how they will act; "For this to work, here is what I will need..." Talk it out whenever you can. Go over your assumptions with someone you trust who can give you a different perspective.

DECIDING ON POSSIBLE ENTRY POINTS

Your answers to the nine questions in the previous section should give you a fairly complete description of the situation for introducing type. They may also suggest possible points of entry, that is, where, with whom, and how to start introducing type. In a school organization, typical points of entry are: with people responsible for curriculum planning and instructional resources; with the leadership team, focusing on teamwork and management; in the counseling work; in the staff development program; with groups working on changing the organization, such as a school improvement team; or teacher by teacher, classroom by classroom. Your own position in the organization may dictate the point of entry. In each case, except perhaps the latter, you will need to have the leadership endorse and support the entry plan. You may be in a position that allows you only to plant the seeds of type with some person who then takes responsibility for the entry process, perhaps with you serving as a helper.

Analyzing the forces for and against

In whatever point of entry that is being considered, the specific situation of the entry needs to be analyzed. The force field technique for analyzing a situation is very useful in cases like this. There are three basic steps in force field analysis.

1. **Make a Goal statement.** In any situation where one has a desired goal, there are forces working for and forces working against the reaching of the goal. For a successful analysis of the forces, you need a statement of the goal that is clearly focused. It is alright to begin with a fairly general goal such as, "the introduction of type so that it is accepted, used, and disseminated from the point of entry." Then the task is to decide what forces at this possible point of entry are working for and against the reaching of the goal.

2. **List the forces.** Begin the force field analysis with two lists, side by side, of forces for and forces against. For example, in the case of the community college senate leadership team, I asked questions about the situation until I had a fairly clear picture of forces for and forces against a constructive use of type. Because I was not a member of the organization, my interest was to plant the seeds, and I wanted to know whether the conditions were favorable for them to grow. When you are a member of the organization, and want to assess to rightness of a possible entry point, your questions to yourself will be to estimate what people and what conditions in the situation would be favorable and unfavorable to the use of type.

3. **Consider the strength of the forces.** The next step in force field analysis, after the lists have been made, is to weigh the relative strength of each force in the equation: Which favorable forces can I strengthen and which unfavorable ones can I weaken, with the resources at hand? What specifically can be done to each? The situation, as it is, is an equilibrium of the forces; to get energy into accomplishing my goal — the acceptance of type through this entry point — I have to change the balance of forces, change the status quo that does not now include uses of type.

An example of analyzing the forces

Consider the situation of a young high school teacher who was eager to extend uses of type in his school. The school had a good record of serving well the academically-oriented, college-bound students, but not doing well with the others. As a distributive education teacher, he taught mainly the latter students. The principal put him on a committee of teachers charged with the task of finding out what was needed to better serve the students who were likely to enter the workforce after graduation, if they made it to graduation. The committee members were given time during the school day to do their work. The young teacher saw this committee work as an entry point for introducing type. Here is part of the force field analysis he did. His goal statement was "to have the committee support type as a way of looking at learning needs of students and improving their instruction."

His list of favorable forces included:

- the committee appreciates my energy and ideas
- the committee has agreed to consider type
- the principal knows about type and supports its use
- type data about _S_P types being disadvantaged by the standard academic programs should help us see ways to improve instruction
- some teachers of academic subjects, and all of the administrators, are concerned about the students who aren't college-bound
- nearly all the teachers are interested in improving instruction
- the other committee members are well known and respected by the faculty
- we have funds to give the MBTI to students and faculty

His list of unfavorable forces included:

- the committee members don't know about type, nor do most others on the faculty
- I am one of the younger teachers and not well known
- the teachers usually resist changing the curriculum and their ways of teaching
- the committee has no idea of how much support its recommendations will receive
- the teachers mostly ignored some learning styles work (not type) we did on an inservice day two years ago

He went through his lists to see what favorable forces could be strengthened and what unfavorable ones could be weakened. For our purposes here, we don't need the details of his analysis.

His conclusions were:

1. The committee is a good point of entry, because the other members are open to ideas and I have credibility with them.
2. I will need to go step by step, first introducing type to the committee, and getting their approval to collect some type data on students.
3. Although most of the faculty didn't know me well, the teachers of ninth graders do, and I probably can get their OK and the principal's approval to administer the MBTI to all freshmen, and have the teachers of ninth graders take it too. I expect to get some data that will show the committee the value of using type in their work and including it in their recommendations to the faculty.
4. Because two committee members are department heads, the next step would be for the committee to try out ideas, including type, on all the heads.

These conclusions were the basis for his entry plan. After the committee members took the MBTI and got an orientation to type, they supported taking data on the freshman class. Administering the MBTI to the ninth graders and their teachers did provide some data of importance. Most interesting was the fact that over one third of the students were reported as _S_P types, while only three teachers (less than 10% of them) were _S_Ps. These entry activities opened the door for a wider introduction of type into the school.

Once an entry has been made, as in this case, the situation usually needs a revised force field analysis because the forces change, and the goal statement may need to be changed as the goal is pursued into the next phase of introducing type into the organization.

DECIDING ON STRATEGY — THE LONG VIEW

All of the analysis you have done to this point suggests a strategy, a big-picture plan. Strategy is a military term. It is distinguished from tactic, a plan for action within the strategy. A tactic is consistent with the strategy and is one part of carrying out the strategy.

Write out your strategy. It can begin with summary statements from the analysis you have done and with your ideas for entry. When you have it written fully, I suggest you try to boil it down to a few phrases or sentences. As your plan progresses, and you bring others into the planning of next steps, the strategy statement in its brief form (perhaps amended by the base group) will serve to keep everyone's eye on the target. The young high school teacher had a beginning strategy, through the committee and the department heads.

DECIDING ON TACTICS — AN ACTION PLAN

An action plan deals with details, who will do what, when, and how. This is the aspect of planning most of us know well, even though we often neglect to plan the details well. I have nothing fresh to add to this technique of planning except some details about introducing type to people.

Essential details: Setting up appropriate conditions for introducing type.

I suggest you use the following questions as a checklist whenever you are planning to administer the MBTI and/or explain type to people. Some of the details concern ethical issues. The last section of the chapter deals specifically with guidelines for the ethics of using type. Administering the MBTI and interpreting the results should be done by a qualified person, one who understands type and the limits and appropriate uses of psychological tests. If you are not qualified, read the Epilogue following this chapter. It includes more information about this and suggestions for locating a qualified person. If you do get someone else, it is important for you to use the guidelines here to be sure that all the details are attended to.

1. **The people taking the MBTI:** What do *they* see as:
   a. the purpose for taking it? Watch for hidden agendas and misunderstandings. Don't rely just on reasons and reported perceptions given to you by an intermediary whose motives you don't know.
   b. the potential value of it? You may need to clarify their understanding.
   c. their option of taking it or not? What do they see as the consequences of not taking it?
   d. the uses to be made of the type report itself?
   e. their control over the MBTI results?
   f. the leaders' expectations of them that are implied in introduc-

ing type to members of the organization? The ethics guidelines that follow this section will help you form specific answers to all of these questions.

2. **The formats and approaches used:** How shall I fit the administration of the MBTI and the type explanation to the people? You will want to anticipate the dynamics of the group and fit the introduction to the members. Design the explanation session around their purpose for taking the MBTI. For example, if work-team dynamics is the theme, then the session should give the team members opportunities to practice using type in team dialogue, and they will need to discuss their types with each other. When type is introduced appropriately into the team-building process, team members report that type concepts provide a concrete, objective way for them to talk about their personality differences in teamwork — their differences in perception, decision style, pace, priorities, etc. — without getting personal, that is, without feeling that the mention of differences constitutes a personal attack.

If the purpose of introducing type is to examine learning and teaching styles, there are many activities in this book that can be used. Whatever the purpose they understood was being served by learning about type, it is important that participants in the session have opportunities to practice using type for that purpose.

3. **Administration and scoring of the MBTI:** What options fit your situation? Whether it is administered in a group session or individually, during work hours, or filled out at home, it is important to follow the guidelines for administration and scoring given in the user's guide (Manual: *A Guide to the Development and Use of the Myers-Briggs Type Indicator,* 1985, Myers and McCaulley).

4. **Resources and follow-up support:** What materials will the participants need to have during the type explanation session, to take home as a reference, and to have available in a resource library within your organization? What resource people may be needed to help them learn type-related skills and to explore type beyond your knowledge? Their continued and constructive uses of type will depend on such follow-up support.

At a minimum they will need a sheet of words and phrases that characterize the type preferences, a report of their MBTI results, and a set of the full descriptions of the 16 types. That is the basic set for any explanation session and for taking home. In addition they should have handouts related to their purpose for taking the MBTI. Publications for the resource library can be found in the catalogs available from CPP and CAPT.

ETHICAL GUIDELINES FOR USING THE MBTI

The Association for Psychological Type has adopted a statement of ethical principles for using the MBTI. I have extracted the most basic ones to supplement the guidelines already mentioned.

Voluntary. The client has the choice of taking the MBTI or not. Even subtle pressure should be avoided. In situations where the success of using it depends on every member trying out the ideas of type, as in teams or families, I offer the MBTI to all members, score it for those who choose to take it, and then provide a group type explanation to all, including anyone who didn't take it. After the explanation and during introductory activities, those who didn't take it nearly always are willing to hypothesize a type for themselves and ask to take the MBTI.

Confidential. The practitioner gives the MBTI results directly to the person and not to anyone else. An individual's type does not go to the boss or into a personnel file unless he or she offers to give the information. People usually are comfortable talking about their type, but the MBTI outcome is theirs to reveal or not.

Enhance, not restrict. MBTI results and type concepts are used only to enhance someone's understanding and opportunities, not to restrict their options. The career counselor, for example, does not counsel a client away from a particular occupation because his or her type is rare in that occupation, but provides the information in the context of discussing the opportunities and challenges of the that career in relation to the strengths of the client's type.

Face-to-face explanation. The MBTI respondent always gets a face-to-face explanation of type from the practitioner. He or she always has an opportunity for dialogue about the results and for exploring the ideas to find a best-fit type. For that reason they never get their results through the mail or second hand.

Full type description. The respondent always gets a full type description to accompany the MBTI scored results. I always give them a resource booklet such as Myers' *Introduction to Type* that includes not only a full description of their reported type, but also all the other types — which some may want to explore to find a better fit.

Respondents need good resource materials in their hands when they are later considering type or explaining it to family or colleagues.

What's indicated, what's not. In explaining MBTI results and the type concepts, the practitioner needs to distinguish between what the Indicator indicates and what it does not: type characteristics are tendencies, not imperatives; they are preferences, not abilities or achievement potential; and they represent one view of personality, not a panacea. And the MBTI indicates types, not stereotypes.

Finally, before you start to introduce type into your organization, revisit Chapter 5, "Type is a four-letter word." It will help you spot pitfalls you will want to avoid.

EPILOGUE — NEXT STEPS

There is a community of people who use the Myers-Briggs Type Indicator that has expanded rapidly since the first edition of *People Types and Tiger Stripes* was published in 1979. Many of them stay in contact with each other and with new ideas about type through the Association for Psychological Type, a membership organization formed that same year. APT membership is open to all persons interested in type.

APT has developed a number of ways of spreading knowledge about type. It helps create local chapters whose members meet to "talk type." It sponsors regional conferences and, in the odd-numbered years, an international conference. APT members exchange ideas through APT's quarterly newsletter, *Bulletin of Psychological Type*, and through the *Journal of Psychological Type*, published four times a year. These publications, and a membership directory, are member benefits. APT members join one or more interest areas — Careers and Occupations, Counseling and Psychotherapy, Education, Cross-cultural Issues, Management and Organizational Development, Psychological Theory, Religious and Spiritual, and Research. For information or a membership application, write the APT membership coordinator, APT Headquarters, 9140 Ward Parkway, Kansas City, MO, 64114. Or call (816) 444-3500.

In 1985 APT initiated a training program designed to provide participants with the basic knowledge needed for ethical use of the MBTI. Minimum requirements to purchase the MBTI are established by its publisher, Consulting Psychologists Press, Inc., and include: professional use of the instrument, and completion of course work in psychological tests and measurement (or equivalent documented training in tests and measurement). CPP accepts the APT training as equivalent documented training. Similar training is provided by other organizations, and they also conduct training on applications of type in the areas of use represented in the preceding paragraph.

There are several firms that distribute (mainly by catalog) books and other resource materials related to psychological type, and some of them conduct training. One is the publisher of the MBTI, Consulting Psychologists Press, Inc. Its address is 3803 E. Bayshore Road, Palo Alto, CA 94303. Phone 800-624-1765. Another is the publisher of this book, the Center for Applications of Psychological Type, a non-profit research and service organization founded by Isabel Myers and Mary McCaulley. CAPT distributes MBTI-related materials, and publishes many training aids and a bibliography of all literature involving the MBTI that is updated regularly. CAPT's address is 2815 N W 13th Street, Gainesville, FL 32609. Phone 800-777-2278.

Isabel Myers' book, *Gifts Differing* (1980), is a most important resource for a deeper understanding of type. I believe it will become an American classic. The MBTI *Manual* (1985) by Myers and McCaulley is essential for anyone who uses the MBTI. The are a number of useful publications dealing with teaching and learning. Here are four I recommend. *Applications of the MBTI in Higher Education* (1987), edited by Provost and Anchors. *Strategies for Success: Using Type to do Better in High School and College* (1992) by Provost. *One of a Kind* (1988) by Neff. *The Developing Child: Using Jungian Type to Understand Children* (1992) by Murphy. Murphy is also co-author of the Murphy-Meisgeier Type Indicator for Children (MMTIC), and has written several related booklets. The MMTIC is validated for children in grades 2 to 8. Hanson Silver Strong and Associates, of Moorestown, NJ, also publish materials concerned with teaching and learning that draw on Jung's theory of types; they take an approach that differs from that of this book.

I am interested in your suggestions, case examples, ideas, exercises, and any other experiences in using type that you might like to see in the next edition of *People Types and Tiger Stripes.* Feel free to contact me through CAPT. Best wishes for your explorations into type.

Gordon Lawrence

APPENDIX

INTRODUCTION TO TYPE

ISABEL BRIGGS MYERS

CONSULTING PSYCHOLOGISTS PRESS, INC.
3803 Bayshore Road, Palo Alto, CA 94303

CONTENTS

Foreword I
Opposite Kinds of Perception and Judgment 2
Effects of the Combinations of Perception and Judgment 3
Making Full Use of Perception and Judgment 4
Mutual Usefulness of Opposite Types 5
Remaining Preferences and Summary 6
Effect of the Combinations of All Four Preferences in Young People 7-8
Descriptions of Well Developed Adult Types
    Extraverted Thinking, ESTJ and ENTJ 9
    Introverted Thinking, ISTP and INTP 10
    Extraverted Feeling, ESFJ and ENFJ 11
    Introverted Feeling, ISFP and INFP 12
    Extraverted Sensing ESTP and ESFP 13
    Introverted Sensing, ISTJ and ISFJ 14
    Extraverted Intuition, ENTP and ENFP 15
    Introverted Intuition, INTJ and INFJ 16
Effect of Each Preference in Work Situations 17-18
Type Table with Favorite and Auxiliary Processes 19
    (and space for entry of friends whose types are known)

FOREWORD

The questions in the Myers-Briggs Type Indicator are not important in themselves, but they do indicate basic preferences that have far-reaching effects. There is no right or wrong to these preferences. They simply produce different kinds of people who are interested in different things, are good in different fields and often find it hard to understand each other.

People with preferences opposite to yours tend to be opposite to you in many ways They are likely to be weak where you are strong, and strong where you are weak. Each type has its own set of strengths and abilities.

An understanding of type in general and your own type in particular can help you choose your career. It can also help you deal with the problems and people in your life. The following pages provide a number of ways for you to explore your own preferences and verify your own type. The Indicator reports your type by four letters that show how you came out on each of the four preferences. You can check these letters against the explanations of the separate preferences (pages 2 and 6), the effect of the combinations of perception and judgment (page 3), the effects of the combinations of all four preferences in young people (pages 7-8), the adult descriptions (pages 9-16), and the effect of each preference in work situations. (pages 17-18).

If the description of your reported type makes you feel comfortably understood, your four letters are probably right. If it does not fit you, one or more of the letters may be wrong. Sometimes people are not sure what they do prefer, or they disown their real preference for fear they ought to prefer the opposite, or their answers are affected by chance factors. If your reported type does not seem right to you, read the descriptions for the types that differ from it by a letter or two, and see which one comes closest to being a satisfactory description of yourself.

OPPOSITE KINDS OF PERCEPTION AND JUDGMENT

The Type Indicator is concerned with the valuable differences in people that result from the way they like to perceive and the way they like to judge. Succeeding at anything takes both perception and judgment. First you have to find out what the problem or situation is and what are the various things you might do about it. Then you have to decide which to do. Finding out is an exercise of perception. Deciding is an exercise of judgment. You have two basic ways of finding out and two basic ways of deciding.

Opposite ways of finding out: sensing and intuition. One way to find out is through your *sensing* (S). Your eyes and ears and other senses tell you what is actually there and actually happening. Sensing is especially useful for gathering the facts of a situation. The other way to find out is through your *intuition* (N) which shows you meanings and relationship and possibilities that are beyond the reach of your senses. Intuition is especially useful for seeing what you might do about a situation. You use both sensing and intuition, of course, but not both at once and not, in most cases, with equal liking.

If you like sensing better than intuition, you make more use of sensing, get to be more skillful with it, and grow expert at noticing all the observable facts. You tend to become realistic, practical, observant, fun-loving, and good at remembering a great number of facts and working with them.

If you like intuition better than sensing, you make more use of intuition, get to be more skillful with it, and grow expert at seeing a new possibility or solution. You tend to value imagination and inspirations, and to become good at new ideas, project and problem solving

Opposite ways of deciding: thinking and feeling. One way to decide is through your *thinking* (T). Thinking predicts the logical result of any particular action you may take. Then it decides impersonally, on the basis of cause and effect. The other way to decide is through your *feeling* (F). Feeling takes into account anything that matters or is important to you or to other people (without requiring that it be logical), and decides on the basis of personal values. You use both thinking and feeling, of course, but not both at once and not, in most cases, with equal confidence.

If you trust thinking more than feeling and use it more, you grow to be most skillful in dealing with that part of the world which behaves logically (like machinery) with no unpredictable human reactions. You yourself tend to become logical, objective and consistent, and to make your decisions by analyzing and weighing the facts, including the unpleasant ones

If you trust and use feeling more than thinking, you grow most skillful in dealing with people. You tend to become sympathetic, appreciative and tactful and to give great weight, when making any decisions, to the personal values that are involved, including those of other people.

The kind of perception you prefer to use, either sensing or intuition, can team up with whichever kind of judgment you prefer to use, either thinking or feeling. So there are four possible combinations, each producing a different set of characteristics—different interest, different values, different needs, different habits of mind and different surface traits.

Your own combination of perception and judgment makes a lot of difference in the kind of work you will do best and enjoy. If your daily work has most need for the kind of perception you naturally prefer, you will handle the job better and find it more satisfying. If your daily work has most need for the kind of deciding that comes naturally to you, your decisions will be better and will be made with more confidence. In choosing among careers, find out how much chance each will give you to use *your own combination of perception and judgment.*

EFFECTS OF THE COMBINATIONS OF
PERCEPTION AND JUDGMENT

Sensing plus Thinking. ST people are mainly interested in facts, since facts are what can be collected and verified directly by the senses — by seeing, hearing, touching, etc. And they make decisions on these facts by impersonal analysis, because the kind of judgment they trust is thinking, with its step-by-step process of reasoning from cause to effect, from premise to conclusion.

Sensing plus Feeling. SF people are also interested in facts, but make their decisions with personal warmth, because the kind of judgment they trust is feeling, with its power to weigh how much things matter to themselves and others.

Intuition plus Feeling. NF people make decisions with the same personal warmth. But, since they prefer intuition, their interest is not in facts but in possibilities, such as new projects, things that have not happened yet but might be made to happen, new truths that are not yet known but might be found out, or, above all, new possibilities for people.

Intuition plus Thinking. NT people share the interest in possibilities. But, since they prefer thinking, they approach these possibilities with impersonal analysis. Often the possibility they choose is a theoretical or technical one, with the human element more or less ignored.

The columns below present some of the results of these combinations.

ST SENSING + THINKING	SF SENSING + FEELING	NF INTUITION + FEELING	NT INTUITION + THINKING
Facts	Facts	Possibilities	Possibilities
Impersonal analysis	Personal warmth	Personal warmth	Impersonal analysis
Practical and matter-of-fact	Sympathetic and friendly	Enthusiastic & insightful	Logical and ingenious
Technical skills with facts and objects	Practical help and services for people	Understanding & communicating with people	Theoretical technical developments
Applied science Business Production Construction Etc.	Patient care Community service Sales Teaching Etc.	Behavioral science Research Literature & art Teaching Etc.	Physical science Research Management Forecasts & analysis Etc.

If you can tell which column comes closest to describing you, you can tell which two of the four process (sensing, intuition, thinking and feeling) you naturally use most.

One of those two will be your "favorite" process. The other is the "auxiliary" which supplies perception if the favorite is a judging process (T or F), or supplies judgment if the favorite is a perceptive process (S or N). Your greatest strengths come from the two you like, and it is important to trust and develop them. However, for some purposes, your less-liked kinds of perception and judgment will serve you much better — if you remember (and take the trouble) to use them.

MAKING FULL USE OF PERCEPTION AND JUDGMENT

To make full use of your perception and judgment, you need to use both kinds of perception and both kinds of judgment, each for the right purpose. This is a skill you can acquire by practice. Whenever you have a problem, a decision to make, a situation to deal with, try exercising each process by itself, consciously, purposefully, so that each can make its own contribution to the solution without interference from any other process. Start with your perceptive process (S and N). Perception should always come before judgment.

1. Use your sensing for facing the facts, being realistic, finding exactly what the situation is, what you are doing, what other people are doing. Try to put aside all wishful thinking or sentiment that may blind you to the realities. Ask yourself how the situation would look to a wise, impartial bystander.

2. Use our intuition to discover all the possibilities, all the ways in which you might change the situation or your handling of it or other people's attitudes toward it. Try to put aside your natural assumption that you have been doing the one and only obviously right thing.

3. Use your thinking-judgment in an impersonal analysis of cause and effect. Include all the consequences of the alternative solutions, pleasant and unpleasant, those that weigh against the solution you prefer as well as those in its favor. Try to count the full cost of everything. Examine every misgiving you may have been suppressing out of loyalty to someone or liking for something or reluctance to change your stand.

4. Use your feeling-judgment to weigh just how deeply you care about the things that will be gained or lost by each of the alternative solutions. Make a fresh appraisal, trying not to let the temporary outweigh the permanent, however agreeable or disagreeable the immediate prospect may be. Consider also how the other people concerned will feel about the various outcomes, even if you think it unreasonable of them. And include their feelings and your own feelings along with the other facts, in deciding which solution will work out best.

You will probably choose, as usual, a solution that appeals to your favorite process, but on a sounder basis than usual because you will have considered facts, possibilities, consequences and human value. Ignoring any of these can lead to trouble. Intuitives may base a decision on some possibility without discovering the facts that will make it impossible. Sensing types may settle for a faulty solution to a problem because they assume no better one is possible. Thinking types may ignore human values and feeling types may ignore consequences.

You will find some steps in this exercise easier than others. The ones that use your best processes are rather fun. The others are harder, but worth while. If feeling is your favorite process, the attempt to see *all* the consequences of an act may show you that even the best intentions can go wrong unless thought through. If thinking is your favorite process the attempt to learn how others *feel* about your plans may show why you meet so much opposition.

What makes the hard steps hard is that they call for the strengths of types opposites to yours. When your problem is important, you may be wise to consult someone to whom these strengths come naturally. It is startling to see how different a given situation can look to a person of opposite type, but it will help you to understand and use the neglected opposite side of yourself.

MUTUAL USEFULNESS OF OPPOSITE TYPES

The clearest vision of the future comes only from an intuitive, the most practical realism only from a sensing type, the most incisive analysis only from a thinker, and the most skillful handling of people only from a feeling type. Success for any enterprise demands a variety of types, each in the right place.

Opposite types can supplement each other in any joint undertaking. When two people approach a problem from opposite sides, each sees things not visible to the other. Unfortunately, they seldom see each other's point of view. Too much oppositeness makes it hard for people to work well together. The best teamwork is usually done by people who differ on one or two preferences only. This much difference is useful, and the two or three preferences they have in common help them to understand each other and communicate.

When extreme opposites must work or live together, an understanding of type does much to lessen the friction. Disagreement is less irritating when Smith recognizes that it would hardly be normal for Jones to agree. Jones is not being willfully contrary. He is simply being an opposite type, and opposite types can be tremendously useful to each other when given the chance. The lists below show some of the specific ways.

INTUITIVES NEED SENSING TYPES:

- To bring up pertinent facts
- To apply experience to problems
- To read the fine print in a contract
- To notice what needs attention now
- To have patience
- To keep track of essential details
- To face difficulties with realism
- To remind that joys of the present are important

SENSING TYPES NEED INTUITIVES:

- To bring up new possibilities
- To supply ingenuity on problems
- To read the signs of coming change
- To see how to prepare for the future
- To have enthusiasm
- To watch for new essentials
- To tackle difficulties with zest
- To show that the joys of the future are worth looking for

FEELING TYPES NEED THINKERS:

- To analyze
- To organize
- To find the flaws in advance
- To reform what needs reforming
- To hold consistently to a policy
- To weigh "the law and the evidence"
- To fire people when necessary
- To stand firm against opposition

THINKERS NEED FEELING TYPES:

- To persuade
- To conciliate
- To forecast how others will feel
- To arouse enthusiasm
- To teach
- To sell
- To advertise
- To appreciate the thinker

REMAINING PREFERENCES AND SUMMARY

Outer world or inner world: E or I. Your main fields of interest are apt to be directly related to the kind of perception and kind of judgment you prefer, that is, to your SN and TF preferences. But the sort of work you will most enjoy doing within those fields may depend on your EI preference — whether you like to use your favorite process extravertedly (E) in the outer world of people and things, or introvertedly (I) in the inner world of concept and ideas.

Take the ST people for example. The introverts among them (IST) like to organize facts and principles related to a situation, which is the useful thing to do in economics or law. The extraverts among them (EST) like to organize the situation itself (including any idle bystander) and get it moving which is the useful thing to do in business or industry.

Jung, who invented the terms looked upon extraversion and introversion as valuable opposites, which everyone uses but not with equal ease. Extraverts tend to be more interested and comfortable when they are working actively with people or things. Introverts tend to be more interested and comfortable when their work involves ideas and requires a good deal of their activity to take place quietly inside their heads.

Judging attitude or perceptive attitude toward the outer world: J or P. The final preference, JP, is between the use of perception and the use of judgment in dealing with the outer world. The J people rely mainly on a judging process for this purpose (thinking or feeling, whichever they prefer), and live in a planned, decided, orderly way, wanting to regulate life and control it. The P people rely mainly on a perceptive process (sensing or intuition) for dealing with the outer world, and live in a flexible, spontaneous way, wanting to understand life and adapt to it.

This JP preference works differently with extraverts and introverts. With extraverts the favorite process is, by definition, the one they prefer to use in the outer world. Therefore the extraverts' favorite process governs their JP preference. Extraverts whose *favorite process* is a judging one come out J. Extraverts whose favorite process is a perceptive one come out P.

With introverts the favorite process is, by definition, the one they prefer to use in the inner world. They do their extraverting mostly with their auxiliary. Their *auxiliary process* therefore, is what governs their JP preference. Introverts whose favorite process is a judging one come out P because their auxiliary is perceptive. And introverts whose favorite process is a perceptive one come out J.

Summary of the four preferences.

Your type is the result of your own combination of preferences, which can be stated for convenience in four letters. For example, ISTJ means an introvert liking sensing and thinking and a mainly judging attitude toward the outer world. ENFP means an extravert liking intuition and feeling and a mainly perceptive attitude toward the outer world. (N is used for intuition because I stands for introversion.) The Type Table on the back cover shows the favorite and auxiliary processes for each of the sixteen types. Brief sketches are given on pp. 7-8, longer descriptions on pp.9-16

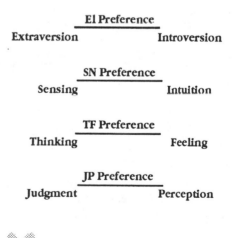

EI Preference

| Extraversion | Introversion |

SN Preference

| Sensing | Intuition |

TF Preference

| Thinking | Feeling |

JP Preference

| Judgment | Perception |

EFFECTS OF THE COMBINATIONS OF ALL

SENSING TYPES

WITH THINKING   **WITH FEELING**

ISTJ Serious, quiet, earn success by concentration and thoroughness. Practical, orderly, matter-of-fact, logical, realistic and dependable. See to it that everything is well organized. Take responsibility Make up their own minds as to what should be accomplished and work toward it steadily, regardless of protests or distractions. Live their outer life more with thinking, inner more with sensing.	**ISFJ** Quiet, friendly, responsible and conscientious. Work devoted to meet their obligations and serve their friends and school. Thorough, painstaking, accurate. May need time to master technical subjects, as their interests are not often technical. Patient with detail and routine. Loyal, considerate, concerned with how other people feel. Live their outer life more with feeling, inner more with thinking.
ISTP Cool onlookers, quiet, reserved, observing and analyzing life with detached curiosity and unexpected flashes of original humor. Usually interested in impersonal principles, cause and effect, or how and why mechanical things work. Exert themselves no more than they think necessary, because any waste of energy would be inefficient. Live their outer life more with sensing, inner more with thinking.	**ISFP** Retiring, quietly friendly. sensitive, modest about their abilities. Shun disagreement, do not force their opinions or values on others. Usually do not care to lead but are often loyal followers May be rather relaxed about assignments or getting things done, because they enjoy the present moment and do not want to spoil it by undue haste or exertion. Live their outer life more with sensing, inner more with feeling.
ESTP Matter-of-fact, do not worry or hurry, enjoy whatever comes along. Tend to like mechanical things and sports, with friends on the side. May be a bit blunt or insensitive. Can do math or science when they see the need. Dislike long explanations. Are best with real things that can be worked, handled, taken apart or put back together. Live their outer life more with sensing, inner more with thinking.	**ESFP** Outgoing, easygoing, accepting, friendly, fond of a good time. Like sports and making things. Know what's going on and join in eagerly. Find remembering facts easier than mastering theories. Are best in situations that need sound common sense and practical ability with people as well as with things. Live their outer life more with sensing, inner more with feeling.
ESTJ Practical realists, matter-of-fact, with a natural head for business or mechanics. Not interested in subjects they see no use for, but can apply themselves when necessary. Like to organize and run activities. Tend to run things well, especially if they remember to consider other people's feelings and points of view when making their decisions. Live their outer life more with thinking, inner more with sensing.	**ESFJ** Warm-hearted, talkative, popular, conscientious, born cooperators, active committee members. Always doing something nice for someone. Work best with plenty of encouragement and praise. Little interest in abstract thinking or technical subjects. Main interest is in things that directly and visibly affect people's lives. Live their outer life more with feeling, inner more with sensing.

Left margin (top to bottom): **INTROVERTS** — JUDGING / PERCEPTIVE; **EXTRAVERTS** — PERCEPTIVE / JUDGING

FOUR PREFERENCES IN YOUNG PEOPLE

SENSING TYPES
WITH FEELING   **WITH THINKING**

INFJ	**INTJ**
Succeed by perseverance, originality and desire to do whatever is needed or wanted. Put their best efforts into their work. Quietly forceful, conscientious, concerned for others. Respected for their firm principles. Likely to be honored and followed for their clear convictions as to how to best serve the common good. Live their outer life more with feeling, inner more with intuition.	Have original minds and great drive which they use only for their own purposes. In fields that appeal to them they have a fine power to organize a job and carry it through with or without help. Skeptical, critical, independent, determined, often stubborn. Must learn to yield less important points in order to win the most important. Live their outer life more with thinking, inner more with intuition.
INFP	**INTP**
Full of enthusiasms and loyalties, but seldom talk of these until they know you well. Care about learning ideas, language, and independent projects of their own. Apt to be on yearbook staff, perhaps as editor. Tend to undertake too much, then somehow get it done. Friendly, but often too absorbed in what they are doing to be sociable or notice much. Live their outer life more with intuition, inner more with feeling.	Quiet, reserved, brilliant in exams, especially in theoretical or scientific subjects. Logical to the point of hair-splitting. Interested mainly in ideas, with little liking for parties or small talk. Tend to have very sharply defined interests. Need to choose careers where some strong interest of theirs can be used and useful. Live their outer life more with intuition, inner more with thinking.
ENFP	**ENTP**
Warmly enthusiastic, high-spirited, ingenious, imaginative. Able to do almost anything that interests them. Quick with a solution for any difficulty and ready to help anyone with a problem. Often rely on their ability to improvise instead of preparing in advance. Can always find compelling reasons for whatever they want. Live their outer life more with intuition, inner more with feeling.	Quick, ingenious, good at many things. Stimulating company, alert and outspoken, argue for fun on either side of a question. Resourceful in solving new and challenging problems, but may neglect routine alignments. Turn to one new interest after another. Can always find logical reasons for whatever they want. Live their outer life more with intuition, inner more with thinking.
ENFJ	**ENTJ**
Responsive and responsible. Feel real concern for what others think and want, and try to handle things with due regard for other people's feelings. Can present a proposal or lead a group discussion with ease and tact. Sociable, popular, active in school affairs, but put time enough on their studies to do good work. Live their outer life more with feeling, inner more with intuition.	Hearty, frank, able in studies, leaders in activities. Usually good in anything that requires reasoning and intelligent talk, such as public speaking. Are well informed and keep adding to their fund of knowledge. May sometimes be more positive and confident than their experience in an area warrants. Live than outer life more with thinking, inner more with intuition.

JUDGING

INTROVERTS

PERCEPTIVE

PERCEPTIVE

EXTRAVERTS

JUDGING

EXTRAVERTED THINKING TYPES

ESTJ AND ENTJ

Extraverted thinkers use their thinking to run as much of the world as may be theirs to run. They organize their facts and operations well in advance, define their objectives and make a systematic drive to reach these objectives on schedule. Through reliance on thinking, they become logical, analytical, often critical, impersonal and unlikely to be convinced by anything but reasoning.

They enjoy being executives, deciding what ought to be done, and giving the necessary orders. They have little patience with confusion, inefficiency, halfway measures, or anything aimless and ineffective, and they know how to be tough when the situation calls for toughness.

They think conduct should be governed by logic, and govern their own that way as much as they can. They live according to a definite formula that embodies their basic judgments about the world. Any change in their ways requires a deliberate change in the formula.

Like other judging types, they run some risk of neglecting perception. They need to stop and listen to the other person's side of the matter, especially with people who are not in a position to talk back. They seldom find this easy, but if (repeat, *if*) they do not manage to do it, they may judge too hastily, without enough facts or enough regard for what other people think or feel.

Feeling is their least developed process. If they suppress or neglect it too long, it can explode in damaging ways. They need to make some conscious use of feeling, preferably in appreciation of other people's merits — an art that comes less naturally to thinkers than to feeling types. Thinkers can, if they will, "make it a rule" in their formula to mention what is well done, not merely what needs correcting. The results will be worthwhile, both in their work and in their private lives.

ESTJ
With sensing as auxiliary

Look at things with their sensing rather than their intuition. Hence are most interested in realities perceived by their five senses, which makes them matter-of-fact, practical, realistic, factually-minded, concerned with here and now. More curious about new things than new ideas. Want ideas, plans and decisions to be based on solid fact.

Solve problems by expertly applying and adapting past experience.

Like work where they can achieve immediate, visible and tangible results. Have a natural bent for business and industry, production and construction. Enjoy administration and getting things organized and done. Do not listen to their own intuition very much, so tend to need an intuitive around to sell them on the value of new ideas.

ENTJ
With intuition as auxiliary

Look at things with their intuition rather than their sensing, hence are mainly interested in seeing the possibilities beyond what is present or obvious or known. Intuition heightens their intellectual interest, curiosity for new ideas, tolerance for theory, taste for complex problems, insight, vision and concern for long range consequences.

Are seldom content in jobs that make no demand on intuition. Need problems to solve and are expert at finding new solutions. Interest is in the broad picture, not in detailed procedures or facts. Tend to choose like-minded intuitives as associates. Also tend to need someone with sensing around to keep them from overlooking relevant facts and important details.

INTROVERTED THINKING TYPES

ISTP AND INTP

Introverted thinkers use their thinking to analyze the world, not to run it. They organize ideas and facts, not situations or people unless they must. Relying on thinking makes them logical, impersonal, objectively critical, not likely to be convinced by anything but reasoning. Being introverts, they focus their thinking on the principles underlying things rather than on the things themselves. Since it is hard to switch their thinking from ideas to details of daily living, they lead their outer lives mainly with the preferred perceptive process, S or N. They are quiet, reserved, detachably curious and quite adaptable — till one of their ruling principles is violated, at which point they stop adapting.

If (repeat, *if*) they do not develop their perception, they will have too little knowledge or experience of the world. Their thinking will have no real relationship to the problems of their time, and not very much will come of it.

In the field of ideas they are decisive, though socially they may be rather shy except with their best friends. Their special problem is to make their ideas understood. Wanting to state exact truth, they tend to state it in a way too complicated for most people to follow. If they will use simple statements, even if they think the point is too obvious to be worth making, their ideas will be much more widely understood and accepted.

Feeling is their least developed process. They are not apt to know, unless told, what matters emotionally to another person. They should recognize that most people do care about having their merits appreciated and their point of view respectfully considered. And they should act accordingly. Both their working life and personal life will go better if they take the trouble to do two simple things — say an appreciative word when praise is honestly due, and mention the points where they agree with another person *before* they bring up the points where they disagree.

ISTP
With sensing as auxiliary

See the realities. Create capacity for facts and details. Good at applied science and at mechanics and the properties of materials and things. With nontechnical interests, can use general principles to bring order out of masses of confused data and meaning out of unorganized facts. May be analysts of markets, sales, securities or statistics of any kind.

Likely to be patient, accurate, good with their hands, fond of sports and outdoors, and have a gift of fun.

Great believers in economy of effort, which is an asset if they judge accurately how much effort is needed, and do efficiently what the situation demands. If not, economy of effort can become mere laziness and little will get done.

INTP
With intuition as auxiliary

See the possibilities. Value facts mainly in relation to theory. Good at pure science, research, math, and the more complicated engineering problems. With nontechnical interests, make scholars, teachers, abstract thinkers in economics, philosophy, psychology, etc.

Apt to have insight, ingenuity, quick understanding, intellectual curiosity, fertility of ideas about problems. More interested in reaching solutions than in putting them into practice, which others can do as well.

Need to check out even their most attractive intuitive projects against the facts and the limitations these impose. Otherwise may squander their energies in pursuing impossibilities.

EXTRAVERTED FEELING TYPES
ESFJ and ENFJ

Extraverted feeling types radiate warmth and fellowship. Reliance on feeling gives them a very personal approach to life, since feeling judges everything by a set of personal values. Being extraverts, they focus their feeling on the people around them, placing a very high value on harmonious human contacts. They are friendly, tactful, sympathetic, and can almost always express the right feeling.

They are particularly warmed by approval and sensitive to indifference. Much of their pleasure and satisfaction comes not only from other's warmth of feeling but from their own; they enjoy admiring people and so tend to concentrate on a person's most admirable qualities. They try to live up to their ideals and are loyal to respected persons, institutions and causes.

They are unusually able to see value in other people's opinions. And even when the opinions are conflicting, they have faith that harmony can somehow be achieved and often manage to bring it about. Their intense concentration on other people's viewpoints sometimes makes them lose sight of the value of their own. They are best at jobs that deal with people and any situation where the needed cooperation can be won by good will. They think best when talking with people and enjoy talk. It takes special effort for them to be brief and businesslike.

Being judging types, they like to have matters settled and decided, but they do not need or want to make all the decisions themselves. They have many "shoulds" and "should nots" and may express these freely. They are conscientious, persevering, orderly even in small matters, and inclined to expect others to be the same.

If (repeat, *if*) they do not develop their perception, they will, with the best of intentions, act on assumptions that turn out to be wrong. They are especially likely to be blind to the facts when there is a situation that is disagreeable or a criticism that hurts. It is harder for them than for other types to see things they wish were not true. If they fail to face disagreeable facts, they will sweep their problems under the rug instead of finding good solutions.

ESFJ
With sensing as auxiliary

Look at things with their sensing, which makes them practical, realistic, matter-of-fact, concerned with here and now. Appreciate and enjoy their material possessions and details of direct experience. Like to base plans and decisions upon known facts.

Enjoy variety, but usually adapt excellently to routine.

Compassion and awareness of physical conditions often attract them to nursing (where they provide warmth and comfort as well as devoted care) and to health professions in general.

ENFJ
With intuition as auxiliary

Look at things with their intuition rather than their sensing, hence are mainly interested in seeing the possibilities beyond what is present or obvious or known. Intuition heightens their understanding, long range vision, insight, curiosity about new ideas, love of books and tolerance for theory.

Likely to have a gift of expression, but may use it in speaking to audiences rather than in writing. Interest in possibilities for people attracts them often to counseling in the fields of career choice or personal development.

INTROVERTED FEELING TYPES
ISFP and INFP

Introverted feeling types have a wealth of warmth and enthusiasm, but may not show it till they know you well. Reliance on feeling leads them to judge everything by personal values; being introverts, they choose these values without reference to the judgment of others. They know what is most important to them and protect it at all costs. Loyalties and ideals govern their lives. Their deepest feelings are seldom expressed, since their tenderness and passionate conviction are masked by their quiet reserve.

Their feeling being introverted, they conduct their outer lives mainly with their preferred perceptive process, either sensing or intuition. This makes them open-minded, flexible and adaptable — until one of the things they value most deeply seems in danger — at which point they stop adapting. Except for the sake of their work they have little wish to impress or dominate. The friends who mean most to them are the people who understand their values and the goals they are working toward.

They are twice as good when working at a job they believe in; their feeling puts added energy behind their efforts. They want their work to contribute to something that matters to them — human understanding or happiness or health, or perhaps to the perfecting of some project or undertaking. They want to have a purpose beyond their paycheck, no matter how big the check. They are perfectionists wherever their feeling is engaged and are usually happiest at some individual work involving their personal values.

Being idealists, they measure their accomplishments against an inner standard of perfection, instead of what is actually possible. They may suffer from too great self-demand, feeling that the contrast between their inner ideal and outer reality is somehow their fault. They need to find something they really care about, and then work to achieve it. With an ideal to work for, and good development of perception to help them recognize realistic difficulties and possible solutions, they can achieve a high degree of self-confident drive.

If (repeat, if) they do not find a way to use their energies in the service of an ideal, they tend to become oversensitive and vulnerable, losing confidence in life and in themselves. If their perception is undeveloped, they may have so little realism that they aspire to the impossible and achieve frustratingly little.

ISFP
With sensing as auxiliary

See the realities. Mildly resemble ESFP, especially in seeing and meeting the need of the moment. Can pay close, unbroken attention for long periods, when work requires monitoring or close observation.

Show their warmth more by deeds than words. Compassionate toward all helpless creatures. Work well at jobs requiring devotion. Gentle, considerate, retiring. Consistently underestimate and understate themselves. May find satisfactory outlets in fields where taste, discrimination and a sense of beauty are of value.

INFP
With intuition as auxiliary

See the possibilities. Mildly resemble ENFP, especially in liking to concentrate on projects and disliking details not related to a deep interest. Understanding, tend to have insight and long-range vision. Curious about new ideas, fond of books and language. Apt to have skill in expressing themselves.

Ingenious and persuasive on the subject of their enthusiasms. Especially interested in possibilities for people. Enjoy counseling and teaching. With high ability, may excel in literature art, science , or psychology.

EXTRAVERTED SENSING TYPES
ESTP and ESFP

Extraverted sensing makes the adaptable realists, who good-naturedly accept and use the facts around them, whatever these are. They know what the facts are, since they notice and remember more than any other type. They know what goes on, who wants what and who doesn't. And they do not fight those facts. There is a sort of effortless economy in the way they deal with a situation, never taking the hard way when an easier one will work.

Often they can get other people to adapt, too. Being perceptive types, they look for the satisfying solution, instead of trying to impose any "should" or "must" of their own, and people generally like them well enough to consider any compromise that they suggest "might work". They are unprejudiced, open-minded, and usually patient, easygoing and tolerant of everyone — including themselves. They enjoy life. They don't get wrought up. Thus they may be very good at easing tense situations and pulling conflicting factions together.

Their expert sensing may show itself: (a) in a gift for machinery and the handling of tools and materials for craft or artistic purposes, or in ability to recognize quality, line, color, texture or detail; (b) in a capacity for exact facts, even when separate and unrelated, and the ability to absorb, remember and apply them; (c) in a continuous awareness, an ability to see the need of the moment and turn easily to meet it.

They are strong in the art of living, appreciate and enjoy their material possessions, and take the time to acquire and care for these. They value enjoyment, from good food and good clothes to music, art and all the products of the amusement industry. Even without these helps, they get fun out of life, which makes them fun to be with.

Being realists, they get more from first-hand experience than from study, are more effective on the job than on written tests, and doubly effective when on familiar ground. Seeing the value of new ideas, theories and possibilities may well come a bit hard, because intuition is their least developed process.

Their net effectiveness depends on whether they develop their judgment to the point where it can balance their easygoing sensing and give some direction to their lives. If (repeat, *if*) their judgment is not good enough to give them any character or stick-to-it-iveness, they may adapt mainly to their own love of a good time, and become lazy, unstable and generally shallow.

ESTP
With thinking as auxiliary

Like to make decisions with their thinking rather than their feeling. Hence are more aware of the logical consequences of an act or decision.

Thinking gives them more grasp of underlying principles, helps with math and theory and makes it easier for them to get tough when the situation calls for toughness.

ESFP
With feeling as auxiliary

Like to make decisions with their feeling rather than their thinking. Feeling gives them tact, sympathy, interest in people, ease in handling human contacts, and may make them too easy as disciplinarians.

Feeling also makes for artistic taste and judgment, but is no help with analysis.

INTRODUCTED SENSING TYPES
ISTJ and ISFJ

Introverted sensing types are made particularly dependable by their combination of preferences. They use their favorite process, sensing, in their inner life, and base their ideas on a deep, solid accumulation of stored impressions, which gives them some pretty unshakable ideas. Then they use their preferred kind of judgment, thinking or feeling, to run their outer life. Thus they have a complete, realistic, practical respect both for the facts and for whatever responsibilities these facts create. Sensing provides the facts. And after the introvert's characteristic pause for reflection, their judgment accepts the responsibilities.

They can remember and use any number of facts, but want them all accurate. They like everything kept factual, clearly stated, not too complex. Not till you know them very well do you discover that behind their outer calm they are seeing the facts from an intensely individual, often delightfully humorous angle. Their private reaction, the way a thing will strike them, is quite unpredictable.

But what they actually do about it will be sound and sensible because what they do is part of their outer life and so is governed by their best judgment. No type is more thorough, painstaking, systematic, hard-working, or patient with detail and routine. Their perseverance tends to stabilize everything with which they are connected. They do not enter into things impulsively, but once in, they are very hard to distract, discourage or stop. They do not quit unless experience convinces them they are wrong.

As administrators, their practical judgment and memory for detail make them conservative, consistent, able to cite cases to support their evaluations of people and methods. They will go to any amount of trouble if they "can see the need of it," but hate to be required to do anything that "doesn't make sense." Usually it is hard for them to see any sense in needs that differ widely from their own. But once they are convinced that a given thing does matter a lot to a given person, the need becomes a fact to be respected and they may go to generous lengths to help satisfy it, while still holding that it doesn't make sense.

Their effectiveness depends on their developing adequate judgment for dealing with the world. If (repeat, *if*) judgment remains childish, the world is not dealt with, the person retreats into silent preoccupation with inner reactions to sense-impressions, and not much of value is likely to result.

ISTJ
With thinking as auxiliary

Mildly resemble the extroverted thinking types.

Thinking stresses analysis, logic and decisiveness.

In their personal relationships, they may need to take extra pains to understand and appreciate. They will then be in no danger of overriding people less forceful than they are, and will find themselves richly repaid both in their work and in their private lives.

ISFJ
With feeling as auxiliary

Mildly resemble the extraverted feeling types.

Feeling stresses loyalty, consideration and the common welfare.

They are sympathetic, tactful, kind and genuinely concerned, which traits make them very supportive to persons in need of support. They are often attracted to fields where systematic attention to detail is combined with a care for people as in the health professions.

EXTRAVERTED INTUITIVE TYPES
ENTP and ENFP

The extraverted intuitives are the enthusiastic innovators. They are always seeing new possibilities — new ways of doing things, or quite new and fascinating things that might be done — and they go all out in pursuit of these. They have a lot of imagination and initiative for originating projects, and a lot of impulsive energy for carrying them out. They are wholly confident of the worth of their inspirations, tireless with the problems involved, and ingenious with the difficulties. They get so interested in the current project that they think of little else.

They get other people interested too. Being perceptive types, they try to understand people rather than to judge them; often, by putting their minds to it, they achieve an uncanny knowledge of what makes a given person tick, and use this to win support for their project. They adapt to other people in the way they present their objective, but never to the point of giving it up. Their faith in their intuition makes them too independent and individualistic to be conformists, but they keep a lively circle of contacts as a consequence of their versatility and their easy interest in almost everything.

In their quieter moments, their auxiliary gives them some balancing introversion and adds depth to the insights supplied by their intuition. At its best, their insight, tempered by judgment, may amount to wisdom.

Their trouble is that they hate uninspired routine and find it remarkably hard to apply themselves to humdrum detail unconnected with any major interest. Worse yet, even their projects begin to seem routine and lose attraction as soon as the main problems are solved and the rest seems clear sailing. They may discipline themselves to carry through, but they are happiest and most effective in jobs that permit one project after another, with someone else taking over as soon as the situation is well in hand.

If their judgment and self-discipline are *not* developed, they will throw themselves into ill-chosen projects, leave them unfinished, and squander their inspirations, abilities and energies on unimportant, half-done jobs. At their worst, they will be unstable, undependable, fickle and easily discouraged.

ENTP	ENFP
With thinking as auxiliary	**With feeling as auxiliary**
More independent, analytical and critical of their inspirations, more impersonal in their relations with people, more apt to consider only how others may affect their projects and not how the projects may affect others.	More enthusiastic, more concerned with people and skillful in handling them. Much drawn to counseling, where each new person presents a fresh problem to be solved and fresh possibilities to be communicated.
May be inventors, scientists, troubleshooters, promoters, or almost anything that it interests them to be.	May be inspired and inspiring teachers, scientists, artists, advertising or sales people, or almost anything that it interest them to be.

INTROVERTED INTUITIVE TYPES
INTJ and INFJ

The introverted intuitives are the great innovators in the field of ideas. They trust their intuitive insights as to the relationships and meanings of things, regardless of established authority or popular beliefs. They trust their vision of the possibilities, regardless of universal skepticism. And they want to see their ideas worked out in practice, accepted and applied.

Consequently, they have to deal firmly with the outer world, which they do by means of their preferred kind of judgment, either T or F. Thus they back up their original insight with the determination, perseverance and enduring purpose of the judging types. When they are driving to turn an inspiration into a reality, problems stimulate rather than discourage them. The impossible takes a little longer-but not much.

Certain dangers arise from their single-minded concentration. They see their goal so clearly that they may not even look for the other things they need to see — the things that conflict with their goal. They may not take the trouble to learn the details of the situation they propose to change. Since sensing is their least developed process, they can easily overlook relevant facts and the limitations these facts impose.

They may not consider the opposition they will meet, its strength or source or probable grounds. They may not consider the possibility that something is wrong with their idea. In scientific research or engineering design, a trial of their boldly ingenious ideas will visibly succeed — or fail and show where the idea *has* to be revised. They need to be particularly alert for flaws in their ideas in those fields where their insights cannot be tested so clearly.

Their auxiliary process, if adequately developed, can supply needed criticism of their ideas. Judgment can be used to foresee difficulties and decide what needs to be done about them. Most original inspirations need to be modified in the light of facts. Ideas need to be worked out and perfected to lessen objections. The best ideas still need to be presented to the world in terms understandable to other types.

If (repeat, *if*) their judgment is *not* developed, they cannot criticize their own inner vision, and they tend to reject all judgment from outside. As a result, they cannot shape their inspirations into effective action. Their ideas will go to waste, and they may be regarded only as visionaries or cranks.

<table>
<tr><td>

INTJ
With thinking as auxiliary

Most individualistic and most independent of all the types.

Resemble extraverted thinkers in organizing ability and a tendency to ignore the views and feelings of those who don't agree with them.

Logical, critical, decisive, determined, often stubborn.

Tend to drive others almost as hard as they drive themselves.

Apt to be effective, relentless reorganizers. Can be efficient executives, rich in ideas.

</td><td>

INFJ
With feeling as auxiliary

Less obviously individualistic, more apt to win cooperation than to demand it.

Resemble extraverted feeling types in their sympathetic handling of people and in a tendency to ignore harsh and uncongenial facts.

May apply their ingenuity to problems of human welfare on their own and in their own way.

Can be successful executives, especially where affairs can be conducted on a personal basis.

</td></tr>
</table>

INTRODUCTION TO TYPE　　　*A - 16*

EFFECTS OF EACH PREFERENCE IN WORK SITUATIONS

EXTRAVERTS

Like variety and action.

Tend to be faster, dislike complicated procedures.

Are often good at greeting people.

Are often impatient with long slow jobs.

Are interested in the results of their job, in getting it done and in how other people do it.

Often do not mind the interruption of answering the telephone.

Often act quickly, sometimes without thinking.

Like to have people around.

Usually communicate freely.

INTROVERTS

Like quiet for concentration.

Tends to be careful with details, dislike sweeping statements.

Have trouble remembering names and faces.

Tend not to mind working on one project for a long time uninterruptedly.

Are interested in the idea behind their job.

Dislike telephone intrusions and interruptions .

Like to think a lot before they act, sometimes without acting.

Work contentedly alone.

Have some problems communicating.

THINKING TYPES

Do not show emotion readily and are often uncomfortable dealing with people's feelings.

May hurt people's feelings without knowing it.

Like analysis and putting things into logical order. Can get along without harmony.

Tend to decide impersonally, sometimes paying insufficient attention to people's wishes.

Need to be treated fairly.

Are able to reprimand people or fire them when necessary.

Are more analytically oriented — respond more easily to people's thoughts.

Tend to be firm-minded.

FEELING TYPES

Tend to be very aware of other people and their feelings.

Enjoy pleasing people, even in unimportant things.

Like harmony. Efficiency may be badly disturbed by office feuds.

Often let decisions be influenced by their own or other people's personal likes and wishes.

Need occasional praise.

Dislike telling people unpleasant things.

Are more people-oriented — respond more easily to people's values.

Tend to be sympathetic.

SENSING TYPES

Dislike new problems unless there are standard ways to solve them.

Like an established way of doing things.

Enjoy using skills already learned more than learning new ones.

Work more steadily, with realistic idea of how long it will take.

Usually reach a conclusion step by step.

Are patient with routine details.

Are impatient when the details get complicated.

Are not often inspired, and rarely trust the inspiration when they are.

Seldom make errors of fact.

Tend to be good at precise work.

INTUITIVE TYPES

Like solving new problems.

Dislike doing the same thing repeatedly.

Enjoy learning a new skill more than using it.

Work in bursts of energy powered by enthusiasm, with slack periods in between.

Reach a conclusion quickly.

Are impatient with routine details.

Are patient with complicated situations.

Follow their inspirations, good or bad.

Frequently make errors of fact.

Dislike taking time for precision.

JUDGING TYPES

Work best when they can plan their work and follow the plan.

Like to get things settled and finished.

May decide things too quickly.

May dislike to interrupt the project they are on for a more urgent one.

May not notice new things that need to be done.

Want only the essentials needed to begin their work.

Tend to be satisfied once they reach a judgment on a thing, situation, or person.

PERCEPTIVE TYPES

Adapt well to changing situations.

Do not mind leaving things open for alterations.

May have trouble making decisions.

May start too many projects and have difficulty in finishing them.

May postpone unpleasant jobs.

Want to know all about a new job.

Tend to be curious and welcome new light on a thing, situation, or person.

INTRODUCTION TO TYPE   *A - 18*

TYPE TABLE

		INTROVERTS	INTROVERTS	EXTRAVERTS	EXTRAVERTS
		JUDGING	PERCEPTIVE	PERCEPTIVE	JUDGING
INTUITIVES	WITH THINKING	**INTJ** Introverted Intuition with thinking	**INTP** Introverted Thinking with intuition	**ENTP** Extraverted Intuition with thinking	**ENTJ** Extraverted Thinking with intuition
INTUITIVES	WITH FEELING	**INFJ** Introverted Intuition with feeling	**INFP** Introverted Feeling with intuition	**ENFP** Extraverted Intuition with feeling	**ENFJ** Extraverted Feeling with intuition
SENSING TYPES	WITH FEELING	**ISFJ** Introverted Sensing with feeling	**ISFP** Introverted Feeling with sensing	**ESFP** Extraverted Sensing with feeling	**ESFJ** Extraverted Feeling with sensing
SENSING TYPES	WITH THINKING	**ISTJ** Introverted Sensing with thinking	**ISTP** Introverted Thinking with sensing	**ESTP** Extraverted Sensing with thinking	**ESTP** Extraverted Thinking with sensing

INTROVERTS: JUDGING — PERCEPTIVE EXTRAVERTS: PERCEPTIVE — JUDGING

APPENDIX